DIFFERENT PATHS TO CURBING CORRUPTION: LESSONS FROM DENMARK, FINLAND, HONG KONG, NEW ZEALAND AND SINGAPORE

RESEARCH IN PUBLIC POLICY ANALYSIS AND MANAGEMENT

Series Editor: Evan Berman

Interim Series Editor: Clay Wescott

RESEARCH IN PUBLIC POLICY ANALYSIS AND
MANAGEMENT   VOLUME 23

DIFFERENT PATHS TO CURBING CORRUPTION: LESSONS FROM DENMARK, FINLAND, HONG KONG, NEW ZEALAND AND SINGAPORE

EDITED BY

JON S. T. QUAH

Anti-Corruption Consultant, Singapore

United Kingdom − North America − Japan
India − Malaysia − China

Emerald Group Publishing Limited
Howard House, Wagon Lane, Bingley BD16 1WA, UK

First edition 2013

Copyright © 2013 Emerald Group Publishing Limited

British Library Cataloguing in Publication Data
A catalogue record for this book is available from the British Library

ISBN: 978-1-78190-730-6
ISSN: 0732-1317 (Series)

ISOQAR certified
Management System,
awarded to Emerald
for adherence to
Environmental
standard
ISO 14001:2004.

Certificate Number 1985
ISO 14001

INVESTOR IN PEOPLE

CONTENTS

LIST OF CONTRIBUTORS

Gerald E. Caiden	Sol Price School of Public Policy, University of Southern California, Los Angeles, CA, USA
Robert Gregory	School of Government, Victoria University of Wellington, Wellington, New Zealand
Michael Johnston	Department of Political Science, Colgate University, Hamilton, NY, USA
Jon S. T. Quah	Anti-Corruption Consultant, Singapore
Ari Salminen	University of Vaasa, Vaasa, Finland
Ian Scott	University of Hong Kong, Hong Kong, SAR
Krishna K. Tummala	Kansas State University, Manhattan, KS, USA
Daniel Zirker	School of Social Sciences, University of Waikato, Hamilton, New Zealand

ABOUT THE AUTHORS

Gerald E. Caiden, Ph.D., a native of London, is an Emeritus professor at the Price School of Public Policy, University of Southern California, USA. He has served on the faculties of universities in Australia, Canada, Israel, and the United States. He has published over 30 books and monographs and over 300 journal articles, and was an editorial consultant to several public policy and administration journals, and a reader for notable publishers. He was also a consultant, researcher, and administrator for many organizations, ranging from the World Bank and the United Nations to local authorities and public utilities.

Robert Gregory, Ph.D., is an Emeritus Professor of political science at the School of Government, Victoria University of Wellington, New Zealand. He has published widely on public administration, public management, and public policy, particularly on issues of accountability and responsibility. Among his latest publications is his chapter 'Accountability in Modern Government' in Peters, B. G. & Pierre, J. (Eds.) (2012) *The Sage Handbook of Public Administration*, second edition. His 1995 article on "The Peculiar Tasks of Public Management" won the Sam Richardson Award for the most important article in that year's volume of the *Australian Journal of Public Administration*.

Michael Johnston, Ph.D., is the Charles A. Dana professor of political science at Colgate University in Hamilton, New York, USA. He has studied corruption, democratization, and reform for many years, with an emphasis on comparing differing syndromes of corruption. He has been a consultant for several governmental and international bodies, including the World Bank, United Nations, United States Agency for International Development, and the Organization of American States. His forthcoming book, *Corruption, Contention, and Reform*, which will be published by Cambridge University Press, explores ways of building social and political foundations for corruption control.

Jon S. T. Quah, Ph.D., was a professor of political science at the National University of Singapore and coeditor of the *Asian Journal of Political*

Science until his retirement in June 2007. He was a vice-president of the Asian Association for Public Administration (2010–2012) and is now an anti-corruption consultant based in Singapore. His major publications are: *Curbing Corruption in Asian Countries: An Impossible Dream?* (2011, 2013); *Taiwan's Anti-Corruption Strategy: Suggestions for Reform* (2010); *Public Administration Singapore-Style* (2010); *Combating Corruption Singapore-Style: Lessons for Other Asian Countries* (2007); and *Curbing Corruption in Asia: A Comparative Study of Six Countries* (2003).

Ari Salminen, Ph.D., is a professor of public management at the University of Vaasa, Finland. He is the author of several books on the welfare state and ethical governance. He regularly presents his research in such annual international conferences as the European Group of Public Administration. His articles on the accountability of public servants, European welfare states, trust, integrity violations, good governance, and public service ethos have appeared in the *International Review of Administrative Sciences, International Journal of Public Administration, International Journal of Public Sector Management, Journal of European Social Policy,* and *Public Integrity.*

Ian Scott, Ph.D., is an Emeritus professor of political science at Murdoch University and a visiting professor in the Department of Politics and Public Administration at the University of Hong Kong. He was a chair professor of politics and public administration at the University of Hong Kong from 1990 to 1995 and at Murdoch University from 1995 to 2002. He is the author of *The Public Sector in Hong Kong* (2010) and coeditor of *Gaming, Governance and Public Policy in Macao* (2011). His present research focuses on public service ethics and corruption.

Krishna K. Tummala, Ph.D., is Emeritus professor and a director of the Graduate Program in Public Administration from 1988 to 2011 at Kansas State University in Manhattan, Kansas, USA. He was a council member of the American Society for Public Administration, the National Association of Schools of Public Affairs and Administration, and national President of *Pi Alpha Alpha.* He received the Paul H. Appleby Award for "Distinguished Service to the Indian Institute of Public Administration and Public Administration" in 2011 the Fred Riggs Award for "Lifetime Scholarly Achievement in Comparative and International Administration" in 2008, and the ASPA Don Stone Award for "dedicated Service and exemplary contributions" in 2005. He has published extensively in many national and international journals.

Daniel Zirker, Ph.D., is a professor of politics at the University of Waikato, New Zealand. He was a former US Peace Corps volunteer in Northeast Brazil (1970–1972), and a Fulbright senior lecturer at the University of Dar es Salaam in Tanzania (1989–1990). He chaired the Research Committee on Armed Forces and Society of the International Political Science Association from 1999 to 2005, and has published on democratization, economic development, corruption, and civil–military relations. He has coedited two books on democratization in Europe and Central Asia, including *The Military and Society in the Former Eastern Bloc* (1999).

LIST OF FIGURES

LIST OF TABLES

CHAPTER 1

INTRODUCTION: DIFFERENT PATHS TO CURBING CORRUPTION

Jon S. T. Quah

PURPOSE OF BOOK

Corruption is a serious problem in many countries around the world, according to Transparency International's 2012 Corruption Perceptions Index (CPI) and the World Bank's 2011 Control of Corruption governance indicator. Indeed, an analysis of the scores of 176 countries included in the 2012 CPI in Table 1 shows that 50 countries (28.4 percent) scored between 30 and 39, 35 countries (19.9 percent) had scores between 20 and 29, and 26 countries (14.8 percent) had scores between 40 and 49. At the other extreme in the top two categories, only Denmark, Finland, and New Zealand had scores of 90, and nine other countries had scores between 80 and 89.

Table 2 shows that some countries like Denmark, Finland, New Zealand, Singapore, and Hong Kong SAR have consistently performed better on these two indicators than other countries. While Denmark, Finland, and New Zealand are the top three countries for both indicators, Singapore and Hong Kong are perceived as the two least corrupt countries in Asia. More specifically, Denmark, Finland, and New Zealand are ranked joint first

Different Paths to Curbing Corruption: Lessons from Denmark, Finland, Hong Kong, New Zealand and Singapore
Research in Public Policy Analysis and Management, Volume 23, 1–22
Copyright © 2013 by Emerald Group Publishing Limited
ISSN: 0732-1317/doi:10.1108/S0732-1317(2013)0000023001

Table 1. Performance of 176 Countries by CPI Score, 2012.

2012 CPI Score	No. of Countries	Percentage
90–100	3	1.7
80–89	9	5.1
70–79	12	6.8
60–69	16	9.1
50–59	13	7.4
40–49	26	14.8
30–39	50	28.4
20–29	35	19.9
10–19	9	5.1
0–9	3	1.7
Total	176	100.0

Source: Compiled from http://cpi.transparency.org/cpi2012/results/.

Table 2. Performance of Five Countries on the 2012 Corruption
Perceptions Index and 2011 Control of Corruption.

Country	2012 Corruption Perceptions Index Rank & Score	2011 Control of Corruption (Percentile Rank)
Denmark	1st (90)	100.0
New Zealand	1st (90)	99.5
Finland	1st (90)	98.6
Singapore	5th (87)	96.2
Hong Kong SAR	14th (77)	94.3

Sources: Compiled from http://cpi.transparency.org/cpi2012/results/ and http://info.world-bank.org/governance/wgi/mc_chart.asp

among the 176 countries included in the 2012 CPI, and Denmark's percentile rank is 100 in the World Bank's Control of Corruption indicator for 2011, followed by New Zealand, with a percentile rank of 99.5, and Finland, which has a percentile rank of 98.6. In contrast, Singapore and Hong Kong are ranked 5th and 14th, respectively, on the 2012 CPI and have respective percentile ranks of 96.2 and 94.3 on the 2011 Control of Corruption indicator.

Why have these five countries performed better than other countries on the 2012 CPI and 2011 Control of Corruption indicator? The answer to this question is important because these countries have different policy contexts and pursued different paths to curb corruption. As the reasons for their effectiveness in corruption control might be different, an analysis of their successful experiences in combating corruption will be instructive for those countries which are concerned with ameliorating their rampant corruption. To address this question, it is necessary to analyze their policy contexts and their anti-corruption strategies in order to explain why they are more effective than other countries in minimizing corruption. The purpose of this book is thus twofold: (1) to explain why these five countries have succeeded in combating corruption, and (2) to identify the lessons that other countries can learn from their successful experiences in curbing corruption.

The following literature review confirms that while there are many country studies on corruption in Denmark, Finland, Hong Kong, New Zealand, and Singapore, there is, however, no comparative book on how these five countries have succeeded in curbing corruption or an analysis of the lessons that could be learnt by other countries from their experiences. Hence, this book will be of great interest to scholars as it serves to rectify an important gap in the literature. Furthermore, policy-makers, anti-corruption practitioners, and civil society activists in those countries afflicted by widespread corruption will also be interested in learning how the five countries have succeeded in combating corruption and the relevant lessons that they can extrapolate to minimize corruption in their own countries. Finally, this volume will serve as a useful textbook or resource book for undergraduate and graduate courses on corruption and governance in universities as well as for training courses on anti-corruption strategies conducted by anti-corruption agencies and international organizations in various countries.

REVIEW OF LITERATURE

Comparative Studies

A review of the literature reveals that while research has been done on the five countries, there is no existing comparative study on how they have succeeded in curbing corruption and the lessons to be learnt by other countries from their experiences. This book rectifies an important research gap in the literature as there is no comparative analysis of anti-corruption strategies in Asian and European countries in a single volume. The closest attempt is the edited book by Bull and Newell (2003), which focuses on corruption in

11 European countries, the United States, and Japan.[1] Among the European countries included were the "quite corrupt" countries of Greece, Italy, and Spain; the "somewhat corrupt" countries of Belgium, France, Germany, and Portugal; and the "least corrupt" countries of Ireland, Netherlands, Sweden,[2] and the United Kingdom. Another relevant book is the comparative analysis of the local integrity systems in the following seven cities: Amsterdam, Antwerp, Hamburg, Hong Kong, London, New York City, and Sydney in Huberts, Anechiarico, and Six (2008).

The pioneering study by Little and Posada-Carbo (1996), which analyzes political corruption in four European countries (France, Italy, Spain, and the United Kingdom) and four Latin American countries (Brazil, Mexico, Paraguay, and Venezuela), was followed by Tulchin and Espach's book, *Combating Corruption in Latin America* (2000), which includes chapters on Brazil and Italy. In contrast, the comprehensive book edited by Caiden, Dwivedi, and Jabbra (2001) consists of six country chapters on Australia, Canada, China, France, South Africa, and the United States, and five regional chapters on the Asia-Pacific region, central and eastern Europe, Latin America, Middle East, and West Africa.

There are many comparative works on corruption in Asian countries. The first effort to compare systematically the anti-corruption strategies in Hong Kong, India, and Indonesia was initiated by Palmier (1985). It was followed a year later by the publication of the comparative analysis of the patterns of bureaucratic corruption in Hong Kong, Malaysia, Nepal, Philippines, Singapore, South Korea, and Thailand in Carino (1986). Quah has compared anti-corruption measures in South Korea and Thailand (1999a), as well as in Hong Kong, India, Mongolia, Philippines, and Singapore (1999b), and examined the impact of democratization on corruption in the Philippines and South Korea (2004). Pedro (2001) has included case studies on corruption in Hong Kong, Indonesia, Malaysia, Philippines, Singapore, and Thailand in his book. Similarly, Campos (2001) analyzes the "predictability" of corruption and its impact on investment in China, Indonesia, Malaysia, Philippines, South Korea, and Thailand during the 1997 East Asian financial crisis. The problem of crony capitalism in the Philippines and South Korea is examined by Kang (2002). Lindsey and Dick (2002) analyze the problems of governance and corruption in Indonesia and Vietnam. Arvis and Berenbeim (2003) focus on anti-corruption initiatives from private sector firms in Hong Kong, Japan, Philippines, Singapore, and South Korea. Kidd and Richter's (2003a, 2003b) two books deal respectively with corruption and governance and fighting corruption in Asian countries. Quah (2003a) analyzes the anti-corruption measures in Hong Kong, India, Mongolia, Philippines, Singapore, and South Korea. Bhargava and Bolongaita (2004) provide an analytical framework for enhancing the effectiveness of anti-corruption policies and programs in Indonesia, Philippines, South Korea, and Thailand. The national integrity systems of Cambodia, China, Hong Kong, Japan, Philippines, Singapore, South Korea, Thailand, and Vietnam were evaluated by Quah (2007a). Finally, Quah (2011) has also assessed the effectiveness of the anti-corruption measures in the following 10 Asian countries: Hong Kong, India, Indonesia, Japan, Mongolia, Philippines, Singapore, South Korea, Taiwan, and Thailand.

Among the five countries, so far only comparative research has been conducted on the anti-corruption strategies in Singapore and Hong Kong because of the well-known effectiveness of the Corrupt Practices Investigation Bureau (CPIB) and the Independent Commission Against Corruption (ICAC) in combating corruption in both city-states. Law (1985) initiated comparative research on the anti-corruption measures in Hong Kong and Singapore for his M.Soc.Sc. dissertation at the University of Hong Kong. Law's pioneering effort was followed by several comparative studies on corruption in both city-states by Quah (1995, 2010a, 2012, 2013) and Johnston (1999).

Country Studies

As noted by Michael Johnston in Chapter 2, there are few academic studies in English on corruption and corruption control in Denmark. Jorgan Gronnegaard Christensen (1994, 1995) has published two important works: one on the rewards of high public office, and the other is a case study on politicians and private interests in Denmark. Adam Lindgreen (2004) has provided a set of Danish guidelines for corruption and unethical behavior, and Denmark's Ministry of Justice (2007) has prepared a short article on "How to avoid corruption." Alina Mungiu-Pippidi's 2011 historical case study of corruption in Denmark is useful, while Peter Rordam (2012) has discussed "The myth of Denmark as a corruption-free country." Denmark's national integrity system's capacity to prevent corruption and maintain integrity was assessed in 2011 by Transparency International Denmark (2012).

On the other hand, much more research has been done on corruption in Finland, beginning with Matti Joutsen's pioneering 1975 study, followed by Joutsen and Keranen (n.d., p. 1), who provide data on the extent of corruption and explain why Finland is "a country with little corruption." Finland's Ministry of Foreign Affairs (2006) has prepared a booklet that identifies the four strengths of Finnish society in preventing corruption. In addition to the two studies on police corruption by Puonti, Vuorinen, and Ivkovic (2004) and Juntunen and Kayhko (2008), research has also been conducted on good governance and corruption in Finland by Salminen, Lammi, and Rautio (2003) and Tiihonen (2003). Salminen, Viinamaki, and Ikola-Noorbacka (2007) examine the legal and institutional measures for controlling corruption in Finland, while Darren Zook (2009, p. 166) analyzes the strengths of the Finnish model of anti-corruption policy and argues that it is "exportable, affordable, and in many ways adaptable to different political cultures." Finally, Salminen, Ikola-Noorbacka, and Mantysalo conducted the national integrity assessment of Finland in 2011 to "systematically assess Finland's integrity system, identify potential weaknesses, and suggest improvements for strengthening the system" (Transparency Suomi, 2012, pp. 1, 3).

In the case of New Zealand, Charles Sturt (1996), the founding director of the Serious Fraud Office (SFO), presented a paper on the structure, functions, and independence of the SFO at the Seventh International Anti-Corruption Conference in Beijing in October 1995. Anand Satyanand (2001), who was the Ombudsman from 1995 to 2005, highlighted the key role of the SFO and Ombudsman in ensuring good governance in New Zealand. Unlike the two major studies by Larry Hill (1976) and Bryan Gilling (1998), which did not focus on the Ombudsman's role in curbing corruption, Satyanand (2005) dealt with this aspect in the paper he presented at the Sixth International Training Course on Corruption Control in Criminal Justice at the United Nations Asia and Far East Institute for the Prevention of Crime and Treatment of Offenders (UNAFEI) in Fuchu, Japan, in November 2003. New Zealand's national integrity system was also evaluated by John Henderson, Shaun Cave, and Murray Petrie (2003) during the same year.

Robert Gregory's research focuses on why governmental corruption is not a serious problem in New Zealand. While "hard-core" corruption involving bribery or fraud is not common, he cautions that such cases appear to be increasing in New Zealand with changing social circumstances and structural and cultural changes to the civil service (Gregory, 2002, pp. 34–35; 2006, p. 136). Even though the remuneration of public officials in New Zealand is lower than private sector salaries, Gregory (2003, p. 101) contends that, unlike China, New Zealand's low level of corruption can be attributed to its egalitarian culture and "strong culture of compliance in both the public and private sectors, based on formal, rules-centred controls." Finally, Gregory, Zirker, and Scrimgeour (2012, p. 2) confirm New Zealand's reputation as a "non-corrupt" country, but warn against complacency as Iceland's ranking on the CPI has declined from its joint 1st position (with Finland and New Zealand) in 2006 to 13th position in 2011 as a result of its national banking collapse in 2008.

The many research studies on corruption in Hong Kong fall into two categories. The first category, which focuses generally on Hong Kong's anti-corruption strategy and integrity system, include Cheung (2008); Downey (1976); Lee (1981); Palmier (1985, part II); de Speville (1997, 1999); Lai (2001, 2002); Law (2008); J. M. K. Lo (2001); Lo (2003); Chan (2003); Quah (2003a, pp. 129–149; 2011, pp. 237–268); Manion (2004, pp. 26–83); Le Corre (2006); and Scott and Leung (2012). In view of the ICAC's success in combating corruption, it is not surprising that the second category consists of the following 10 studies on the ICAC and its functions: King (1980); Wong (1981); Lethbridge (1985); Clark (1986); Scott, Carstairs, and Roots (1988); Skidmore (1996); Chan (1997); de Speville (2010); and Scott (2011, 2013).

Similarly, research on corruption in Singapore has focused on several themes, beginning with Singapore's anti-corruption strategy by Tien (1973), Mohan (1987), Quah (1989; 2003a, pp. 106–128), Tan (1999), Ali (2000), Chua (2001, 2005), and Tan (2001). Second, Ho (2003), Tan (2003), and Tay (2006) have examined its national integrity system, while the relevance of Singapore's experience in combating corruption for other Asian countries is analyzed in several publications by Quah (1999c, 2001, 2003b, 2007b, 2009), who contends that these countries can emulate Singapore's example "if their citizens do not tolerate corruption and if they show such intolerance by electing into public office honest political leaders who are committed to clean and honest government" (Quah, 2007b, p. 47). The remaining three types of studies focus on the anti-corruption measures (Quah, 1978, 2010b), the CPIB (2003, 2012), and police corruption (Quah, 1979, 2006).

SUMMARY OF CHAPTERS

This book is divided into nine chapters. Following this introductory chapter, the next six chapters focus in turn on the five countries and India, which is also included in this book in Chapter 7 because of its unfavorable policy context and ineffective anti-corruption strategy. Chapter 8 discusses the problem of accounting for the success of anti-corruption measures, and Chapter 9 compares the three different paths pursued by the six countries in their war on corruption and identifies relevant lessons for other countries.

Corruption Control in Denmark

Michael Johnston analyzes in Chapter 2 Denmark's success story in corruption control by examining the impact of both domestic and international factors. While Denmark has performed well on the 2012 CPI and 2011 Control of Corruption indicator, he correctly reminds us that it is not possible to ascertain accurately whether Denmark has fewer corruption problems than other countries because both indicators are based on perceptions. Moreover, Denmark's performance on these indicators might also be adversely affected if Greenland were to be included in view of the increasing importance of its mining and wind-power industries, which could enhance the opportunities for corruption.

Denmark is a relatively small country with a land area of 43,075 sq km, a small population of 5.8 million persons, and a high GDP per capita of US$59,928. It is a parliamentary democracy and well-governed with an effective civil service, free press, and independent judiciary. While it might not be possible for other countries to replicate Denmark's small size, social homogeneity, and extensive social capital, Johnston contends that they should emulate the modest lifestyles of Danish political leaders and civil servants and the important roles played by the civil service, independent judiciary, Ombudsman, Public Accounts Committee, and Auditor-General's Office in ensuring accountable and honest government.

Johnston presents four hypotheses to explain Denmark's low level of perceived corruption, and tentatively concludes that as its quality of government is associated with its social homogeneity, extensive equality, and political competition, "a good recipe for accountability and effective corruption control" is "to govern impartially and well." Furthermore, as ethnic fragmentation can result in less impartial administration by increasing inequality and political competition, governments should introduce policies to reduce income inequalities and encourage more competitive politics to ensure impartiality in public administration.

While larger countries with internal cleavages might not be able to attain Denmark's enviable level of social homogeneity and consensus, Johnston nevertheless recommends that these countries should begin incrementally "by governing well and fairly" in a few service sectors to show that improvements are possible in order to nurture the public's trust in each other and in those leaders who govern well. In the final analysis, Denmark's effective corruption control is a reflection of its emphasis on good governance and its consensual, communal, and egalitarian political culture.

Corruption Control in Finland

Like Denmark, Finland, which has a much larger territory but smaller population and lower GDP per capita, has also a low level of perceived corruption, according to the 2012 CPI and 2011 Control of Corruption indicator. In Chapter 3, Ari Salminen provides a profile of the corruption situation and a comprehensive analysis of the anti-corruption measures in Finland. The findings of a national survey of more than 2,000 citizens conducted from 2008 to 2010 confirm that bribery, theft, and fraud are not serious problems. Table 3 in Chapter 3 shows that the number of suspected bribery cases in Finland from 2005 to 2011 is low and ranges from 20 cases in 2007 to 43 cases in 2010. However, these respondents have expressed their concern with the "excessive linkages in business life," nepotism, and old boys' networks, which have adverse consequences for Finnish society.

Finland relies on several watchdog institutions to implement impartially the following nine anti-corruption laws: Constitution of Finland (1999), Penal Code (1889), Government Act (2003), Administrative Procedure Act (2003), State Civil Servants Act (1994), Local Government Act (1995), Act on the Openness of Government Activities (1999), Accounting Act (1997), and Auditing Act (2007). The key watchdog institutions are the Parliamentary Audit Committee, Ombudsman, Chancellor of Justice, National Audit Office, and the media. The low level of perceived corruption in Finland indicates that these watchdog institutions have been effective in implementing the various anti-corruption laws.

In spite of Finland's success in corruption control, Salminen concludes that its anti-corruption measures need to be reformed to meet the three emerging challenges, which require the more active participation of civil society organizations; the prevention of distorted networking in politics, business, and public administration; and the introduction of ethical codes for the public service, local authorities, and politicians.

Hong Kong's Community Relations Strategy

The ICAC was established on February 15, 1974, to implement its three-pronged approach of investigation, prevention, and education to combat corruption in Hong Kong (Quah, 2011, p. 253). As research on the ICAC has emphasized its investigation function, Ian Scott's analysis of its community relations strategy in Chapter 4 shifts the focus to its prevention and education functions instead. He contends that the reliance on its community relations strategy has enhanced the ICAC's effectiveness by enabling the public to report corrupt acts, making its officers more sensitive to the community's attitudes and perceptions on corruption, and facilitating its support for local anti-corruption initiatives.

The ICAC created the Community Relations Department (CRD) in January 1975 with 28 personnel to educate the public against the adverse consequences of corruption and mobilize their support to combat corruption. The CRD was divided into the Media and Education Division to handle publicity and press-relations, and the Liaison Division, which works with the community through its seven regional offices throughout Hong Kong. It was plagued initially with the twin problems of limited funding and difficulty in recruiting senior and middle-level officers. However, these problems were resolved with the increased public support for the CRD's activities.

The ICAC's community relations strategy relies on the three steps of increasing public awareness of its activities; winning their support to fight corruption; and involving civil society, business, and government organizations in its community programs. The ICAC was concerned during its early years with changing public perceptions of corruption as a way of life in Hong Kong in the 1970s, and how to ascertain whether it had succeeded in changing these perceptions. Accordingly, the ICAC initiated liaison programs to change the public's acceptance of corruption by highlighting its negative effects and to enhance public confidence by informing the public about the law and creating communication channels to enable them to obtain information or report corruption offenses.

The mass surveys conducted by the ICAC in the 1980s showed that public attitudes toward corruption had changed with their increased knowledge of its role and the content of the Prevention of Bribery Ordinance. The CRD has transformed its initial "intensive and highly disaggregated" approach to the "maintenance of a more generalized, single community-wide anti-corruption message" that extends beyond the ICAC's original focus on bribery. However, the ICAC has focused its attention recently on four groups: the business community, youth, public service, and new migrants. While its monopoly of community education and publicity on corruption in Hong Kong has enabled it to establish partnerships with many organizations, the ICAC has not encouraged the development of local anti-corruption initiatives to avoid the duplication of its own programs.

Scott concludes that the ICAC's community relations strategy reinforces the importance of four lessons: (1) the critical importance of face-to-face engagement with the public to change their attitudes; (2) the CRD's focus on particular groups has enabled it to tailor its message to them; (3) resource constraints and "message fatigue" make it difficult for the ICAC to sustain its initial intensive campaigns on a long-term basis; and (4) the CRD has relied in recent years on partnerships with various community organizations to spread its anti-corruption message to their members.

Corruption Control in New Zealand

In Chapter 5, Robert Gregory and Daniel Zirker focus on those factors responsible for New Zealand's corruption-free record. They contend that New Zealand's sterling performance on Transparency International's CPI for many years can be attributed not only to its favorable policy context (small population with high GDP per capita) but more importantly to its "strong egalitarian ethos" and rigorous controls over public officials by the Ombudsman and SFO as part of its policy of zero tolerance toward corruption. While Australia and New Zealand share similar cultures and heritages and are parliamentary democracies, New Zealand's CPI scores have consistently been higher than those of Australia's because of the following three important differences: (1) Australia's beginnings as a penal colony and New Zealand's origins as a British settler society; (2) New Zealand's egalitarian culture and Australia's emphasis on individualism and freedom; and (3) police corruption is a problem in Australia but not in New Zealand.

However, Gregory and Zirker have warned New Zealanders not to be complacent about their country's excellent CPI scores in view of its changing corruption profile for three reasons. First, New Zealand's egalitarian ethos has been eroded somewhat by the increase in income inequality since the 1990s. Second, the incidence of financial fraud in New Zealand has increased in recent years as reflected in the finding of the Price Waterhouse Cooper and Office of the Auditor-General 2011 survey that fraud involving more than NZ$100,000 was reported by 8 percent of the respondents.

The same survey also reported that 9.5 percent of the respondents confirmed the occurrence of fraud cases costing between NZ$10,000 and NZ$100,000. The situation is unlikely to improve because of the increasing extent of Asian-based international organized criminal activities in the Pacific region.

Indeed, and this is the third reason, the media has also exposed many corruption scandals in New Zealand during the past five years, including the high-profile scandal involving Kim Dotcom in 2012. The other corruption scandals involved prison guards, police officers, and other government officials, including a former Minister of Justice. Citing the example of Iceland, whose banking collapse of 2008 has resulted in a substantial decline in its CPI rankings and scores from 2006 to 2011, Gregory and Zirker have advised New Zealanders not to take their country's corruption-free record for granted because of these three emerging trends.

Corruption Control in Singapore

Jon S. T. Quah explains in Chapter 6 how Singapore, which is the least corrupt Asian country according to the CPI from 1995 to 2012, has succeeded in minimizing corruption after the enactment by the People's Action Party government of the Prevention of Corruption Act (POCA) in June 1960, which empowered the CPIB to perform its function of corruption control effectively. Corruption was a serious problem during the British colonial period and after the Japanese Occupation because of the lack of political will and the ineffective Prevention of Corruption Ordinance and Anti-Corruption Branch (ACB). The ACB, which was part of the Singapore Police Force, was ineffective because it was understaffed and burdened with multiple functions, and unable to curb police corruption.

Unlike its predecessor, the CPIB focuses solely on corruption control and has been provided with the necessary legal powers, personnel, and budget to perform its functions effectively. The CPIB's effectiveness in curbing corruption in Singapore is manifested in its consistently good performance on the following five indicators: Transparency International's CPI from 1995 to 2012; Political and Economic Risk Consultancy's (PERC's) annual surveys on corruption from 1995 to 2013; World Bank's Control of Corruption indicator from 1996 to 2011; World Bank's Ease of Doing Business Rank from 2007 to 2013; and the *Global Competitiveness Report's* Public Trust of Politicians indicator from 1999 to 2012.

Other countries can draw four lessons from Singapore's effective anti-corruption strategy: (1) political will is needed for effective corruption control; (2) the CPIB has been effective because of its reliance on expertise and the adoption of a total approach to enforcement; (3) corrupt offenders are punished by enforcing the POCA impartially to deter corruption; and (4) Singapore's favorable policy context (small city-state and population; high GDP per capita; and a stable, incorrupt political system with a high level of rule of law) has contributed to the effective implementation of its anti-corruption strategy.

Corruption Control in India

As the second aim of this book is to provide lessons for those countries interested in learning from the successful experiences of Denmark, Finland, Hong Kong, New Zealand, and Singapore, Chapter 7 written by Krishna K. Tummala explores the lessons that India can learn to improve its ineffective anti-corruption strategy. After describing India's unfavorable policy context, he provides details of the major corruption scandals in recent years, including the Commonwealth Games and 2G Spectrum scandals in 2010, and the Coalgate scandal in 2012. The prevalence of these scandals is a reflection of the ineffectiveness of India's two anti-corruption agencies (ACAs): the Central Bureau of Investigation (CBI) and Central Vigilance Commission (CVC).

The CBI as the lead ACA is responsible not only for investigating corruption cases but also for economic and organized crimes, including terrorism. The CVC supervises the functioning of the CBI but is an advisory body without any enforcement powers or jurisdiction over politicians. The CBI is handicapped in curbing the rampant police corruption in India not only because it is a police agency but also by its 5,755 personnel and budget of US$720 million in 2012. Apart from serving several ministries, the CBI also lacks the power to investigate corruption cases at the state level. However, the most serious criticisms of the CBI are its reluctance to investigate prominent persons or politicians, and the public perception that it is not an independent agency but a political pawn of the government. While the judiciary is independent, the judicial process is extremely slow as it takes an average of 15 years to clear a court case.

Tummala concludes that in view of the significant contextual differences between India and the five richer but smaller countries, India has to find its own way to resolve its corruption problem by taking into consideration its many contextual constraints. While India has been ineffective in combating corruption during the past 50 years, he remains optimistic that India will be able to minimize the serious problem of corruption in the future.

Accounting for Success in Combating Corruption

How can success in combating corruption be assessed? This thorny question is addressed by Gerald E. Caiden in Chapter 8. The past record of anti-corruption efforts by governments around the world is spotty but the efforts by the United Nations (UN) to put the corruption issue on the global agenda have resulted in the launching of the UN Compact for Global Business (UNCB) in 2000 and the UN Convention Against Corruption (UNCAC) three years later. While the daily diet of corruption scandals in many countries makes for depressing reading, the success of the 10 least corrupt countries on the 2012 CPI should be recognized as their experiences demonstrate that corruption can be kept at bay if their governments are politically committed to implement impartially effective anti-corruption measures.

Caiden identifies eight major causes of corruption and argues that these causes must be addressed if those countries afflicted with corruption wish to improve their anti-corruption record. Indeed, the success stories of those western European countries and members of the British Commonwealth reflect their ability to rectify these causes.[3] He concludes that, while changing global attitudes and the increased willingness of corruption victims to demand redress for their grievances provide a glimmer of hope, the reality is that in spite of democratization and good governance in some countries, the status quo of business as usual remains intact with global corruption on the increase.

Comparing Different Paths to Curbing Corruption

In Chapter 9, Jon S. T. Quah begins by comparing the diverse policy contexts in Denmark, Finland, Hong Kong, New Zealand, Singapore, and India before describing the three different paths taken by them to curb corruption. He contends that, in contrast to India's unfavorable policy context for corruption control, the more favorable policy contexts of the other five countries have enhanced their effectiveness in minimizing corruption. Unlike Singapore and Hong Kong, which have relied on a single ACA like the CPIB and the ICAC to spearhead their anti-corruption strategies, Denmark, Finland, and New Zealand have depended instead on other institutions like the Ombudsman in all three countries, the Chancellor of Justice in Finland, and the SFO in New Zealand to enforce their policy of zero tolerance for corruption. The third path to curbing corruption is taken by India, which has relied on the ineffective strategy of relying on multiple ACAs like the CBI, CVC, and their branches at the state level for the past 50 years.

Five lessons can be learnt by other countries from the successful anti-corruption efforts of Denmark, Finland, Hong Kong, New Zealand, and Singapore. First, the success of the five countries reaffirms the critical importance of sustained political will and good governance, without which anti-corruption efforts will be doomed to failure. Second, in contrast to the much publicized effectiveness of the CPIB and ICAC, the lower level of perceived corruption in Denmark, Finland, and New Zealand shows that reliance on a single ACA is not necessarily the most effective method of corruption control if there are other institutions to ensure good governance instead. Third, the cultural values of equality and moderation as reflected in the adoption of modest lifestyles by politicians and civil servants have contributed to the corruption-free record of Denmark, Finland, and New Zealand. Fourth, paying adequate salaries to civil servants and ministers is a necessary but insufficient prerequisite for effective corruption controls if other required reforms are not implemented. Finally, even though Denmark, Finland, Hong Kong, New Zealand, and Singapore have enviable anti-corruption records, these countries should remain vigilant constantly to sustain their success in corruption control by dealing with such emerging threats like increasing income inequality, the sophisticated methods of corrupt individuals to avoid detection and prosecution, and the rising incidence of private sector financial fraud.

NOTES

1. Japan was incorrectly classified as "somewhat corrupt" by Bull and Newell even though Rothacher (2003), who wrote the chapter on Japan, had shown that corruption was endemic in Japanese politics. See also Quah (2011, pp. 58–61) for an analysis of Japan's structural corruption.

2. Sweden was ranked fourth with a score of 88 on the 2012 CPI and with a percentile rank of 99.1 for the 2011 Control of Corruption indicator. While Sweden has performed well on the CPI, it has been ranked first only once with a score of 9.3 on the 2008 CPI, unlike Denmark, Finland, and New Zealand, which have been

ranked first on the CPI for many years. For studies on corruption in Sweden, see Andersson (2002, 2003) and Andersson and Bergman (2009).

3. The eight western European countries are Denmark, Belgium, Finland, Luxembourg, Netherlands, Norway, Sweden, and Switzerland. The seven British Commonwealth countries are Australia, Barbados, Canada, Hong Kong, New Zealand, Singapore, and the United Kingdom.

ACKNOWLEDGMENTS

I am extremely grateful to the seven contributors of Chapters 2, 3, 4, 5, 7, and 8 for accepting my invitation to write their respective chapters. This book originated from the three papers on Denmark, New Zealand, and Singapore presented at the panel chaired by me at the Eighth Annual Conference of the Asian Studies Association of Hong Kong (ASAHK) in Hong Kong on March 8−9, 2013. I would like to thank Professor Sonny Lo, Head of the Department of Social Sciences at the Hong Kong Institute for Education and Chairman of the Eighth ASAHK Conference Organizing Committee for accepting my panel proposal; Michael Johnston, Robert Gregory, and Daniel Zirker for presenting their papers on Denmark and New Zealand; and Krishna K. Tummala for serving as the discussant for the panel. Thanks are also due to Ari Salminen for preparing Chapter 3 on Finland, Ian Scott for Chapter 4 on Hong Kong, Krishna Tummala for Chapter 7 on India, and Gerald Caiden for Chapter 8. As I have known and worked with most of the contributors for many years on other projects, it has been a pleasure to work with them again on this book. I thank all the contributors for their professionalism and for facilitating my job as the editor by their cooperation and prompt submission of their chapters.

I am most grateful to Thomas Dark, the Publisher of Emerald Group Publishing for his prompt approval of my book proposal and facilitating the publication of the book, and the Managing Editor, Christopher Harris, for overseeing the production process. I would also like to take this opportunity to acknowledge my appreciation for the excellent collection of books and journals on corruption at the National University of Singapore's Central Library, and to thank Tim Yap Fuan, Associate University Librarian for Information Services, for his assistance in locating relevant sources. Finally, I wish to thank the former RPPAM Series Editor Lawrence R. Jones (with whom I have worked closely on my two previous books) and Clay Wescott, the RPPAM Interim Series Editor, for their friendship and staunch support for my research on corruption.

REFERENCES

Ali, M. (2000). Eradicating corruption – the Singapore experience. Paper presented at the Seminar on International Experiences on Good Governance and Fighting Corruption in Bangkok, Thailand, February 17.

Andersson, S. (2002). *Corruption in Sweden: Exploring danger zones and change.* Ph.D. dissertation, Department of Political Science, University of Umea, Sweden.

Andersson, S. (2003). Political corruption in Sweden. In M. J. Bull & J. L. Newell (Eds.), *Corruption in contemporary politics* (pp. 135–148). Basingstoke: Palgrave Macmillan.

Andersson, S., & Bergman, T. (2009). Controlling corruption in the public sector. *Scandinavian Political Studies, 32*(1), 45–70.

Arvis, J.-F., & Berenbeim, R. E. (2003). *Fighting corruption in East Asia: Solutions from the private sector.* Washington, DC: World Bank.

Bhargava, V., & Bolongaita, E. (Eds.) (2004). *Challenging corruption in Asia: Case studies and a framework for action.* Washington, DC: World Bank.

Bull, M. J., & Newell, J. L. (Eds.) (2003). *Corruption in contemporary politics.* New York, NY: Palgrave Macmillan.

Caiden, G. E., Dwivedi, O. P., & Jabbra, J. (Eds.) (2001). *Where corruption lives.* Bloomfield, CT: Kumarian Press.

Campos, J. E. (Ed.) (2001). *Corruption: The boom and bust of East Asia.* Quezon City: Ateneo de Manila University Press.

Carino, L. V. (Ed.) (1986). *Bureaucratic corruption in Asia: Causes, consequences and control.* Quezon City: JMC Press.

Chan, K. M. (1997). Combating corruption and the ICAC. In J. Y. S. Cheng (Ed.), *The other Hong Kong report* (pp. 102–121). Hong Kong: Chinese University Press.

Chan, K. M. (2003). Current challenges and anti-corruption measures in Hong Kong. In S. S. C. Tay & M. Seda (Eds.), *The enemy within: Combating corruption in Asia* (pp. 109–130). Singapore: Eastern Universities Press.

Cheung, A. B. L. (2008). Evaluation of the Hong Kong integrity system. In L. Huberts, F. Anechiarico, & F. Six (Eds.), *Local integrity systems: World cities fighting corruption and safeguarding integrity* (pp. 105–115). The Hague: BJu Legal Publishers.

Christensen, J. G. (1994). Denmark: Institutional constraint and the advancement of individual self-interest in high public office. In C. Hood & B. G. Peters (Eds.), *Rewards at the top: A comparative study of high public office* (pp. 70–89). London: Sage Publications.

Christensen, J. G. (1995). Denmark. In F. F. Ridley & A. Doig (Eds.), *Sleaze: Politicians, private interests and public reaction* (pp. 102–114). Oxford: Oxford University Press.

Chua, C. Y. (2001). Good people, good laws: Curbing public sector corruption. In *Progress in the fight against corruption in Asia and the Pacific* (pp. 65–66). Manila: Asian Development Bank.

Chua, C. Y. (2005). Corruption control: More than just structures, systems and processes alone. In *UNAFEI.* Resource Material Series, No. 65 (March) (pp. 229–237). Retrieved from http://www. unafei.or.jp/english/pdf/RS_No65/No65_19VE_Yak.pdf. Accessed on July 15, 2013.

Clark, D. (1986). Review article: Corruption in Hong Kong – the ICAC story. *Corruption and Reform, 1*(1), 57–62.

Corrupt Practices Investigation Bureau (CPIB) (2003). *Swift and sure action: Four decades of anti-corruption work.* Singapore.

CPIB (2012). *The journey: 60 years of fighting corruption in Singapore*. Singapore.

de Speville, B. (1997). *Hong Kong: Policy initiatives against corruption*. Paris: Organisation for Economic Cooperation & Development.

de Speville, B. (1999). The experience of Hong Kong, China, in combating corruption. In R. Stapenhurst & S. J. Kpundeh (Eds.), *Curbing corruption: Toward a model for building national integrity* (pp. 51–58). Washington, DC: World Bank.

de Speville, B. (2010). Anti-corruption commissions: The "Hong Kong model" revisited. *Asia-Pacific Review, 17*(1), 47–71.

Downey, B. (1976). Combating corruption: The Hong Kong solution. *Hong Kong Law Journal, 6*(1), 27–66.

Gilling, B. (1998). *The Ombudsman in New Zealand*. Auckland: Dunmore Publishing.

Gregory, R. (2002). Governmental corruption in New Zealand: A view through Nelson's telescope? *Asian Journal of Political Science, 10*(1), 17–38.

Gregory, R. (2003). New Zealand – the end of egalitarianism? In C. Hood, B. G. Peters, & G. O. M. Lee (Eds.), *Reward for high public office: Asian and Pacific rim states* (pp. 88–104). London: Routledge.

Gregory, R. (2006). Governmental corruption and social change in New Zealand: Using scenarios, 1950-2020. *Asian Journal of Political Science, 14*(2), 117–139.

Gregory, R., Zirker, D., & Scrimgeour, F. (2012). A Kiwi halo? Defining and assessing corruption in a "non-corrupt" system. *Asia Pacific Journal of Public Administration, 34*(1), 1–29.

Henderson, J., Cave, S., & Petrie, M. (2003). *National integrity systems Transparency International country study report: New Zealand 2003*. Berlin: Transparency International.

Hill, L. B. (1976). *The model Ombudsman: Institutionalizing New Zealand's democratic experiment*. Princeton, NJ: Princeton University Press.

Ho, P. K. (2003). Singapore's integrity system. In S. S. C. Tay & M. Seda (Eds.), *The enemy within: Combating corruption in Asia* (pp. 261–272). Singapore: Eastern Universities Press.

Huberts, L., Anecharico, F., & Six, F. (Eds.) (2008). *Local integrity systems: World cities fighting corruption and safeguarding integrity*. The Hague: BJu Legal Publishers.

Johnston, M. (1999). A brief history of anti-corruption agencies. In A. Schedler, L. Diamond, & M. F. Plattner (Eds.), *The self-restraining state: Power and accountability in new democracies* (pp. 217–226). Boulder, CO: Lynne Rienner Publishers.

Joutsen, M. (1975). *The potential for corruption*. Helsinki: National Research Institute of Legal Policy.

Joutsen, M., & Keranen, J. (n.d.). *Corruption and the prevention of corruption in Finland*. Helsinki: Ministry of Justice.

Juntunen, A., & Kayhko, E. (2008). Police corruption, ethics and values of police and respondents: A study based on a citizen survey in Finland. Paper presented at the Ethics and Integrity of Governance Conference organized by the European Group of Public Administration in Rotterdam, September 3–6.

Kang, D. C. (2002). *Crony capitalism: Corruption and development in South Korea and the Philippines*. Cambridge: Cambridge University Press.

Kidd, J. B., & Richter, F.-J. (Eds.) (2003a). *Corruption and governance in Asia*. Basingstoke: Palgrave Macmillan.

Kidd, J. B., & Richter, F.-J. (Eds.) (2003b). *Fighting corruption in Asia: Causes, effects and remedies*. Singapore: World Scientific Publishing.

King, A. Y. C. (1980). An institutional response to corruption: The ICAC of Hong Kong. In C. K. Leung, J. W. Cushman, & G. Wang (Eds.), *Hong Kong: Dilemmas of growth* (pp. 115–142). Canberra: Research School of Pacific Studies, Australian National University.

Lai, A. N. (2001). Keeping Hong Kong clean: Experiences of fighting corruption post 1997. *Harvard Asia Pacific Review, 5*(2), 51–54.

Lai, A. N. (2002). Building public confidence in anti-corruption efforts: The approach of the Hong Kong Special Administrative Region. *Forum on Crime and Society, 2*(1), 135–146.

Law, F. (2008). The Hong Kong integrity system. In L. Huberts, F. Anechiarico, & F. Six (Eds.), *Local integrity systems: World cities fighting corruption and safeguarding integrity* (pp. 79–101). The Hague: BJu Legal Publishers.

Law, J. K.-H. (1985). *A comparative study of the anti-corruption measures of Hong Kong and Singapore since 1945.* M.Soc.Sc. in Public Administration dissertation, Department of Politics and Public Administration, University of Hong Kong, Hong Kong.

Le Corre, J. Y. (2006). *National integrity systems Transparency International integrity study report: Hong Kong 2006.* Berlin: Transparency International.

Lee, R. P. L. (Ed.) (1981). *Corruption and its control in Hong Kong: Situations up to the late seventies.* Hong Kong: Chinese University Press.

Lethbridge, H. J. (1985). *Hard graft in Hong Kong: Scandal, corruption, the ICAC.* Hong Kong: Oxford University Press.

Lindgreen, A. (2004). Corruption and unethical behavior: Report on a set of Danish guidelines. *Journal of Business Ethics, 51*(1), 31–39.

Lindsey, T., & Dick, H. (Eds.) (2002). *Corruption in Asia: Rethinking the governance paradigm.* Annandale: Federation Press.

Little, W., & Posada-Carbo, E. (Eds.) (1996). *Political corruption in Europe and Latin America.* Basingstoke: Macmillan Press.

Lo, J. M. K. (2001). Controlling corruption in Hong Kong: From colony to special administrative region. *Journal of Contingencies and Crisis Management, 9*(1), 21–28.

Lo, T. W. (2003). Minimizing crime and corruption in Hong Kong. In R. Godson (Ed.), *Menace to society: Political-criminal collaboration around the world* (pp. 231–256). New Brunswick, NJ: Transaction Publishers.

Manion, M. (2004). *Corruption by design: Building clean government in Mainland China and Hong Kong.* Cambridge, MA: Harvard University Press.

Ministry of Foreign Affairs, Finland. (2006). *Combating corruption: The Finnish experience.* Helsinki: Ministry of Foreign Affairs, Finland.

Ministry of Justice, Denmark. (2007). *How to avoid corruption.* Copenhagen, 16 pages. Retrieved from http://www.justitsministeriet.dk. Accessed on March 27, 2013.

Mohan, S. C. (1987). *The control of corruption in Singapore* (Vols. 1–2). Ph.D. thesis, Faculty of Law, School of Oriental and African Studies, University of London, UK.

Mungiu-Pippidi, A. (2011). Becoming Denmark: Understanding historical achievers. In A. Mungiu-Pippidi (Ed.), *Contextual choices in fighting corruption: Lessons learned* (pp. 57–70). Berlin: Hertie School of Governance. Retrieved from http://www.against corruption.en/uploads/norad/Becoming-Denmark-Historical-Lessons-Learned.pdf. Accessed on August 12, 2012.

Palmier, L. (1985). *The control of bureaucratic corruption: Case studies in Asia.* New Delhi: Allied Publishers.

Pedro, A. C., Jr. (Ed.) (2001). *Combating corruption in East Asia.* Manila: Yuchengco Center, De La Salle University.

Puonti, A., Vuorinen, S., & Ivkovic, S. K. (2004). Sustaining police integrity in Finland. In C. B. Klockars, S. K. Ivkovic, & M. R. Haberfeld (Eds.), *The contours of police integrity* (pp. 95−115). Thousand Oaks, CA: Sage Publications.

Quah, J. S. T. (1978). *Administrative and legal measures for combating bureaucratic corruption in Singapore.* Occasional Paper No. 34. Department of Political Science, University of Singapore, Singapore.

Quah, J. S. T. (1979). Police corruption in Singapore: An analysis of its forms, extent and causes. *Singapore Police Journal, 10*(1), 7−43.

Quah, J. S. T. (1989). Singapore's experience in curbing corruption. In A. J. Heidenheimer, M. Johnston, & V. T. LeVine (Eds.), *Political corruption: A handbook* (pp. 841−853). New Brunswick, NJ: Transaction Publishers.

Quah, J. S. T. (1995). Controlling corruption in city-states: A comparative study of Hong Kong and Singapore. *Crime, Law and Social Change, 22,* 391−414.

Quah, J. S. T. (1999a). Combating corruption in South Korea and Thailand. In A. Schedler, L. Diamond, & M. F. Plattner (Eds.), *The self-restraining state: Power and accountability in new democracies* (pp. 245−256). Boulder, CO: Lynne Rienner Publishers.

Quah, J. S. T. (1999b). Comparing anti-corruption measures in Asian countries: Lessons to be learnt. *Asian Review of Public Administration, 11*(2), 71−90.

Quah, J. S. T. (1999c). Singapore's anti-corruption strategy: Some lessons for South Korea. *Korean Corruption Studies Review, 4*(December), 173−193.

Quah, J. S. T. (2001). Combating corruption in Singapore: What can be learnt? *Journal of Contingencies and Crisis Management, 9*(1), 29−35.

Quah, J. S. T. (2003a). *Curbing corruption in Asia: A comparative study of six countries.* Singapore: Eastern Universities Press.

Quah, J. S. T. (2003b). Singapore's anti-corruption strategy: Is this form of governance transferable to other Asian countries? In J. B. Kidd & F.-J. Richter (Eds.), *Corruption and governance in Asia* (pp. 180−197). Basingstoke: Palgrave Macmillan.

Quah, J. S. T. (2004). Democratization and political corruption in the Philippines and South Korea. *Crime, Law and Social Change, 42*(1), 61−81.

Quah, J. S. T. (2006). Preventing police corruption in Singapore: The role of recruitment, training and socialization. *Asia Pacific Journal of Public Administration, 28*(1), 59−75.

Quah, J. S. T. (2007a). *National integrity systems Transparency International regional overview report: East and Southeast Asia.* Berlin: Transparency International.

Quah, J. S. T. (2007b). *Combating corruption Singapore-style: Lessons for other Asian countries.* Baltimore, MD: School of Law, University of Maryland.

Quah, J. S. T. (2009). Curbing corruption in a one-party dominant system: Learning from Singapore's experience. In T. Gong & S. K. Ma (Eds.), *Preventing corruption in Asia: Institutional design and policy capacity* (pp. 131−147). London: Routledge.

Quah, J. S. T. (2010a). Defying institutional failure: Learning from the experiences of anti-corruption agencies in four Asian countries. *Crime, Law and Social Change, 53*(1), 23−54.

Quah, J. S. T. (2010b). Combating corruption. In *Public administration Singapore-style* (pp. 171−198). Bingley: Emerald Group Publishing.

Quah, J. S. T. (2011). *Curbing corruption in Asian countries: An impossible dream?* Bingley: Emerald Group Publishing.

Quah, J. S. T. (2012). Combating public sector corruption in Singapore and Hong Kong: Lessons for the private sector in Asian countries. *Public Administration and Policy, 15*(1), 35−62.

Quah, J. S. T. (2013). Curbing corruption and enhancing trust in government: Some lessons from Singapore and Hong Kong. In J. Liu, B. Hebenton, & S. Jou (Eds.), *Handbook of Asian criminology* (pp. 25–47). New York, NY: Springer Science & Business Media.

Rordam, P. (2012). The myth of Denmark as a corruption-free country. *Copenhagen Post*, November 16.

Rothacher, A. (2003). Political corruption in Japan. In M. J. Bull & J. L. Newell (Eds.), *Corruption in contemporary politics* (pp. 106–119). Basingstoke: Palgrave Macmillan.

Salminen, A., Lammi, K., & Rautio, V. (2003). Good governance as an ethical issue: The case of Finland. Paper presented at the European Group for Public Administration Annual Conference in Oeiras, Portugal, September 3–6.

Salminen, A., Viinamaki, O.-P., & Ikola-Norrbacka, R. (2007). The control of corruption in Finland. *Administratie si Management Public (Administration and Public Management Review)*, 9, 81–95.

Satyanand, A. (2001). Institutional safeguards for good governance: The New Zealand experience. In *Progress in the fight against corruption in Asia and the Pacific* (pp. 197–201). Manila: Asian Development Bank.

Satyanand, A. (2005). The role of Ombudsman and its connection with the control of corruption. In *UNAFEI*. Resource Material Series, No. 65 (March) (pp. 213–228). Retrieved from http://www.unafei.or.jp/english/pdf/RS_No65/No65_18VE_Satyanand.pdf. Accessed on July 10, 2013.

Scott, I. (2011). The Hong Kong's ICAC's approach to corruption control. In A. Graycar & R. G. Smith (Eds.), *Handbook of global research and practice in corruption* (pp. 401–415). Cheltenham: Edward Elgar.

Scott, I. (2013). Institutional design and corruption prevention in Hong Kong. *Journal of Contemporary China, 22*(79), 77–92.

Scott, I., & Leung, J. Y. H. (2012). Integrity management in post-1997 Hong Kong: Challenges for a rule-based system. *Crime, Law and Social Change, 58*(1), 39–52.

Scott, T., Carstairs, A., & Roots, D. (1988). Corruption prevention: The Hong Kong approach. *Asian Journal of Public Administration, 10*(1), 110–119.

Skidmore, M. J. (1996). Promise and peril in combating corruption: Hong Kong's ICAC. *Annals of the American Academy, 547*(September), 118–130.

Sturt, C. (1996). The fight against corruption: New Zealand's answer. In Academic Office of the 7th International Anti-Corruption Conference Secretariat (Ed.), *Anti-corruption for social stability and development* (pp. 305–311). Beijing: Hong Qi Publishing House.

Tan, A. L. (1999). The experience of Singapore in combating corruption. In R. Stapenhurst, & S. J. Kpundeh (Eds.), *Curbing corruption: Toward a model for building national integrity* (pp. 59–66). Washington, DC: World Bank.

Tan, T. K. (2001). Mandarins, masses and mnemonic devices: Combating corruption in Singapore. In A. C. Pedro (Ed.), *Combating corruption in East Asia* (pp. 3–16). Manila: Yuchengo Center for East Asia, De La Salle University.

Tan, T. K. (2003). Masters, mandarins and mortals: The constitution of Singapore's national integrity system. In S. S. C. Tay & M. Seda (Eds.), *The enemy within: Combating corruption in Asia* (pp. 291–326). Singapore: Eastern Universities Press.

Tay, S. S. C. (2006). *National integrity systems Transparency International country study report: Singapore 2006*. Berlin: Transparency International.

Tien, A. (1973). *How Singapore stops corruption*. Insight, January, 16–19.

Tiihonen, P. (2003). Good governance and corruption in Finland. In S. Tiihonen (Ed.), *The history of corruption in central government* (pp. 99–118). Amsterdam: IOS Press.

Transparency International Denmark (2012). *National integrity assessment: Denmark*. Copenhagen: Transparency International Denmark.

Transparency Suomi (2012). *National integrity assessment: Finland*. Helsinki: Transparency International Finland.

Tulchin, J. S., & Espach, R. H. (Eds.) (2000). *Combating corruption in Latin America*. Washington, DC: Woodrow Wilson Center Press.

Wong, J. K. H. (1981). The ICAC and its anti-corruption measures. In R. P. L. Lee (Ed.), *Corruption and its control in Hong Kong: Situations up to the late seventies* (pp. 45–72). Hong Kong: Chinese University Press.

Zook, D. C. (2009). The curious case of Finland's clean politics. *Journal of Democracy, 20*(1), 157–168.

CHAPTER 2

THE GREAT DANES: SUCCESSES AND SUBTLETIES OF CORRUPTION CONTROL IN DENMARK

Michael Johnston

ABSTRACT

Denmark's apparent success at controlling corruption is likely both real and more complex than it may appear. This chapter reviews a series of hypotheses about the extent and sources of corruption control in Denmark, emphasizing both domestic and international factors. Some possible vulnerabilities are discussed, including whether Greenland — which is usually excluded from Danish governance ratings — might introduce corruption via its mining industries, and whether the growing wind-power industry (in some senses, another extractive enterprise) might also encourage corruption. A simple data analysis, using the Gothenburg University Quality of Government Impartiality Index, suggests that small social scale, a homogeneous population, competitive politics, and extensive international connectedness might well help check Danish corruption, but relationships among the variables are complex and marked by considerable simultaneity. Denmark illustrates two

Different Paths to Curbing Corruption: Lessons from Denmark, Finland, Hong Kong, New Zealand and Singapore
Research in Public Policy Analysis and Management, Volume 23, 23–56
Copyright © 2013 by Emerald Group Publishing Limited
All rights of reproduction in any form reserved
ISSN: 0732-1317/doi:10.1108/S0732-1317(2013)0000023002

subtleties often overlooked: the importance of "soft controls" — social values, a working consensus, an emphasis on fairness, and common goals — for corruption control, and the question of whether advanced market societies really control corruption or merely reduce incentives to engage in it, as a result of business-friendly policies and institutions. A final issue involves dependent variables: better indirect measures of corruption might well be obtained by gathering and benchmarking indicators of government performance.

INTRODUCTION

Amid the widespread public concern with serious corruption, and in light of the indifferent — at best — record of the international anti-corruption movement when it comes to sustained national-level corruption control, it can be difficult to come to terms with the apparent success stories. Whatever the drawbacks of mainstream national-level corruption indices, it is undeniable that some countries are widely regarded as doing an effective job of corruption control, and have been seen in such terms for a number of years. Such cases are few in number, however, and often appear to be unrepresentative of the larger universe of societies. Moreover, much of our theory and data serve better to explain problems and failures than to interpret success: after all, it is a genuine analytical challenge to account for corruption that *does not* occur. How real are the few apparent success stories? What lessons, if any, can we take away to aid reform efforts elsewhere?

This chapter on Denmark lays out the basic ideas to address the questions above. It does not reach definite conclusions regarding successful corruption control anywhere, much less provide a full explanation of Denmark's record. Rather, the agenda is to sort through some of the complexities of understanding apparent success stories, and to develop propositions and hypotheses that might guide further work. For several key ideas solid evidence can be scarce, as we shall see. Still, it is important to develop a better understanding of what successful corruption control looks like in practice.

SMALL, PROSPEROUS — AND WELL-GOVERNED?

With a population of 5.8 million, Denmark is located on the Jutland peninsula, north of Germany, and includes several sizeable islands as well

(Schwab, 2012, p. 383). Denmark is a thoroughly North European society as it became a North Atlantic Treaty Organization (NATO) member in 1949 and joined the European Union (EU) (or European Economic Community, as it was at the time) in 1973. It was, for a time, one of the most enthusiastic members of the EU, but in recent years has exempted itself from some provisions of the Maastricht Treaty, has kept the Krone as its national currency in preference to the Euro, and has shown considerable skepticism about the EU Constitution project. When Denmark ratified the Treaty of Lisbon in 2008, it did so by parliamentary action rather than by popular referendum. The country is party to many international and EU treaties, conventions, and agreements. About a quarter of the population live in metropolitan Copenhagen, and the nation as a whole enjoys an enviable standard of living: its GDP per capita in 2011 was US$59,928 (Schwab, 2012, p. 384) and its Gini coefficient of 24.8 reflects a striking degree of economic equality.

Denmark is formally a constitutional monarchy but operates, on a day-to-day level, as a European-style parliamentary democracy. In its Folketing or unicameral assembly the center-right Liberal Party and the center-left Social Democrats are in rough parity, the former receiving 26.7 percent of the vote in the 2011 elections and the latter, 24.9 percent; the third largest party is the populist, right-wing Danish People's Party (DPP), at around 12 percent. The DPP stands somewhat outside the governing consensus with its monarchist views and its objections to immigration, and like its counterparts in other European democracies has made an issue of whether, and how much of, the country's repertoire of social benefits should be available to recent arrivals. The bureaucracy is generally regarded as high in quality and capacity: on the World Bank's Government Effectiveness Index the nation receives a score of 2.17, and on Regulatory Quality, 1.93 – both scores ranking near the top of the scale (World Bank, 2013). There is a free press and an independent judiciary; Supreme Court members are nominally appointed by the monarch and are well-respected.

Denmark consists of more than Jutland and its immediate surroundings, however. The Faroe Islands, located in the North Atlantic halfway between Norway and Iceland, are under Danish control. So, in most respects, is Greenland – the world's largest island, and part of North America. Over the years Greenland's 60,000 or so residents have been given increasing self-government powers, but Copenhagen retains sovereign authority and is responsible for international affairs. As we shall see, the question of whether or not "Denmark" includes Greenland has become a part of the discussion about the country's favorable corruption-control reputation.

It is also relevant to the issue of what does, and does not, make for more corruption: much Greenlandic economic activity revolves around mining, and extractive industries are often seen as adding to the challenges of corruption control in countries where they are economically significant.

At times during Danish history corruption has indeed been a major concern.[1] During the early 19th century, for example, a large number of civil servants were caught embezzling government funds, often from governmental units at the local and regional levels. That outbreak of corruption was part of a major economic depression and outbreak of inflation that followed the Napoleonic Wars, in which Denmark allied with France. At war's end Denmark was forced to yield control of present-day Norway to the Swedes; as a consequence land values and economic activity declined sharply, and many civil servants experienced significant cuts in pay and purchasing power. Citizens suffering the consequences of such official theft could and did complain to the King, who acted decisively to suspend and jail the offenders. By around 1830 the surge of embezzlements was brought to an end, and corruption levels remained low (with only a few exceptions) thereafter. It is interesting to note that, in connection with speculations on the implications of Danish democracy that appear elsewhere in this chapter, sound corruption controls were effectively in place *before* the rise of parliamentary politics in 1849. Thus, while legitimate and effective democratic processes very likely enhance government accountability in Denmark, its successes in checking corruption cannot be reduced to the fact of democracy itself (on these and many other issues see Jensen, 2013).

HOW HONEST IS DENMARK'S GOVERNMENT?

The best-known reform success stories are those of two small city-states: Singapore and the Hong Kong SAR. Denmark, while physically larger, is no more populous than those two cases. Singapore and Hong Kong are also prosperous; their GDP per capita in 2011 was US$34,049 for Hong Kong and US$49,271 for Singapore (Schwab, 2012, p. 384). Denmark, with its Gini coefficient of 24.8, is considerably more egalitarian compared to the global average (39.0), the United States (45.0), Singapore (47.3), or Hong Kong (53.3) (World Factbook, 2013). All three societies are immersed in regional and global trade, and thus part of a system that might check corruption in some respects (Treisman, 2000) and encourage it in other ways.

When it comes to the essential question of how much corruption takes place in Denmark, there is a simple answer: no one knows. With respect to how the country is perceived, however, there is a clear verdict: Denmark ranks at or near the top, year after year, on governance indices (see, as just one example of Denmark's positive reputation, Gilani, 2012). Its Transparency International (TI) Corruption Perceptions Index (CPI) scores and rankings for recent years are shown in Table 1.

The World Bank Institute's World Governance Indicators (WGI), which includes a "Control of Corruption" measure, reflects similar results for Denmark, as can be seen in Table 2. The WGI scores range from roughly +2.5 (very effective corruption control) to −2.5 (very ineffective), with a mean of zero; the percentile rankings indicate that Denmark's score ranked at the top among 215 countries, year after year. The WGI scores are based in part upon many of the same perception surveys incorporated into the CPI, but include other evidence as well and are calculated in a more sophisticated manner.

Table 1. Denmark's CPI Scores and Rankings, Selected Years.

Year	Score/Maximum Points	Rank/Countries in Index
2012	90/100	T1/176
2010	9.3/10	T1/178
2005	9.5/10	4/158
2000	9.8/10	2/90
1995	9.32/10	2/41

Source: http://cpi.transparency.org/cpi2012/results/.
"T", tied in rank.

Table 2. Denmark's WGI Control of Corruption Scores and Rankings, Selected Years.

Year	Score	Percentile Rank
2011[a]	2.42	100
2008	2.47	100
2004	2.52	100
2000	2.52	100
1996	2.37	100

Source: World Bank (2013).
[a]Latest data available.

Neither the CPI not the WGI figures measure corruption directly. Both − particularly the CPI − have their critics. These data are included here only to make the point that Denmark's low-corruption reputation is no short-term fluke; indeed, given the amount of publicity the country receives annually for its rankings, we can be fairly confident that any significant outbreak of corruption would impair these positive perceptions at least temporarily. At the same time, it is worth noting that neither data series includes Greenland. The surveys on which the CPI results draw apparently do not invite judgments of Greenland, either as a part of Denmark nor on its own. The WGI results show no data for Greenland between 1996 and 2008, but beginning in 2009 Greenland received scores of 1.17 (2009), 1.19 (2010), and 1.22 (2011). Those are much-above-average results − good for an 85th percentile ranking in all three years − but, depending upon how one might weigh the Greenland contribution to Danish governance overall, would reduce the country's score by some amount. We will return to the Greenland question below.

So far so good, at least as far as Denmark's enviable international reputation is concerned. Few would contend that the indices are wholly wrong; in every outward respect Denmark appears to be a well- and honestly governed society.

One factor − a very nice problem to have, in one sense − complicating any study of Danish corruption is a lack of readily available cases. There are few academic studies in English − that linguistic limitation is my own − of corruption, or corruption control, in Denmark (one welcome exception is Lindgreen, 2004). Journalistic accounts are scarce as well; most items are opinion pieces (see, e.g., Delingpole, 2012; Rørdam, 2012), or reports of Denmark's moves to suspend development aid in highly corrupt societies (see, for Uganda, Namulando, 2012; Reuters, 2012) and of the five-point anti-corruption program of Danish International Development Agency (DANIDA), the nation's foreign aid agency (Villarino, 2013). News items on contemporary corruption cases are few, which we might hope reflects an absence of the problem itself but might also be open to other interpretations. The risk, as a result, is that any attempt to explain the absence of corruption will end up confusing assumptions with conclusions, in the absence of evidence that might disprove the former or point unambiguously to the latter.

Nevertheless, we can offer some general hypotheses as a starting point. Four hypotheses on the extent to which anything is, or is not, rotten in the state of Denmark are analyzed in the following four sections.

DIFFERENT PATHS TO CURBING CORRUPTION: LESSONS
FROM DENMARK, FINLAND, HONG KONG, NEW...; ED. BY
JON S.T. QUAH.   Cloth   255 P.
LONDON: EMERALD GROUP PUBL, 2013
SER: RESEARCH IN PUBLIC POLICY ANALYSIS AND
MANAGEMENT; V. 23.
TITLE CONT: ZEALAND AND SINGAPORE. COLLECTION OF
NEW ARTICLES COMPARING SUCCESSFUL POLICIES.

ISBN 1781907307   **Library PO#** GENERAL APPROVAL

		List	114.95	USD
5461 UNIV OF TEXAS/SAN ANTONIO		**Disc**	17.0%	
App. Date 2/05/14 PAD.APR	6108-11	**Net**	95.41	USD

SUBJ: 1. POLITICAL CORRUPTION--PREVENTION. 2.
CORRUPTION--PREVENTION.

CLASS JF1081   DEWEY# 364.1323   LEVEL ADV-AC

YBP Library Services

DIFFERENT PATHS TO CURBING CORRUPTION: LESSONS
FROM DENMARK, FINLAND, HONG KONG, NEW...; ED. BY
JON S.T. QUAH.   Cloth   255 P.
LONDON: EMERALD GROUP PUBL, 2013
SER: RESEARCH IN PUBLIC POLICY ANALYSIS AND
MANAGEMENT; V. 23.
TITLE CONT: ZEALAND AND SINGAPORE. COLLECTION OF
NEW ARTICLES COMPARING SUCCESSFUL POLICIES.

ISBN 1781907307   **Library PO#** GENERAL APPROVAL

		List	114.95	USD
5461 UNIV OF TEXAS/SAN ANTONIO		**Disc**	17.0%	
App. Date 2/05/14 PAD.APR	6108-11	**Net**	95.41	USD

SUBJ: 1. POLITICAL CORRUPTION--PREVENTION. 2.
CORRUPTION--PREVENTION.

CLASS JF1081   DEWEY# 364.1323   LEVEL ADV-AC

HO: There Is No Way of Knowing Whether Denmark Has Fewer Corruption Problems than Other Countries

This is not a null hypothesis, strictly speaking, in the sense that "Denmark has not more and no fewer corruption problems than other societies," but that sort of approach runs directly into basic problems of measurement. Simply put, no one knows how much corruption, or just what balance of various types of it, takes place in any country, partly because of a lack of settled definitions and in part because such activities tend to be clandestine. In addition, as I will suggest below, in advanced market democracies, a category that includes not only Denmark but also most other societies that score well on perception indices, it can be surprisingly hard to say exactly what is or is not corruption, and many activities that involve what might be seen as the abuse of public trust for private benefit are not illegal. Yet another complication is that an unknown but likely significant portion of corrupt activities involving such societies actually takes place, or at least comes to light, elsewhere – often, coloring perceptions of less-developed countries as a result of schemes originating, or serving key interests in, the affluent North and West (for a longer discussion of such issues, see Johnston, 2013, Chapter 7). Compounding the problem is that our most widely used corruption indices rely on perceptions – not the same thing as corruption – and collapse a wide range of potential variations into a one-dimensional, more-versus-less numerical scale. Both the measurement issue and our understandable tendency to think of corruption primarily in terms of clear-cut rule- or law-breaking make any assessment of Denmark's over-all corruption problems a matter of your educated guess versus mine.

It may also be that the perceptions underlying such indices are distorted by outward characteristics of a society like Denmark. Many casual observers, unfortunately, are likely to associate corruption with poverty, political instability, recent experience as a colony, social divisions, and even violence (along with, at the worst end of the stereotype scale, a tropical climate). Indeed, some of the opinion surveys that factor into perception indices use questions inviting and drawing upon such associations. Denmark, much to its good fortune, presents none of those appearances: it is affluent, politically stable, socially homogeneous, egalitarian (Uslaner, 2007, p. 15), and at peace with its neighbors and with itself. Its climate is decidedly un-tropical.

A related concern about index scores is that they may tap into the overtness and openness of corruption, rather than its overall pervasiveness or seriousness (Johnston, 2009). Might Denmark's consensual style – for example, "Danish Labor Market" policies of tripartite cooperation and negotiation among labor, employers, and government (Andersen & Svarer, 2006) – conceal serious corruption or discourage whistle-blowing? In all likelihood we will never know, although it must be noted that little if any evidence exists, at present, for (or directly against) that scenario.

H1: Denmark Is More Corrupt than the Corruption Indicators Suggest

Perhaps Denmark has more serious corruption problems than the indices might suggest. While evidence is scarce at present, a hidden Danish corruption problem might reflect several realities.

First, as noted earlier, Greenland is generally left out of accounts of the state of governance in Denmark. The fragmentary WGI scores for Greenland, since only 2009, do not suggest vast governance abuses on the world's largest island, but Transparency Greenland (the Greenlandic candidate chapter for full membership in Transparency International) has alleged significant corruption involving Alcoa's aluminum smelter in Maniitsoq. Greenland's Bureau of Minerals and Petroleum is seen by some critics as caught in a conflict of interest, charged as it is with both regulating and promoting the growth of mining. A Transparency Greenland board member has voiced concerns that policies making it easier for mining companies to import inexpensive labor will likewise lead to abuses, stating that "Greenland will be known as a place where money talks and human rights do not have to be taken seriously" (Weaver, 2012).

Another possible area for scrutiny is the growing wind-power industry: not surprisingly, Denmark's geography and its strong preferences for non-fossil fuel energy make it a prime location for windmill farms. Strictly speaking, wind power is not an extractive industry, since generating power does not deplete the wind, but like mining, it involves major capital investments tied to specific locations, offers major potential profits, and brings industry and public officials into close interaction. One report (Rørdam, 2012) has it that wind-power firms have falsified data on the noise and other environmental effects of power generation windmills in order to win construction approvals and pay neighboring land-holders smaller compensation. Legislators went along with wind industry proposals, we are told, even though they were aware – or had good reason to be aware – of industry deceptions. Rørdam does not allege that legislators were bribed – the industry's leverage, he says, came via threats to move jobs and investments to other countries — which if true would put this case on the boundaries of what most would call corruption per se. But Rørdam does argue that the industry's conduct is corrupting in a larger sense of undermining the moral quality and authority of governing institutions, and of weakening democratic accountability, in the name of company profits. Indeed, contemporary market societies feature numerous business-related activities that break no laws, yet turn political leverage into major profits and can be viewed as abusing public trust (on that issue, see Johnston, 2013, Chapter 7; Lessig, 2011).

Other possibilities for a hidden Danish corruption problem might be that serious misconduct is hidden away at high levels in government and business, and/or that while Denmark may control corruption effectively at home it might export it elsewhere through its international corporations and aid programs. Both, of course, are highly speculative ideas. "High levels" of government and business do exist and interact in Denmark, just as they do elsewhere, but in both spirit and in actual distributions of wealth and power the nation is admirably egalitarian, and its various elites seem closely tied to the rest of society. We have already noted Denmark's remarkably low Gini coefficient. Another rough indicator of political equality is the fact that in most years nearly 40 percent of the membership of the Folketing, the national parliament of Denmark, is made up of women (Index Mundi, 2013), ranking Denmark 13th in the world out of 190 countries (Inter-Parliamentary Union, 2012). Gilani (2012) strikes a similar note, based on his interviews with Danish politicians and anti-corruption activists, when he suggests that the "modest lifestyles" of politicians enable them to serve as role models for other elites. The Speaker of the Parliament, for example, commutes to and from his office by bicycle. However symbolic such conduct might seem, it could both reflect and reinforce values of egalitarianism, accountability, and service, and that political figures taking large sums of money in defiance of such values might well become conspicuous rather quickly.

Similarly, we can never know for sure how much, if any, Danish corruption is exported to poorer parts of the world. Whatever their backgrounds or intentions, Danes working in the wider world are not likely to be exempt from the corrupting pressures and incentives that can arise in various settings; Wang and Rosenau (2001, p. 41), for example, cite data from an unnamed poll taken in the late 1990s suggesting that 74 percent of Danish business people working abroad claimed to have paid bribes in pursuit of contracts. Still, Copenhagen's aggressive steps to cut off aid to corrupt regimes, and DANIDA's strict anti-corruption controls within its own aid programs, suggest that on the whole the nation's international record is a positive one (Namulando, 2012; Reuters, 2012; Villarino, 2013).

H2: Denmark Has Little Corruption Because of Domestic Factors

If Denmark does have less serious corruption problems than many other countries, what is it about the society that might explain such outcomes? Here again, causality is difficult to establish — not least because the supposed low levels of corruption remain a matter of perception and indirect evidence — and there is always the risk of working backward from positive outcomes to some favorite hypothesis or social characteristic and pronouncing it a key cause. At the same time, however, theory and empirical evidence can point to some possibilities. For the purposes of this chapter, I propose a rough division of such characteristics into factors we cannot affect — and therefore, cannot recommend for emulation elsewhere — and others that we can affect and, therefore, might commend to other countries.

Difficult or Impossible Factors to Emulate

Several "natural" aspects of Danish society might contribute to its success at controlling corruption. One is its small scale and social homogeneity. Small size can ease some of the logistical challenges of governance and law enforcement, for example. Social homogeneity might contribute to a strong social consensus on right and wrong, and on the role and conduct of government. Both factors might reduce the likelihood of deep social divisions of the sort that could convert politics into disjointed processes of patronage, and of related grievances that might justify, for some, bending or breaking rules of political procedure. Daniel Kaufmann has speculated on the connections between a society's size and its corruption problems, as one 2006 news report recounts:

> "Larger countries have high levels of corruption on average," said Dani Kaufmann, director of the Global Governance at the World Bank Institute and co-author of [a recent] study report. "This is not a steadfast rule," Dani, however, said, replying to a question. He added that there are some differences — some small countries have [the] worst form[s] of corruption and lack of governance. (United News of Bangladesh, 2006)

In addition, Denmark is regarded as having deep and extensive social capital, perhaps as an outgrowth, again, of its small size and extensive homogeneity (Laursen, Andersen, & Laursen, 2011). Social capital may help people check the activities of officials, and can add force to consensus values. While "building up civil society" is a frequent anti-corruption recommendation, where social capital is extensive it would seem more likely to be because of historical and cultural factors than any result of conscious reform efforts, and thus it falls into our category of factors that are difficult to emulate elsewhere. A related influence is the nation's political culture, which is relatively consensual, communal, and egalitarian in nature. Uslaner (2007, p. 15) has discussed those dimensions of political culture at some length, and while he places great emphasis on the value of extensive political and social trust, he suggests that avoiding an "inequality trap" is even more fundamental. In that connection, egalitarian Denmark might well benefit from corruption-inhibiting, good-governance encouraging influences. At the same time, consensus might create drawbacks of its own to the extent that it might inhibit whistleblowing, or increase incentives for elites and journalists to downplay corruption in order to maintain a clean international image for the nation as a whole. Either way, "soft" values-based corruption controls, the forces creating and sustaining them, and their perhaps-surprising weakness in larger and more diverse democracies such as the United States (Johnston, 2012; Maesschalck, 2004) may be a comparative dimension worth further scrutiny.

Denmark's modest experiences as an imperial power — with the exception of Greenland, as discussed above — might also be a positive factor, in the sense that Danish governments have had to produce positive economic results without resort to cheap colonial labor or resources, and without preferential access to colonial markets. In addition, to the extent that a string of colonies might encourage casual attitudes toward accountability, sound governance, human rights, and the rule of law, or could create privileged access and influence in Copenhagen for certain business interests (particularly extractive industries in various colonies), not being an imperial power might spare a country from some of the incentives and distractions that could contribute to corruption.

Along similar lines, Denmark's lack of resource dependence could marginally inhibit corruption. Here too, we do not know what that situation would be like if the country had been, say, an oil state, but we should probably watch the development of Greenlandic mining and the political activities of the wind-power industry — as discussed above — closely in the future.

Corruption Controls That Could be Exported and Emulated
Of the short list of corruption-checking factors in this section, not all can be exported everywhere, for some would seem to be connected to other

influences such as consensus, social homogeneity, small size, and social capital. Larger and more diverse societies might well have to look elsewhere for corruption-control opportunities. Still, the general soundness and legitimacy of the Danish state, courts, law enforcement, and parliament seem likely to produce legislation and other formal controls that would be well-accepted and congruent with social values and expectations. Clearly we cannot simply demand or proclaim such legitimacy elsewhere, but one possibility is that government, by governing in demonstrably fair and effective ways on a day-to-day basis, can build up trust and support for its laws, rules, and processes (that theme is explored in Johnston, 2011). Similarly, Rothstein (2011) places great emphasis on *impartiality* as a component of high-quality government. Rothstein and Uslaner (2005) add that "universal" social policies — not those targeted at the poor but rather those distributing resources and increasing opportunities across whole societies in demonstrably fair and accepted ways — help build trust:

> We argue that social trust is caused by two different, yet interrelated types of equality, namely, economic equality and equality of opportunity. This argument has important implications for public policy because universal social policies are more effective than selective ones in creating both types of equality and thereby social trust. (Rothstein & Uslaner, 2005, pp. 42–43)

Taking a variety of such ideas together, it is tempting to suggest that a well-run social democracy might enjoy a number of anti-corruption advantages, particularly in the context of a small and relatively homogenous society.

Another point often noted about Denmark is that its top political and administrative leaders lead decidedly modest lifestyles, and that the visible perquisites of political leadership are quite limited (Gilani, 2012). The parliamentary Speaker who commutes on a bicycle has already been noted. While the Danish royal family enjoys considerable outward prestige the political leadership is much less given over to cults of personality or the symbolism of power. It would seem plausible that offices thus constituted might attract a different sort of aspirant from those seeking office in some other societies, or at least might draw officials into an elite political culture that discourages ostentation while emphasizing service and accountability. As with many other such arguments there are real chicken-and-egg questions here: a low-key top officialdom might inhibit corruption in some ways and effectively draw upon social consensus, but at the same time we should ask what are the causes of such expectations and styles of leadership.

The way in which Parliament — the Folketing — is elected is important as well. A complicated system of proportional representation divides the nation into three "electoral provinces," and then into 10 multimember constituencies. Another 40 seats out of the total of 175 are filled through an allocation system reflecting overall party strength. Votes are counted by a "Hare System plus largest remainder" process, with any party winning two percent of the vote or more guaranteed at least some representation in the seat allocation (Folketinget, 2011, pp. 4–5). The result is a competitive parliamentary election system – one of the most truly proportional in the world, as judged by correspondence between vote percentages and the final allocations of seats. Eight parties currently hold seats, yet none controls much more than a quarter of the seats, and only about 0.9 percent of the electorate's preferences did not yield seats in the final results (Folketinget, 2011, p. 10). Both competition and cross-party cooperation are encouraged by the system; arguably such a system creates incentives for parties to scrutinize each other while operating within a framework of broadly shared values. In addition, election campaigns are publicly financed. That approach is not without potential costs in terms of democratic values (Van Biezen, 2004), to the extent that it might reduce the need for parties to cultivate and advocate the interests of a mass base, but it clearly does reduce exposure to pressure from contributors.

While these arrangements appear to work admirably well in Denmark, they are hardly a surefire plan for accountable and honest government. Elsewhere such power-sharing arrangements encourage cross-party collusion, or inflexible *Proporz*-style accommodations, that can weaken popular influence over policy and the conduct of government. In those settings the two largest parties can end up clinging to each other for mutual support, while a somewhat frustrated electorate becomes increasingly open to extreme alternatives as successive elections appear to produce little change. From the standpoint of corruption control, the ideal would be that the parties monitor each other and bring corruption issues to the fore, but it is also easy to imagine how leaders of such a system might find it advantageous to conceal ethical problems behind a guise of cooperation, consensus, and periodical electoral competition that in some countries might be more apparent than real. Precisely why that has not happened in Denmark will require further research.

Two other factors deserve mention too. One is the overall effectiveness of government: the WGI for 2011 gives Denmark a score of +2.17 on Government Effectiveness, and a +1.93 on Regulatory Quality. Both scores are good for a percentile ranking of 100 (tied with New Zealand for top scores) out of the 215 countries rated (World Bank, 2013). Those accomplishments are likely aided by small scale, social homogeneity, a strong working consensus, and, in recent generations, broad-based affluence. Danish government *works,* and works well, for most; incentives to circumvent rules or to build extra-systemic networks of influence are likely reduced by that fact. Affluence, after all, was not always part of the overall scene; during the 1930s, for example, Denmark suffered from some of the worst and most intractable unemployment problems in Western Europe (Judt, 2005). By now the direct memory of that era will have faded, but as recently as the early 1980s through the mid-1990s Danish unemployment ranged between 8 and 12 percent (Andersen & Svarer, 2006, p. 2). Perhaps there is a shared sense — similar to what one might expect to find in Singapore and Hong Kong — that whatever its shortcomings at any one time, the current system delivers a high quality of life, is likely to continue to do so, and that undermining its rules and procedures might be risky indeed. Similarly, economic development can be usefully regarded not just as a process of accumulating and distributing wealth, but one of *institution-building* as well (Sun & Johnston, 2010): banking, regulatory, taxation, social services, and other institutions, where they are strong, effective, and legitimate, not only foster affluence but make it more likely that an economy will withstand stresses and work according to consistent rules. We might well expect most Danes to feel a relatively strong stake in that system, particularly as they contemplate the realities of life as a very small country in a very big world.

Finally, of course, there are specific aspects of Danish anti-corruption controls. Those, broadly speaking, emphasize (and underline the legitimacy of) extensive state involvement in and scrutiny of economic activities, rather than the sort of vestigial state so often advocated by neoliberal thinkers during the 1980s and 1990s. While I have yet to review the country's corruption control policies in great detail, the general impression that emerges is that Denmark succeeds less because its control mechanisms are distinctive (indeed, in that connection EU policies probably constrain the options somewhat) than because those controls are well-enforced and widely accepted as legitimate (Business Anti-Corruption Portal, 2013; Chêne, 2011; Transparency International, 2013).

The nation's independent judiciary and the generally high quality of its bureaucracy are positive points too. The Parliamentary Ombudsman — an office established in 1955 and further defined by legislation in 1996 — fields citizen complaints of many sorts regarding the activities of national or local governments. In most years the office processes around 4,000 cases, including but not limited to questions of possible corruption. The

Ombudsman, who is required by law to be a law graduate and forbidden to serve on any local council, is appointed by and serves at the pleasure of the Folketing, and files an annual public report each Autumn. The Ombudsman is also empowered to initiate investigations of his or her own; while opinions and recommendations issued by the office do not in themselves have the force of law, they are given considerable weight by the Ombudsman's parliamentary mandate, and are generally taken very seriously. Precisely what effect the Ombudsman's office has had on corruption over the years is impossible to say, but it is worth noting that the Danish/Scandinavian model of an Ombudsman empowered to monitor government performance has been emulated, with widely varying degrees of success, in several other countries around the world.[2] Similarly, the Public Accounts Committee (some, but not all of whose, members are drawn from the Folketing) and the Auditor General's Office, also empowered by the Folketing, oversee the use of public resources and report to both parliament and the public.[3]

Whatever the details of an anti-corruption regime, it seems likely that once it includes the full range of familiar administrative and other controls now familiar to the corruption control movement, the main challenge is that those controls be well- and predictably implemented, and that they be integrated into a demonstrably fair overall system of government. Denmark, by all accounts, meets that standard.

Perhaps the general verdict of this part of the discussion is that controlling corruption is inseparable from the larger challenges of *governing well*, in a fair, predictable, and demonstrably effective manner. That, of course, is no simple matter. It does seem likely that small, affluent, and homogenous societies — and perhaps, social democracies in particular — would enjoy some built-in advantages in that regard. Still, it is not difficult to think of relatively new democracies that are small and homogeneous and yet, perhaps because of recent conflicts and continuing economic difficulties, are still struggling with the quality of government. Once again it is difficult to separate causes and effects. Denmark did not become affluent and well-governed simply because it checked corruption, and it seems equally unlikely that it checked corruption solely because it is affluent and well-governed. Rather, all of those desirable outcomes are likely linked to a range of other cultural and historical developments, many of which may not be open to emulation elsewhere. Denmark presents a favorable anti-corruption profile, but whether there is a "Danish model" that might travel well to other societies is quite a different question.

H3: Denmark Has Little Corruption Because of International, Not Domestic, Factors

A final set of speculations deals with Denmark's role in the world. No society is immune to outside influences, and smaller ones might be particularly open to such forces, be they for good or for ill.

One possible connection involves Denmark's extensive integration with international and intergovernmental organizations. Chief among them, of course, is the EU, but others include the United Nations (and specifically, the UN Convention Against Corruption), Organization for Economic Co-operation and Development, Council of Europe, World Trade Organization, and conceivably NATO and the Organization for Security and Cooperation in Europe (OSCE) as well. The first four in particular lay down anti-corruption policies of various sorts, along with mutual monitoring procedures. NATO and OSCE are relatively unconnected to broader governance agendas, but do emphasize active membership by, and cooperation among, democracies; OSCE also has a significant human-rights agenda. All might help maintain the cross-border, regional, and global scrutiny that is increasingly necessary in response to global corruption: consider efforts to check money-laundering and trafficking in human beings and arms. Between 2006 and 2010 Denmark significantly upgraded its anti-money laundering systems as a result of consultations, and a certain amount of pressure, originating within the Financial Action Task Force (FATF), an international body established by the G-7 governments in 1989.[4] All of those international connections are likely to contribute to the sharing of expertise and information, both of which Denmark's effective governmental system would be well-positioned to accept and employ. The EU's anti-corruption record, however, has not exactly been stellar (Warner, 2007), and behind the liberalization policies that were central to many international organizations' anti-corruption thinking for many years there lurk new, and ever-more-elusive, opportunities to carry out and conceal corrupt schemes.

General integration into the world economy, however, has been cited by Treisman (2000) among others as a positive factor in corruption control, and Denmark certainly meets that test. Indeed, the exigencies of economic survival as a small state among much larger competitors might well encourage sound, effective government; such pressures have arguably contributed to the successes of Singapore and Hong Kong as well. Those influences might include the role of the Danish state as a credible guarantor in trade and aid policy, and the very considerable value of a positive reputation as a destination for foreign direct investment. More will be said about the possible effects of global integration and connectedness in a discussion below.

PUTTING IDEAS TO A TEST: FIRST INDICATIONS

As suggested earlier, most theories and measures of corruption are better-suited to identifying and analyzing governance problems than to explaining success. Accounting for corruption that does not seem to occur is a challenge, if only at a logical level and certainly in terms of amassing a body of valid and reliable evidence. Causality is complicated as well; simultaneities are endemic to virtually all of the propositions offered so far. One major risk is that our explanations will merely confuse our assumptions with our conclusions if we simply use some positive attributes of a society to "explain" positive outcomes. In the long run, most of the ideas proposed so far can only really be tested by detailed case-studies and process-oriented analysis of a sort that lies beyond the scope of this chapter.

Hypotheses 2 and 3 — that characteristics of Danish society, and/or its extensive engagement with the rest of the world, might help check corruption — however are open to some cross-sectional comparison. This section offers a preliminary, and deliberately very simple, data analysis related to those ideas; results tend to support some, if not all, of the propositions offered regarding that hypothesis, and also invite a closer look at some less tangible, but still critical, ways of checking corruption. Specifically, I assembled indicators of social scale and homogeneity (population, area, ethnic fractionalization, and linguistic fractionalization), resource dependence (fuel exports as a percentage of all merchandise exports), and political competition (from the Polity IV dataset) for just over 100 countries. Also included were data on affluence (GDP per capita) and the security of property rights (Heritage Foundation index). A final indicator is the Index of Global Connectedness compiled by DHL, the German-based international shipping firm. Details and sources for all of those indicators are listed in the appendix.

But what can we use for a dependent variable? While the TI CPI and the WGI Control of Corruption indicator have their strengths and definite uses, neither is a measure of corruption as such. An interesting alternative, however, is a survey-based index of *impartial public administration* gathered by the Quality of Government (QoG) Institute at the University of Gothenburg, Sweden (Dahlström, Lapuente, & Teorell, 2011; see also data

source details in the appendix). As noted earlier, Rothstein and his colleagues have made a strong case that impartiality is a core principle of high-
quality government. The QoG index is based on an expert survey (much
like the CPI in recent years), and thus is subject to all of the *caveats* offered
with respect to the other corruption indices: at the very least, it is worth
remembering that it does not measure the *fact* or actual extent of impartiality in government, but rather some informed judgments as to how impartial
a country's public administration is. Like perceptions of corruption such
judgments are open to influences of many sorts, not least of which the
evaluators' general impressions of a society's level of governmental attainment. Still, it has some advantages: impartiality is not only a positive aspect
of high-quality government, which is the real outcome we are trying
to account for in the case of Denmark, but is also a much more specific
attribute, with a widely shared meaning and interpretation, than is "corruption." That latter idea is notoriously hard to define and, quite likely, can be
influenced by an even wider range of impressions and influences.

A further *caveat* is that cross-sectional data analysis, even when we are
confident of our measures, tells us only about relationships among variables
across a large number of cases. Even if the results are strong and clear-cut
for those cases, that does not prove that the indicated relationships are the
reasons why corruption appears to be uncommon *in Denmark*. Testing
of any causal claims for that society would require detailed case studies.
A final problem is that as with many data-driven analyses of governance,
the concepts, and variables in question are rife with simultaneity. Simply
put, causes and effects are deeply entangled, and thus claims of causality are
difficult to validate. Thus, the following analysis is offered only as a preliminary way of asking whether our thoughts about good government in
Denmark are worth further investigation.

Correlates of Impartial Public Administration

The QoG impartiality variable (hereafter, "QoG"), available for 107 countries, does not produce results identical to the major corruption indices, but
neither does it produce surprising or strongly counterintuitive assessments.
The simple correlation between QoG and the TI CPI is .866; with the WGI
Control of Corruption indicator it is .874 ($p = \sim.000$ for both correlations).
The scatterplot below shows that the relationship between QoG impartiality and TI CPI is positive and largely consistent across all values of both
variables, although the relationship is somewhat tighter at the upper (high

impartiality/low corruption) end of the two survey variables. That may reflect a greater familiarity on the part of the experts with many of those apparently well-governed countries. The two clearest outliers are the United Arab Emirates (ARE) and Puerto Rico (PRI); the latter was excluded from the analysis, in the end, because of missing values on other indicators (Fig. 1).

Two other indicators gathered for the analysis — GDP per Capita, and Security of Property Rights — were also strongly correlated with the QoG scores (.749 and .866, respectively; $p = \sim.000$ for each coefficient). In part because of that very strong covariation, but mostly because both might just as easily be interpreted as *results* of low levels of corruption/high-quality government, as well as, or instead of, as causes, I have not included them in further analysis. That decision reflects the general simultaneity problem noted above, but does not mean that affluence and security of property rights are off the table as important factors in the discussion. Instead, they will likely be better studied in the context of more specific case and process studies. What relationships stand out between the Impartiality scores and our other data, then? Some simple correlations are presented in Table 3.

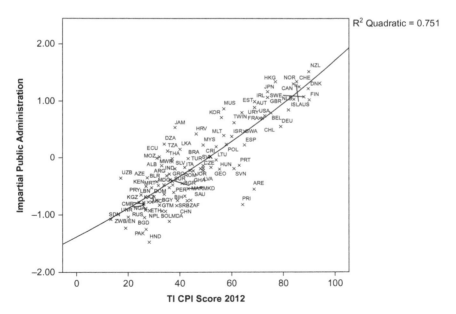

Fig. 1. Scatterplot of QoG Impartiality and TI CPI Scores.

Table 3.   Simple Correlations among Variables.

	Impartial Pub Admin (QoG)	Ethnic Fractional-ization	Linguistic Fractional-ization	Population (log)	Area (log)	GINI
Ethnic fractionalization (Alesina et al.)	−.383 .000					
Linguistic fractionalization (Alesina)	−.248 .006	.666 .000				
Population (log)	−.239 .008	.118 .120	.197 .024			
Area (log)	−.181 .035	.247 .006	.168 .046	.708 .000		
Gini coefficient	−.375 .000	.392 .000	.136 .087	.160 .050	.287 .002	
Political Competition 2011 (Polity IV)	.505 .000	−.262 .004	−.239 .008	−.209 .018	−.231 .010	−.050 .311

$N = 101$; probabilities are one-tailed tests.

These results provide some initial support for the notion that smaller and more homogeneous societies might have better luck in controlling corruption or maintaining high-quality government. For the 101 countries for which all indicators were available, small populations and areas, and low levels of ethnic and linguistic fractionalization, are associated with judgments of high levels of impartiality in public administration. So too are lower levels of income inequality (Gini). Much the strongest predictor of Impartiality scores is Political Competition: competitive political processes are positively correlated with judgments of impartial administration, negatively related to greater size and area, and − perhaps surprisingly − negatively related to ethnic and linguistic fractionalization (more on those connections to come, below). The biggest surprise at this stage of the analysis was the *weakness* of the Fuel Exports variable: it was not related significantly to the Impartiality index, or indeed to other variables of interest, either in terms of simple correlations or in the regressions to be discussed below. Fuel as a share of exports may well be a flawed resource-dependency measure, even though it does return high values for the usual "resource curse" suspects; thus, for now the notion that Denmark's lack of resource dependence makes for better-quality government remains without support or, depending upon how we view the fuel-exports variable, untested.

Simple linear regression (OLS) simplified the analysis somewhat (see Table 4): indicators of social scale (logged values of both population and area, as well as population density) dropped out as significant predictors, as did linguistic fractionalization – not surprising because of its close correlation with the somewhat stronger ethnic fractionalization variable. The remaining variables lend support to the argument that Denmark's quality of government may indeed be linked to social homogeneity, extensive equality, and political competitiveness. Low levels of ethnic fractionalization, and of income inequality, are statistically linked to high QoG scores; the strongest single predictor, again, is political competition. These results suggest, but of course cannot by themselves prove, that high levels

Table 4. Regression Analysis.

R	R-Square	Adjusted R-Square	Std. Error of Estimate	df1	df2	Significance
.567	.321	.301	.60375	3	101	.000

Analysis of Variance

	Sum of Squares	df	Mean Square	F	Significance
Regression	17.429	3	5.810	15.938	.000
Residual	36.816	101	.365		
Total	54.245	104			

Coefficients

Model	Unstandardized Coefficients		Standardized Coefficients	t	Significance
	B	Std. Error	Beta		
(Constant)	.034	.326		.104	.917
Ethnic fractionalization (Alesina et al)	−.754	.264	−.254	−2.852	.005
Gini coefficient	−.016	.007	−.209	−2.400	.018
Political Competition 2011 – Polity IV	.100	.024	.353	4.206	.000

$N = 104$; dependent variable: QoG Index of Impartial Public Administration.

of political competition within homogeneous and egalitarian societies may be effective in holding governments accountable to widely shared standards and expectations. In that sort of setting, political competition would seem less likely to revolve around delivering particularistic benefits for specific constituencies than to emphasize better government performance generally. In that connection the strong simple correlations between Impartiality Scores, on the one hand, and GDP per capita and secure property rights on the other (noted at the start of this section) might reflect a tendency for all three variables to measure strongly similar attributes of effective government, but they could also suggest that competing to govern impartially *and well* in a society where the day-to-day meanings of such outcomes are matters of consensus is a good recipe for accountability and effective corruption control. More subtle qualitative and case-oriented research could help us distinguish more clearly among affluence, secure property rights, the rule of law, and impartial administration.

In themselves, these findings are not particularly surprising. It must also be acknowledged that the statistical strength of the equation (adjusted R-square of .301) leaves much to be accounted for. Moreover, straightforward policy prescriptions are few: encouraging political competition is likely a good thing in itself, within agreed rules and limits of course, but can also bring corruption risks of its own (Johnston, 2005, Chapter 4). No one would seriously propose redrawing the map to create small countries as a corruption-control strategy, and ethnic cleansing in the name of reform is, to put it politely, an utter non-starter. But there may be a subtler, and more workable, anti-corruption strategy behind the data too. Consider a path analysis among the variables in the equation above, as presented in Fig. 2.

These results suggest − not surprisingly − that ethnic fragmentation can contribute to less-impartial administration both directly and (weaker in

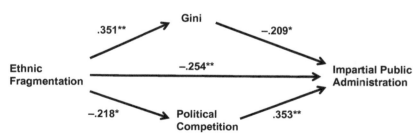

Fig. 2.   Path Analysis. $**p = <.01$; $*p = <.05$.

statistical terms) indirectly, by fostering greater inequality and through political competition. Differing segments of society, particularly if they are unequal in terms of wealth and other resources, and (the data suggest) if they contend in the political sphere, seem likely to demand and obtain contrasting, and less-than-impartial, treatment by government. The negative relationship between Ethnic Fragmentation and Political Competition might seem surprising in itself; on its face the Polity IV indicator of competition seems tilted somewhat in favor of the kind of competition seen in democracies, so perhaps we are picking up the effect of factors over and above the simple fact of competition, such as strong political rules, legitimate institutions, and the like. But there is some evidence that greater ethnic fragmentation inhibits political competition in various regions of Russia (Lazarev, 2011), and in African nations as well (Keefer, 2010). Moreover, deep ethnic divisions might be linked to conflict and violence rather than to political competition as such. The upshot of the path diagram above might be that contending ethnic factions might find it more effective to seek administrative advantages directly, be it through corruption or various sorts of ethnic ties and appeals to officials, than to go through the cumbersome processes of politics. The positive relationship between ethnic fragmentation and greater inequality might also suggest that in divided societies many groups simply lack the resources to compete effectively in the political arena. Here again, the data raise some tantalizing possibilities that cannot be directly confirmed here.

But they also raise two further questions. First, whatever a society's level of ethnic fractionalization, could taxation, spending, and other policies aimed at reducing income inequalities over time, and could political-finance, electoral-system, and party laws encouraging more competitive politics, at least marginally counteract the corruption/partiality implications of ethnic divisions? Over the long-term such policies might well give smaller and less-influential ethnic factions ways and means with which to check less-than-impartial administration. The second question is this: how, in practice, do more homogeneous and egalitarian societies encourage and reward impartial government? Active political competition seems to be a part of the answer, but even there the question remains of how and why more competitive politics might stay focused on effective government. The broader, and more tantalizing, possibility − one requiring much more rigorous testing than cross-sectional data can provide − might have to do with the strength of "soft," or values-based, corruption controls (Johnston, 2012; Maesschalck, 2004). At the homogeneous and egalitarian end of the social scale, we might be seeing consensus, shared values, and a common identity at work, quite likely accompanied by significant levels of political and social trust. I did not include trust data in this analysis, in part, because here too it is difficult to say whether trust is a cause or an effect of high-quality government, but mostly because the sorts of trust data available across large numbers of societies strike me as dubious in their validity and reliability. Trust, I would argue, is one more part of the picture best assessed in qualitative, highly detailed ways.

Can any of these corruption-inhibiting, impartiality-building factors — all of which are still matters mostly of speculation here — be applied in societies where they are not already in place long since, and where significant corruption has yet to be checked? Consensus and shared identity cannot simply be proclaimed, and trust must be carefully cultivated and *earned*. For competing political parties and candidates the immediate incentives to mobilize specific constituencies will be compelling, regardless of high-flown rhetoric and calls for unity. Still, one possibility is that even in fragile and deeply divided societies, trust can be built, and expectations of better government deepened, by demonstrably improving government performance, even (at first) in just a few important service sectors (see, e.g., Johnston, 2011). Showing that government can do a few things central to a better quality of life — building roads, providing public utilities — in effective and fair ways, and that it can *demonstrate* those tendencies and accomplishments by publishing evidence of performance, may be a valuable step toward better government. It could help build trust in officials and credibility of policies and agencies; reduce the sense among citizens that they are engaged in zero-sum competition, based on favoritism, with each other; and encourage expectations that government, its performance, and the day-to-day quality of life can be improved. The trust to be gained in that way — and it will likely build only slowly at first — may never approach Danish levels: it is after all a long-established society. Moreover, most countries will be considerably larger in scale, making for more internal divisions as well as practical challenges of governing and delivering services; but then in much larger societies a Danish level of homogeneity and consensus might not only be improbable, but also undesirable, in some respects. Still, there is a reform strategy visible here: *begin as you mean to continue*. Begin by governing well and fairly, even if only in a few service sectors. Demonstrate that improvements are taking place. Show citizens that trusting each other, and backing leaders who seem likely to govern well, can be a way to improve the quality of life — not just a way to watch others gain unfair advantages. Then, as the history of Denmark (founded, by many accounts, in the year 1167) suggests, stay with that strategy for a very long time.

Engagement with the World

A second hypothesis on which some fragmentary data are available is that having to do with "global connectedness": the extent, diversity, and breadth of a country's interactions with the rest of the world. Conceivably such engagement might facilitate the diffusion of reform values, "best practices," and expectations of trustworthiness (the classic argument that repeated interactions can build cooperation and trust is that of Axelrod, 1984). Equally, for a country – particularly a smaller one, we might speculate – to be *able* to engage in trade and other interactions, to capitalize upon such links and transactions, maintain its policies, and defend its own interests and that of its citizens and business firms, it must develop strong institutions and a working consensus on how things are to be done. Extensive global engagement might be linked to more impartial administration by a number of paths.

As a preliminary test of such ideas I used the DHL Global Connectedness Index (Ghemawat & Altman, 2012). The index is derived from extensive data on a variety of kinds of exchange activities – trade, information, people, and capital – and assigns scores to over a hundred countries based on the depth (share of aggregate economic activity that is international in scope) and breath (geographic reach) of their international connections. An important advantage of the index is that it is derived from data on actual exchange activity, rather than inferred from information on factors such as sound banking and legal frameworks that might *enable* international engagement. Thus, the index is not just measuring sound institutions and governance by another name. On the downside, however, it is easy to imagine that our impartiality rankings might be positively biased by the sorts of affluence and international prestige that might accompany extensive global connectedness. Thus, a good deal of caution is still in order about the results reported here. While the Connectedness Index has been calculated and published for 2012 (Ghemawat & Altman, 2012), the exact numerical results for that year are apparently being held as proprietary data, and are reported to the general public using only graphs without precise values. Thus, I have used the 2011 figures, which are reported numerically.

Nonetheless, those results are striking in statistical terms. The simple correlation between the QoG impartiality index and the Global Connectedness Index is $+.661$ ($N = 101$, $p = \sim.000$): whatever the possible causal connections or varieties of simultaneity involved, greater global engagement and more impartial public administration are quite likely found in the same societies. Entering the Connectedness variable into the regression analysis above significantly increased the R-square (to .536) for the 99 countries for which all variables were available; not only was the effect of connectedness strong, it seems to hold true regardless of ethnic divisions and inequality: both the fractionalization variable and the Gini index dropped out of the equation, with only political competition remaining as another positive predictor of QoG impartiality scores (see Table 5).

To the extent that we place credence in these data, even relatively divided and unequal societies are seen as practicing more impartial administration when they are extensively engaged with the rest of the world, and enjoy competitive domestic politics. Causality (if any) is complex and likely riddled with simultaneities, as I have noted at several points. Moreover, connecting with the rest of the world, particularly on a favorable and productive basis, is no simple task. Institutions must be built, along with facilities; legal frameworks must be strengthened, international affiliations extended, and expectations − both domestic and on the part of possible

Table 5. Regression Analysis Incorporating Global Connectedness Indicator.

R	R-Square	Adjusted R- Square	Std. Error of the Estimate
.732	.536	.517	.50758

Analysis of Variance

	Sum of Squares	df	Mean Square	F	Significance
Regression	28.316	4	7.079	27.477	.000
Residual	24.476	95	.258		
Total	52.792	99			

Coefficients

Model	Unstandardized coefficients		Standardized coefficients	t	Significance
	B	Std. Error	Beta		
(Constant)	−2.105	.418		−5.042	.000
Ethnic fractionalization	−.327	.238	−.108	−1.374	.173
Gini coefficient	.005	.006	.062	.743	.459
Political competition	.087	.021	.299	4.153	.000
Global connectedness	.027	.004	.580	6.582	.000

international counterparts − cultivated. Particularly in uncertain times those tasks, along with international engagement in general, may well encounter significant domestic political resistance.

Still, a plot of the QoG and Connectedness Indices lends intriguing, if tentative, support to the notion that once such steps have been taken and connectedness has taken root, a kind of international synergy might become possible, as shown in Fig. 3.

The data suggest that as connectedness to other countries grows, perceptions of impartial public administration increase at a sharply increasing rate. Precisely what causal connections underlie that finding − to the extent that we take it seriously − is a matter of conjecture, although it is tempting to guess that the rewards of international connectedness and exchange relationships are greater where government and administration are more impartial, creating incentives to strengthen such aspects of the quality of government, and that such improvements facilitate further engagement. In the case of Denmark, that account has considerable face validity; but again, establishing its accuracy and understanding it in greater detail would

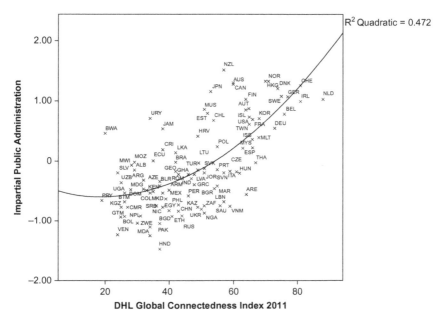

Fig. 3.   Scatterplot of QoG Impartiality and DHL Global Connectedness Indices.

require much more detailed case- and process-oriented evidence. More ambitious statistical techniques could no doubt disentangle some of the simultaneities among our variables, but the limitations of the Impartiality measure — even though it improves upon existing corruption indices in several ways — would remain. While a more sophisticated statistical explanation of variation in the Impartiality index is certainly possible, it is less clear that such work would yield a richer substantive understanding of successful corruption control in general — much less, of the full range of reasons for the apparent success of Denmark, the country that sparked this discussion in the first place.

CONCLUSION: QUESTIONS FOR THE LONGER TERM

The discussion so far has produced much speculation, and few convincing answers, as regards Denmark's apparent success at checking corruption. But perhaps it has helped define useful hypotheses for further research. Such work might well consider broader questions as well. One is whether market democracies, with their favorable corruption-index scores, do not so much control corruption as remove the incentives for it by (in a positive view) offering accountable and fair government, or (more negative) through policies and institutions so friendly to wealth and business interests that bribery is no longer necessary. Denmark's egalitarian style and relatively extensive government apparatus make the latter possibility seem unlikely. But a generally pro-business outlook, or institutionalized cooperation mechanisms such as the "Danish Labor Market" approach might still reduce the incentives to bend or break rules by giving well-institutionalized interests a great deal of what they seek through legitimate channels, and give such favorable outcomes considerable political protection and legitimacy. An even more general proposition is that because of global and regional economic integration, and as a result of the growth of business corporations that seemingly do business everywhere while being held accountable nowhere, corruption is receding into the protective camouflage of global markets — processes that move so quickly and exploit so many opportunities and loopholes around the world that conventional notions and indications of corruption are becoming obsolete. Global business, in that view, might not engage in corruption in Denmark because they have little need for the Danish state or economy to begin with. That, too, remains only speculation at this point, although it will be interesting to watch Danish activities under the OECD convention and UNCAC to get some sense of how the nation is involved in, and responds to, global markets.

A final issue, and one that will be central if the analysis of apparently successful anti-corruption regimes is to proceed, might somewhat melodramatically be called *the quest for a dependent variable*. TI/CPI scores and WGI are interesting and useful, though more extensive and subtle comparisons among such data will be necessary if only to take the size and homogeneity of societies, and the evolving legal and normative climate of the global economy, into account. The QoG impartiality scores draw on more precise and agreed concepts than do corruption indices; moreover, they emphasize a positive element of *good* government, rather than just aiming at the absence of corruption − arguably, an incomplete conception of what high-quality government ought to look like. In my view the QoG data deserve widespread application and testing, but they too suffer the drawbacks of being perception-based survey data. Can we come up with better approaches to measuring corruption itself? Quite possibly we can, as long as we are willing to accept indirect approaches. As I have suggested elsewhere (Johnston, 2009, 2010), indicators and benchmarks of government performance can shed light on the effects of past corruption, and on the incentives sustaining, or inhibiting, it in the here and now. Perhaps a broader construct-validity approach that incorporates such indicators into broader evidence of accountability, impartiality, and legitimacy will prove to be the best approach. That sort of approach might, again, tend to favor more democratic and advanced societies to the extent that they routinely make more public information available. In addition, the results of such work are unlikely to yield any new index values that parse out international rankings out to the nth decimal place − although a case can be made that such apparent precision is usually misleading to begin with. They might, however, both reflect and reinforce a key argument of the discussion thus far, which is that both corruption problems and effective controls are embedded in broader considerations of high-quality government performance, fairness, and justice.

NOTES

1. For this discussion I owe a major debt to Dr. Mette Frisk Jensen, University of Aarhus. Her doctoral research and other studies provide the most complete and authoritative survey of corruption issues through Danish history; the work is at

present available only in Danish (see Jensen, 2013), but she was kind enough to provide me with an English-language overview of some of her key findings. I hope that her work will be published in English translation, as it provides the essential historical context to the whole question of corruption control in Denmark. For a good reference on the general history of Denmark, see Jespersen (2004).

    2. See for example Gellhorn (1966) for an analysis of the functioning of the Ombudsman in Denmark, Finland, New Zealand, Norway, and Sweden.

    3. Descriptions of the Ombudsman, Public Accounts Committee, and Auditor General Office can be found at http:// www.thedanishparliament.dk/About_the_Danish_Parliament/Institutions_of_the_Danish_Parliament.aspx. Retrieved on July 13, 2013.

    4. Details of the FATF in Denmark are available at http://www.fatf-gafi.org/countries/d-i/denmark/. Retrieved on April 2, 2013.

REFERENCES

Andersen, T., & Svarer, M. (2006). *Flexicurity — The Danish labor market model.* Department of Economics, University of Aarhus. Retrieved from http://mit.econ.au.dk/vip_htm/msn/flexicurity_eng.pdf. Accessed on April 3, 2013.

Axelrod, R. (1984). *The evolution of cooperation.* New York, NY: Basic Books.

Business Anti-Corruption Portal. (2013). *Danish public and private anti-corruption initiatives.* Retrieved from http://www.business-anti-corruption.com/anti-corruption-initiatives/partner-initia tives/denmark/. Accessed on April 3, 2013.

Chêne, M. (2011). *What makes New Zealand, Denmark, Finland, Sweden and others 'cleaner' than most countries?* Transparency International, "Space for Transparency," December 7. Retrieved from http://blog.transparency.org/2011/12/07/what-makes-new-zealand-denmark-finland-sweden-and-others-%E2%80%9Ccleaner%E2%80%9D-than-most-countries/. Accessed on April 3, 2013.

Dahlström, C., Lapuente, V., & Teorell, J. (2011). *Dimensions of bureaucracy II: A cross-national dataset on the structure and behavior of public administration.* QoG Working Paper Series 2011:6. Quality of Government Institute, University of Gothenburg, Gothenburg.

Delingpole, J. (2012). Big wind: The most corrupt and corrupting industry in the world. *The Telegraph blogs*, November 19. Retrieved from http://blogs.telegraph.co.uk/news/jamesdelingpole/ 100190461/big-wind-the-most-corrupt-and-corrupting-industry-in-the-world/. Accessed on April 3, 2013.

Folketinget (Danish Parliament). (2011). *The parliamentary electoral system in Denmark.* Copenhagen: Folketinget.

Gellhorn, W. (1966). *Ombudsmen and others: Citizens' protectors in nine countries.* Cambridge, MA: Harvard University Press.

Ghemawat, P., & Altman, S. A. (2012). *DHL global connectedness index 2012.* Bonn: Deutsche Post-DHL. Retrieved from http://www.dhl.com/en/about_us/logistics_insights/studies_research/global_connectedness_index/global_connectedness_index_2012.html. Accessed on April 3, 2013.

Gilani, I. (2012). What makes Denmark corruption-free. *Cocreatenow.org*. Retrieved from http://cocreatenow.org/2012/11/iftikhar-gilani-in-inquilab-about-corruption/. Accessed on February 15, 2013.

Index Mundi. (2013). Retrieved from http://www.indexmundi.com/denmark/seats-held-by-women-in-national-parliament,-percentage.html. Accessed on February 17, 2013.

Inter-Parliamentary Union. (2012, December 31). *Women in national parliaments*. Retrieved from http://www.ipu.org/wmn-e/classif.htm. Accessed on February 17, 2013.

Jensen, M. F. (2013). *Korruption og embedsetik : danske embedsmænds korruption i perioden 1800–1866 (Corruption and official ethics: Danish official corruption in the period 1800–1866)*. Odense: Syddansk Universitetsforlag (University Press of Southern Denmark).

Jespersen, K. J. V. (2004). *A history of Denmark* (I. Hill, Trans.). Basingstoke: Palgrave Macmillan.

Johnston, M. (2005). *Syndromes of corruption: Wealth, power, and democracy*. New York, NY: Cambridge University Press.

Johnston, M. (2009). *Components of integrity: Data and benchmarks for tracking trends in government*. Paris: Organisation for Economic Co-operation and Development. Retrieved from http://www.oecd.org/officialdocuments/displaydocumentpdf?cote = GOV/PGC/GF% 282009%292&doclanguage = en. Accessed on April 3, 2013.

Johnston, M. (2010). Assessing vulnerabilities to corruption: Indicators and benchmarks of government performance. *Public Integrity*, *12*(2), 125–142.

Johnston, M. (2011). *First, do no harm – then, build trust: Anti-corruption strategies in fragile situations*. Background Paper for the 2011 World Development Report, World Bank, Washington, DC. Retrieved from http://siteresources.worldbank.org/EXTWDR2011/Resources/6406082-12838824 18764/WDR_Background_Paper_Johnston.pdf. Accessed on April 3, 2013.

Johnston, M. (2012). Corruption control in the United States: Law, values, and the political foundations of reform. *International Review of Administrative Sciences*, *78*(2), 329–345.

Johnston, M. (2013). *Corruption, contention, and reform: The power of deep democratization*. New York, NY: Cambridge University Press.

Judt, T. (2005). *Postwar: A history of Europe since 1945*. New York, NY: Penguin Press.

Keefer, P. (2010). *The ethnicity distraction? Political credibility and partisan preferences in Africa*. Policy Research Paper 5236, World Bank, Washington, DC. Retrieved from http://elibrary.worldbank.org/content/workingpaper/10.1596/1813-9450-5236. Accessed on April 3, 2013.

Laursen, F., Andersen, T. M., & Laursen, D. J. (2011). *Sustainable governance indicators 2011: Denmark report*. Bertelsman Stiftung, Gütersloh. Retrieved from http://www.sgi-network.org/pdf/SGI11_Denmark.pdf. Accessed on April 3, 2013.

Lazarev, Y. (2011). Ethnic diversity and political competition: Evidence from local elections in Dagestan. Paper presented at the XII HSE International Academic Conference on Economic and Social Development. Retrieved from http://regconf.hse.ru/uploads/79530ca1f9c9d7a0ee013d78bbb e1d7290a4153a.doc. Accessed on April 3, 2013.

Lessig, L. (2011). *Republic, lost: How money corrupts Congress – And a plan to stop it*. New York, NY: Twelve Books.

Lindgreen, A. (2004). Corruption and unethical behavior: Report on a set of Danish guidelines. *Journal of Business Ethics*, *51*(1), 31–39.

Maesschalck, J. (2004). Approaches to ethics management in the public sector: A proposed extension of the compliance-integrity continuum. *Public Integrity*, *7*(1), 21–41.

Namulando, S. (2012). Denmark's [sic] cuts aid to OPM. *The Independent* (Kampala), November 1. Retrieved from http://www.independent.co.ug/news/news/6720-bou-sets-november-cbr-to-125. Accessed on April 3, 2013.

Reuters. (2012). World Bank reassesses Uganda aid after graft allegations. *ChicagoTribune.com*, November 14. Retrieved from http://www.reuters.com/article/2012/11/14/us-uganda-aid-idUSBRE8AD17G20121114. Accessed on April 3, 2013.

Rørdam, P. (2012). The myth of Denmark as a corruption-free country. *The Copenhagen Post*, November 16. Retrieved from http://cphpost.dk/commentary/opinion/opinion-myth-denmark-corruption-free-country. Accessed on April 3, 2013.

Rothstein, B. (2011). *The quality of government: Corruption, social trust and inequality in international perspective*. Chicago, IL: University of Chicago Press.

Rothstein, B., & Uslaner, E. M. (2005). All for all: Equality, corruption, and social trust. *World Politics, 58*(1), 41–72.

Schwab, K. (Ed.) (2012). *The global competitiveness report 2012–2013*. Geneva: World Economic Forum.

Sun, Y., & Johnston, M. (2010). Does democracy check corruption? Insights from China and India. *Comparative Politics, 42*(2), 1–19.

Transparency International. (2013). *Corruption by country/territory: Denmark*. Retrieved from http://www.transparency.org/country#DNK. Accessed on April 3, 2013.

Treisman, D. (2000). The causes of corruption: A cross-national study. *Journal of Public Economics, 76*(3), 399–457.

United News of Bangladesh. (2006). Some OECD countries have high level of corruption: World Bank report. *United News of Bangladesh*, September 15.

Uslaner, E. M. (2007). *Corruption, inequality, and trust*. Unpublished manuscript, University of Maryland. Retrieved from http://www.bsos.umd.edu/gvpt/uslaner/uslanersocialcapitalhandbook elgar.pdf. Accessed on April 3, 2013.

Van Biezen, I. (2004). Political parties as public utilities. *Party Politics, 10*(6), 701–722.

Villarino, E. (2013). Denmark's new aid transparency package: 5 key features. *Devex.com*, January 30. Retrieved from https://www.devex.com/en/news/denmark-s-transparency-package-5-key-features/80221. Accessed on April 3, 2013.

Wang, H., & Rosenau, J. N. (2001). Transparency international and corruption as an issue of global governance. *Global Governance, 7*(1), 25–49.

Warner, C. M. (2007). *The best system money can buy: Corruption in the European Union*. Ithaca, NY: Cornell University Press.

Weaver, R. (2012). In the kingdom of the least corrupt, Greenland remains uncharted territory. *Copenhagen Post*, December 10. Retrieved from http://cphpost.dk/news/national/kingdom-least-corrupt-greenland-remains-uncharted-territory. Accessed on April 3, 2013.

World Bank. (2013). *Worldwide governance indicators*. Washington, DC. Retrieved from http://info.worldbank.org/governance/wgi/index.asp. Accessed on March 29, 2013.

World Factbook. (2013). *Denmark*. Retrieved from https://www.cia.gov/library/publications/the-world-factbook/geos/da.html. Accessed on March 29, 2013.

APPENDIX: DATA SOURCES

(All websites viewed April 3, 2013)
Country population and area: WorldAtlas.com
http://www.worldatlas.com/aatlas/populations/ctypopls.htm

DHL Global Connectedness Index: http://www.dhl.com/en/about_us/
logistics_insights/studies_research/global_connectedness_index/global_
connectedness_index_2012/gci_results.html

Ethnic and Linguistic Fractionalization: reported in Alesina, A., Devleeschauwer, A., Easterly, W., Kurlat, S. & Wacziarg, R. (2003). "Fractionalization." *Journal of Economic Growth, 8* (2) (June), 155–194. Available at http://www.jstor.org/stable/40215942.

Fuel Exports as percentage of all merchandise exports: World Bank
http://data.worldbank.org/indicator/TX.VAL.FUEL.ZS.UN

GDP per capita: World Bank, http://data.worldbank.org/indicator/NY.
GDP.PCAP.CD
Suriname and Taiwan: from *IndexMundi.com*, http://www.indexmundi.
com/g/g.aspx?c = ns&v = 67 and http://www.indexmundi.com/g/g.aspx?c =
tw&v = 67

Gini coefficient data: Unless noted below, Gini data are from *World Factbook* (2013). Available at https://www.cia.gov/library/publications/the-world-factbook/.

Figures for Lebanon, Saudi Arabia, Sudan, UAE are from Global Peace Index, http://economicsandpeace.org/research/iep-indices-data/global-peace-index
Suriname from http://www.tradingeconomics.com/suriname/gini-index-wb-data.html
(latest figure available was for 1998).

Heritage Foundation Security of Property Rights ratings: Heritage Foundation 2013 Index of Economic Freedom, http://www.heritage.org/index/explore

Political Competition 2011: from the Polity IV dataset http://www.systemic peace.org/polity/polity4.htm
Hong Kong's value was estimated as 1, which is that for the People's Republic of China

Iceland's value estimated at 10, consistent with other institutionalized democracies (see also http://www.hks.harvard.edu/m-rcbg/research/r.zeckhauser_jwe_political.competition.pdf for evidence that competition in Iceland does not strongly diverge from that in other democracies)
Malta estimated at 10 on similar grounds: see http://www.maltadata.com/maltavot.htm.

QoG Impartiality Index: Quality of Government Institute, University of Göteborg, Sweden, The QoG Expert Survey: http://www.qog.pol.gu.se/digitalAssets/1379/1379332_qog-expert-survey-codebook-2008-2012.pdf and, for the data files: http://www.qog.pol.gu.se/data/datadownloads/qogexpert-surveydata/.

Transparency International Corruption Perceptions Index, 2012: http://cpi.transparency.org/cpi2012/.

Worldwide Governance Indicators of Control of Corruption, Regulatory Quality, and Government Effectiveness, and three-letter country abbreviations: World Bank Institute, Worldwide Governance Indicators: http://info.worldbank.org/governance/wgi/index.asp.

CHAPTER 3

CONTROL OF CORRUPTION: THE CASE OF FINLAND

Ari Salminen

ABSTRACT

As a Nordic country, Finland is known as a nation with a low level of perceived corruption. This chapter analyzes how corruption is controlled in Finland by asking first, how the different forms of corruption can be identified, including the context and risk areas of corruption; second, what the policies, authorities, and tools for curbing corruption are; and third, how effective are these measures for controlling corruption in Finland. This chapter describes the different aspects of corruption and the corruption control system in Finland, including the level of perceived corruption, anti-corruption regulations, tools and instruments for curbing corruption, and the main watchdog institutions. The main finding is that the control system has worked well so far but it needs reform in the future. The concluding section deals with some challenges facing the control system.

Different Paths to Curbing Corruption: Lessons from Denmark, Finland, Hong Kong, New Zealand and Singapore
Research in Public Policy Analysis and Management, Volume 23, 57–77
Copyright © 2013 by Emerald Group Publishing Limited
ISSN: 0732-1317/doi:10.1108/S0732-1317(2013)0000023003

INTRODUCTION

Finland is a country with a democratic political system, a market economy, and large welfare sector including a strong local self-government. The most important feature is that the public sector still dominates in many areas of society. Publicly financed welfare services cover social security, health care, and education, including reallocated social benefits and high taxation. As a result of political and administrative reforms, more responsibility of public services has been transferred to the market and to the actors of private sector.

Concerning societal development and institutions, Finland represents the Nordic states. As a Nordic country, Finland is known as a nation with a low level of perceived corruption. However, the distinct features of corruption are country-specific and culture-related. Ethics and values in the public sector are based on political and administrative traditions. Finland has a strong legalistic tradition in its public administration. The period after the latter half of the 20th century, the period of the welfare state, has been the time of rapid development of modern welfare state ethics. The values of the welfare state are legalism, equality, openness, and efficiency. Since the 1990s, the market values have gradually been replacing the welfare state values. Profitability, risk-taking, managerialism, and contractualism have become part of the national agenda.

This chapter analyzes how corruption is controlled in Finland. Although the recent academic debate on corruption issues is rather scarce in Finland (see, for example, Peurala, 2011; Salminen, 2010; Salminen & Ikola-Norrbacka, 2011), the topic is largely discussed internationally (see, for example, Andersson & Bergman, 2009; Caiden, 2001a, 2001b; de Graaf & Huberts, 2008; Galtung, 2006; Heidenheimer & Johnston, 2002; Huberts, Lasthuizen, & Peeters, 2006; Johnston, 1999; Langseth, 2006; Quah, 1999).

Both control and corruption are multifaceted phenomena and concepts. What are the functions of control and the control instruments adopted, and on what grounds, in a country? Control is an important topic in organization theory (see Hood, 2000; Sitkin, Cardinal, & Bijlma-Frankema, 2010). As a central function of public administration, control is linked to the hierarchies of decision making, regulation and command, and human resources and performance management. In administrative theory, control is closely connected to governing, coordination, and accountability. Control is used formally and informally, or intentionally and unintentionally. In the context of corruption, control is understood here, on the one hand, as control over corrupt phenomena and, on the other, as control instruments against integrity violations and corruption. Control refers to mechanisms that prevent corruption directly or indirectly.

As abuse of entrusted power for private gain, corruption covers different types of grand and petty corruption. One may ask: which control mechanisms are used to curb corruption in public administration? Three questions are addressed in this chapter, namely (1) How to identify the different forms of corruption in Finland, including the context and risk areas of corruption? (2) What are the policies, authorities, and tools for curbing corruption in Finland? (3) How effective are the measures for controlling corruption in Finland?

LOW LEVEL OF PERCEIVED CORRUPTION IN FINLAND

Finland has scored well in the international comparisons of corruption, as shown in Table 1. Transparency International's Corruption Perceptions Index (CPI) has ranked Finland highly, among other Nordic countries. Within the past 10 years, Finland has been among the top six countries included in the CPI. However, the focus of CPI measurement does not address the problem of old boy networks or institutional corruption, which is an important limitation. Consequently, the results of the CPI should be taken as one perception of the problem because it does not uncover the particularities of corruption in the countries surveyed. Corruption has

Table 1. Finland's Rank and Score on the Corruption Perceptions Index, 2006–2012.

Year	Rank[a]	Score
2012	1st	90/100
2011	2nd	9.4
2010	4th	9.2
2009	6th	8.9
2008	5th	9.0
2007	1st	9.4
2006	1st	9.6

Source: Compiled from http://www.transparency.org.
[a]Indicates joint rank.

special national characteristics and the definition of corrupt characteristics is usually bound to a particular time and place (van Hulten, 2007).

One could also argue that studying the control of corruption in a small, politically stable and homogenous Nordic country, such as Finland, with 5.6 million inhabitants, that consistently receives a high rating for relative freedom from corruption, makes little sense. In other words, what is the reason for studying corruption in Finland? There are reasons to believe that the "gap" between the state and the civil society has not become so far a serious problem in Finland. However, we agree with Huberts et al. (2006) that the high CPI ratings are also a question of reputation, and we might ask further whether good reputation "feeds" and maintains a low level of perceived corruption in Finland.

Checking the readiness of fighting corruption among societal institutions has been the object of the international anti-corruption development work. Transparency International has organized interview-based research in 25 European countries on the basis of national integrity systems. The findings of these reports were published during 2011−2012. Thirteen separate pillars were analyzed in each country on the role, capacity, and governance of the pillars in law and practice level. The national integrity report from Finland broadens the picture on how corruption is controlled in the Finnish society (Transparency Suomi, 2012).

Among the Finnish institutions fighting corruption and strengthening integrity, the weakest institutions were the business sector, civil society, and the absence of an anti-corruption agency; and the strongest institutions were the executive sector, law enforcement organizations, and the Ombudsman. Some of these institutions are discussed further in the later sections.

As part of anti-corruption work, particular recommendations of developing the integrity system for Finland were such topics as increasing the openness of public procurement, preventing double roles in decision making, and considering a national anti-corruption strategy (Transparency Suomi, 2012).

CITIZENS' PERCEPTIONS OF CORRUPTION

In the current era of managerialism, new control instruments are required for checking corrupt behavior in public organizations. New management practices, public-private contracts, and accountability are rapidly changing the context of public administration. Mutual relationships between public sector organizations and private companies have intensified. Too excessive linkages between these organizations may increase the opportunities for corruption. The cultural and country-specific ties make it pertinent to form a special portrait of corruption by referring to examples. Citizens' perceptions of corruption constitute a central point of reference when evaluating their extent and/or harmfulness and their consequences.

Corruption by the judgment of Finnish citizens is presented in Fig. 1. The data are taken from a large national citizens' survey implemented at the University of Vaasa in the years 2008−2010 (Salminen, 2010; Salminen & Ikola-Norrbacka, 2011). The large sample ($N = 5{,}000$) and careful selection of the respondents (Finland as a miniature) have enhanced the validity of the results of the study. More than 2,000 carefully completed questionnaire forms were returned, and the response rate was over 40 percent.

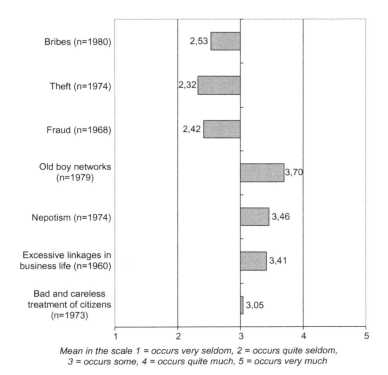

Mean in the scale 1 = occurs very seldom, 2 = occurs quite seldom,
3 = occurs some, 4 = occurs quite much, 5 = occurs very much

Fig. 1. Corruption in Finland: The Views of Citizens. *Source*: Salminen (2010).

The picture of corruption in Finland is not very harsh. In Fig. 1, the grand types of corruption, such as bribery, theft, and fraud, do not occur often. This finding is in line with the results of Transparency International and with other surveys conducted in Finland in recent years. Corruption problems emerge with special risk areas and situations. Such integrity violations as old boys' networks, nepotism, excessive linkages in business life, and maladministration are frequently mentioned in surveys and reports that investigate forms of corruption.

The old boys' networks, like any other forms of corruption, are not easily detected or dissolved, but they are formed in every aspect of society. Citizens do not perceive grand corruption to be a prevalent problem in the politico-administrative system; however, old boys' networks and different forms of favoritism arise as the main concern of citizens. So, even if Finland is considered to be a country with a low level of perceived corruption, there are unethical networks that will lead to more harmful consequences in the long run.

In all societies, the efficiency and achievements of fighting corruption are expected. That is why the control mechanisms should be adjusted to the particular nature of existing corruption in the country. The next section focuses on distorted networking, which is the main corruption problem in Finland (Salminen & Mäntysalo, 2012). It must be kept in mind that there is a thin line between healthy and corrupt networks. Most of networking in society is healthy and acceptable, and network organizations help to dismantle the bureaucratic hierarchies of administration.

DISTORTED NETWORKING

Old boys' networks present a form of distorted networking in society. Their established aims lead to harmful consequences from the citizens' point of view. Fig. 2 presents a simplified illustration of organizing old boys' networks. The lines between the boxes of actors represent the organizational linkages and the nature of interaction or the positions where potential integrity violations occur. In practical sense, the model does not exist but it helps in examining the real situation of corruption in the country.

The distorted networking is based on different interactions between the actors. As described in the illustration, the most typical features are reciprocity, gratitude and loyalty, protection of members, and loyalty and

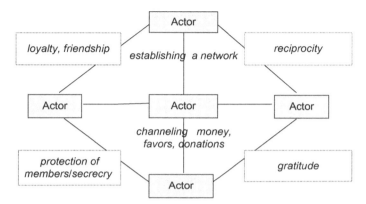

Fig. 2. An Illustration of Distorted Networking. *Source*: Salminen & Mäntysalo (2012).

friendship. It should be noted that the actors of the network do not channel and distribute their own money and other financial benefits. The functioning of the network is long-lasting and personally interactive between the members of the network. As one result of the network is reciprocity among the members, they are all indebted to their co-"old boys," as a response to their services and "returning the favor," even with several years in between the reciprocal exchanges. The policy of publicity in the network is based on mutual agreement of the members: things are kept hidden and private, so there is an agreement, or a "code of silence" (Tallberg, 2009).

The type of networking alters within the old boys' networks, as some of the members are more closely linked than other members. And, there is a common purpose that drives the actors to organize such a network. The organization and origin of the network begins with a common cause that can derive from the dissatisfaction in the contemporary politics in Finland. Theoretically, two types of old boys' networks may emerge: strong ties, where the network is small and dense, and weak ties, where the network is larger and contacts may be loosely organized and broadly diffuse.

Networking encompasses the dimensions of cronyism, favoritism, nepotism, kleptocracy as well protection within a profession, or politicians or businessmen, etc. The corrupt networks exist in several risk areas and situations of Finnish society. The cases are external election funding involving bribery, double roles in political and administrative decision making, wrongdoing in public and private foundations, lack of clarity in public procurement, and the formation of cartels.

How to control corruption through legislation, and which tools and instruments should be selected and to what purposes? These questions are discussed in the following sections.

FRAMEWORK OF REGULATION

As part of corruption control, regulation is based on acts and other codes. In each society, the role of regulation differs in several respects. One of the basic choices is the amount, extent, and details of regulation. The regulatory system can be perceived as either the high road of ethics or the low road of ethics. The first one is typical for Finland, and covers integrity and values. The second one relies on rules and compliance. According to the survey of the members of local councils in Finland in 2012, ethical codes played a minor role in local municipalities, but the need for such codes was recognized (Salminen, Pitkänen & Heiskanen, 2013).

The list of essential laws and acts preventing corruption and improving integrity starts from Constitution and ends with the special acts. The major anti-corruption laws are as follows:

- Constitution of Finland (1999): Citizen rights; conflicts of interests of ministers; and the general qualifications for public office, namely skill, ability, and proven civic merit.
- Penal Code (1889): Giving and accepting bribery; aggravated bribery; bribery of civil servants and bribery of Members of Parliament; bribery in business; election bribery; and abuse of public office.
- Government Act (2003) and Administrative Procedure Act (2003): Conflict of interests of ministers and civil servants; disqualification from decision making; promotion of good administration, quality and efficiency of the public service.
- State Civil Servants Act (1994) and Local Government Act (1995): General responsibilities of a civil servant, declaration of interests and additional income and outside ties; auditing of governance and economy; and conflicts of interest.
- Act on the Openness of Government Activities (1999): Publicity and government actions; citizens' right to access of information; government's duty to promote information and transparency; and grounds for secrecy.

- Accounting Act (1997) and Auditing Act (2007): Good accounting practice; duties of information-giving; and rules and practices on auditing.

Without going into details, some remarks of the nature of regulation could be mentioned. Concerning the control of corruption, two alternatives are available. On the one hand, how to develop integrity and improve ethical conduct in organizations, and, on the other, how to minimize the harms of integrity violations? Regulations, laws, and codes are needed for both directions.

The guarantee of good governance is written down in the Finnish Constitution. The exercise of public powers is based on the law. In the Constitution, it is regulated that ministers have to announce their own liabilities, which might harm their status in the Council of the State. Corresponding regulations are given for the top civil servants and executives in the State Civil Servants Act.

More than fighting corruption directly, the aims of the Administrative Procedure Act are to promote good behavior in public organizations, to improve the relations between citizens and administration, and to prevent maladministration in administrative practices. The scope of the application of this Act is wide from the state and municipal authorities to public enterprises. The main legal principles in this Act emphasize that an authority shall treat the customers of the administration on an equal basis. The actions of the authority shall be impartial and proportionate to their objectives. Principles emphasize the appropriateness of service, which includes appropriate services, organization of services, and that the authority can perform its tasks productively. The principle of advice means that authorities should provide the necessary advice free of charge, and within their competence.

The most important law for curbing corruption in Finland is the Penal Code. Substantial and direct regulations against bribery are written down in the Penal Code. The regulations cover the following eight aspects: giving and accepting bribery; aggravated bribery; giving and accepting a bribe as a Member of Parliament (MP); aggravated bribery as a MP; bribery and aggravated bribery in business; bribery in elections: to vote or not vote; abuse of public office; and negligent abuse of public office.

In the Finnish system, civil servants are also subject to criminal law and they are in a special position in terms of the Penal Code. Applying only to civil servants, there is a group of acts which are separately criminalized as malfeasance, offense in office, and incurring severe punishment, such as dismissal (Ikola-Norrbacka, Salminen, & Viinamaki, 2010).

ANTI-CORRUPTION TOOLS AND INSTRUMENTS: AN OVERVIEW

How can a country be protected from corruption, and what are the main instruments for curbing corruption? Answers to these questions are provided from the development of society and the anti-corruption measures.

The basic explanation comes from the society and its foundations, culture, politics, economics, and values. Balanced society, steady economic growth, fair and free elections, and equality between citizens are the main factors responsible for curbing corruption. The society and political system require openness and transparency. In the civil service, a good level of status is needed for public servants, including a neutral position in relation to politicians. Corporate governance and other good administrative practices should be followed in both public and private organizations.

The effectiveness of the anti-corruption measures is a crucial question as well. In Table 2, the general picture of anti-corruption tools and instruments is presented for a closer look. It includes the areas of tools and instruments, and the related control particulars and characteristics. Seven tools and instruments are listed. Control particulars describe the detailed contents of the tools and instruments. Control is characterized by using three alternatives, which label the differing nature of control, namely promoting integrity, preventing corruption, and the watchdog function (Salminen, Viinamäki, & Ikola-Norrbacka, 2007).

MECHANISMS FOR PROMOTING INTEGRITY AND PREVENTING CORRUPTION

The first control functions are promoting integrity and preventing corruption. Based on the control characteristics in Table 2, the tools and instruments for promoting integrity and preventing corruption are the key anti-corruption acts, good administration, integrity of civil servants, and civil society organizations.

The general qualifications for public office are written down in the Constitution. Conflict of interests and disqualifications are regulated by the Constitution, Government Act, and Local Government Act. The general responsibilities of civil servants are regulated by the Act on State Civil Servants. The core legislation for preventing corruption is the Penal Code.

Table 2. Control Mechanisms in Finland.

Areas of Tools and Instruments	Control Particulars	Control Characteristics
The key anti-corruption acts	Behaving ethically and extensive sanctions of corruption undertakings	"Preventing corruption"
Benefits of good administration	Confidence in public institutions	"Promoting integrity"
Integrity of civil servants	Legalism and loyalty to the office; "danger" of public shame, reputation	"Preventing corruption"/ "Promoting integrity"
Role of Ombudsman, Chancellor of Justice, and other judicial authorities	Maintaining just and clean administrative culture, uncovering integrity violations	"Watchdog function"
Financial and performance audit	Decentralized monitoring; tight financial audits	"Watchdog function"
Civil society and organizations	Trust, morality of society and political culture, awareness raising	"Promoting integrity"
Media	Uncovering integrity violations (cases), investigative journalism	"Watchdog function"

Good governance and good administration are loaded with ethical values. Do the ethical values affect the process of controlling corruption? Since 2003, different surveys and expert interviews conducted at the University of Vaasa have proved that justice and equality, integrity, openness, lawfulness, trustworthiness, expertise, and service-orientation are very frequently mentioned ethical values. These values represent the opposite of corruption, and more particularly, opposition to misbehavior, mismanagement, and maladministration.

A value-led management has been introduced in government during this decade. The results of Finnish surveys (1999 and 2007) in the Finnish ministries and agencies provide evidence for this case. Both surveys show that the most appreciated values are trustworthiness, expertise, openness, and independence. When the public service ethos among Finnish regional and local managers was explored, the different ethical profiles emerged, but the new market values had not infiltrated the traditional value sets of managers as we had expected. Such values as public interest, equality, and integrity are highly appreciated among the managers (Salminen & Mäntysalo, 2013).

Integrity in office is an essential part in curbing corruption. This tradition supports the stable administrative system. For civil service transparency, trust and integrity are guaranteed in different ways. Most civil servants hold their positions after national or local elections and changes in the top management in government agencies. Loyalty in the Finnish civil service is vested in the so-called objective loyalty toward formal position and hierarchy. Loyalty is emphasized in the formal and independent position of civil service and hierarchical statuses (Ikola-Norrbacka et al., 2010).

In daily administrative work, the reporting official researches the matter under advisement, presents alternative proposals, and suggests a final proposal to the decision makers. The system has been seen to serve the prevention of abuse and corrupt behavior. Obligations to provide public argumentation for decisions increase transparency and public trust in governance, and prevent partial and partisan decision-making.

The civil service is regulated in terms of disqualifications and conflicts of interest as well. Public sector office holders are obligated to inform superiors about every connection concerning secondary occupations. Public servants should state their interests before their appointment to office (Tiihonen, 2003, pp. 104–110).

Public tasks and positions are controlled as well. Formal merits in the process of appointments are carefully considered. The jobs of public officials have been secure, and their salary level is relatively good. Everyone has the opportunity to become a public official and make progress in his or her career through personal merit (Ministry for Foreign Affairs, Finland, 2012, p. 137). On paper, only a few posts are formally reserved for political nominations, but in reality, the number of appointments on a political basis is much higher, which is explained by the power-seeking of the leading political parties. This trend does not enhance transparency in administration or trust in politicians among the citizens.

Another powerful tool to prevent corruption is public shame. The shame is enhanced if the case has received a great deal of attention in the media. On some occasions, even the threat of a ruined reputation leads to resignation from office. The offender is remembered for wrongdoing and all the good achievements made before are forgotten. The gates to better jobs are closed (Ikola-Norrbacka et al., 2010). Resignation usually applies in the cases of bribery. However, the examples of politicians and top level civil servants during the past years indicate a trend toward nonresignation rather than resignation.

The Finnish surveys reveal that civil servants face certain corruption-related issues. Civil servants stated that they have regularly or occasionally met unethical behavior in their daily work such as lack of publicity and improper announcements, use of difficult official language, delaying issues, putting self-interest before public interest and making decision without appropriate preparation, presentation, and reporting system. Despite the fact that civil servants in ministries face corruption-related issues, it is emphasized in the survey that forms of grand corruption like taking bribes or gaining financial benefit for the office are still very rare.

Awareness-raising among citizens is a crucial question if corruption is controlled by the civil society organizations. Citizens are active in different roles. This can also be seen in a wider context where citizens are not the subjects of administration but sovereign citizens who can influence things that concern them. A citizen control system may create a forewarning mechanism for public service to follow the rules (Ikola-Norrbacka et al., 2010).

From the citizens' point of view, both transparent and open government and active civil society organizations are required. Such channels as investigations of the Ombudsman, going to the media, and whistle-blowing channels provided by some organizations are available for citizens. For example, Transparency Finland and Finnwatch represent organizations that promote ethical governance, anti-corruption efforts, and corporate responsibility in society.

Alternatively, the maintenance of diverse forms of citizen participation, independent and self-regulated media, a high level of education, public access to official documents, clear-cut roles of appealing institutions, and a possibility to present appeal with professional legal help, are all ways toward a lower level of corruption.

WATCHDOG INSTITUTIONS

Where the watchdog aspect of corruption control is concerned, the main tools are the Ombudsman, Chancellor of Justice and other judicial authorities, audit organizations, and the media. The formal duties of these institutions are described below but other relevant information is available on their websites.

The watchdog functions are implemented by the Finnish Parliament. The Parliamentary Audit Committee oversees the management of government finances and compliance with the budget. The task of the committee is mentioned in the Constitution and the legislative amendment entered into force on 2007. The committee concentrates on the general state and management of government finances as well as on issues of which Parliament ought to be informed.

Another organ is the group of four auditors. The Parliament elects from among its members three auditors and a designated deputy for each auditor. The fourth auditor, who is chosen outside the Parliament, works with a public liability. They audit the finances and administration of the Parliament. The public reports are provided by the auditing activities.

Two institutions represent legal regulation and supervision of legality in Finland. The tasks are written down in the Finnish Constitution. They are the Chancellor of Justice (2013), who reports to the government and to the Parliament, and the Parliamentary Ombudsman (2013). They differ from the administrative courts where cases of integrity violations of public servants are handled, accused, and sentenced.

However, the control function is very strong. Public authorities and officials are required to observe the law and fulfill their duties. Both institutions publish their annual reports. Although the tasks and powers of both institutions are largely the same, there is a special division of labor and work coordination between the Chancellor of Justice and Ombudsman. The division of the duties is prescribed by law. Generally, both judicial authorities perform the following five functions: (1) initiating and implementing investigations and inspections, (2) investigating integrity violations revealed for example by the media, (3) gathering information, (4) supervising other public authorities and servants, and (5) making proposals and providing recommendations of good governance.

The Chancellor of Justice is more concentrated on wrongdoing (disqualification, misuse of public power) cases of public servants than the Ombudsman, who concentrates on violations of the principles of equality and impartiality. Quoted from the formal duty presentations, the aim of Ombudsman is to ensure that the principles of constitutional and human rights and good administration are followed. Examining issues differ between the institutions as well. For example, a complaint can be made either to the Chancellor of Justice or the Ombudsman. They can also transfer complaints from one to the other, but they do not investigate the same case simultaneously.

Alongside investigating complaints, the Chancellor of Justice has the task of overseeing the legality of the government's actions, and hence is present at cabinet sessions and examines the relevant documents beforehand. The Chancellor of Justice attends all the plenary sessions of the government as well as presidential sessions at which the President of the

Republic makes decisions on proposals presented by the government. The review process of the Chancellor of Justice focuses on the consideration of issues of legality, instead of the appropriateness of decisions or resolutions or any other political assessment.

As part of control, both institutions handle complaints. Concerning complaints anyone has the right to turn to the Chancellor of Justice or Ombudsman. The Chancellor of Justice is entitled to perform inspections of those authorities, institutions, offices, and other units that fall within the scope of his supervisory authority. According to the current reports, the Chancellor of Justice has performed about 30 inspections of different authorities each year. Investigating complaints is a central mission for the Ombudsman, which causes a large workload for the agency. More than 4,000 complaints are received every year, and almost the same number of these complaints is annually decided.

Besides, all government agencies have a unit for internal control. If internal units find misuse or references to corruption, they refer the case to the police authorities. Administrative corruption cases have been interesting topics for public debate in the media. Roughly speaking, the amount of both internal and police investigations are increased during the past decade. The data on suspected bribery cases in Finland are presented in the next section.

The National Audit Office (NAO) (2013) is the country's supreme audit institution. It is related to the Finnish Parliament. The formal position and tasks of the NAO is laid down in the Finnish Constitution. The office has several roles in controlling integrity violations and corruption. The audit functions are a direct and intentional part of controlling corruption. The tasks and responsibilities of the NAO are regulated in the Act on the NAO from 2000. As an external auditor, it has an independent position and broad rights to gather information in the Finnish public administration. The audit work covers the whole state economy in the audit areas of fiscal policy, finances, compliance, and performance.

The NAO audits the state's finances, monitors and evaluates fiscal policy, and oversees party and election funding. Through its independent audit work, the NAO ensures that public funds are spent according to Parliament's decisions, in compliance with legislation and wisely, and that fiscal policy is exercised in a sustainable manner. According to the Act on the NAO, a state authority, agency, business enterprise, or state fund must immediately report any abuse of funds or property which it manages or for which it is responsible to the NAO, regardless of confidentiality regulations.

The NAO has a special whistle-blowing instrument for citizens and orga-nizations. As part of the formal audit everyone is able to turn to the NAO concerning complaints about suspected illegalities of financial management of the state, including illegal procedures in state-owned companies. The NAO reports regularly of the audit activities. Most of the audits consist of recommendations of better performance. However, relatively few audits cause further investigations.

The role of the media is important in curbing corruption. Media uncovers integrity violations through investigative journalism, and makes possible public debate of accountability among politicians. Media raises public awareness of corruption and helps public sector authorities to inves-tigate corruption cases. Press freedom is linked to lower levels of corrup-tion. Large circulation of newspapers increases conditions for publicity that reduce corruption in societies (Camaj, 2013).

During the past five years, the Finnish media has revealed several cor-ruption cases or even scandals. Through the methods of investigative jour-nalism, suspected cases are publicly discussed from week to week or month to month. As predicted, the number of the cases which police and judicial authorities have started to investigate is always much lower. There might be a "dark number" of misconduct and certain uncontrolled corruption that can be expected to remain unknown (Huberts et al., 2006, p. 278).

CONTROL OF BRIBERY

How do the anti-corruption legislation and control instruments work in practice? Most often there are differences on how policies and instruments work on paper and in reality. In public administration, there is a difference between those who receive bribes and those who give bribes. Two parties are needed. Corrupt behavior becomes structural if corrupt forms of deci-sion making are approved as a model and a habit.

There are no guarantees that extensive legislation would decrease cor-ruption. It should be noted that bribery is a complicated form of corrup-tion. As mentioned earlier, according to the valid legislation, bribery covers sanctions on bribing, abuse of public office, and violations of official duty. One crucial question is when exactly does a gift become a bribe? Where to draw the line between a bribe and gift, and the question of endangering integrity and impartiality, is not clear cut. Gift-giving per se is about reci-procity (Schultz, 2010) as it is a way of showing respect to others, and acknowledging their social status or a way of common courtesy. But, as the common phrase goes, there is no free lunch, and gift-giving becomes a key determining factor of ethical and acceptable conduct especially in the public realm, where to draw the line between a gift and a bribe, what to accept and what to reject. One indicator against which this line can be weighed upon is reputation and trustworthiness; to consider how does the action influence the perception of integrity, and does it endanger trust and impartiality?

On a more practical level, Table 3 reveals some statistics of suspected bribery cases in Finland since 2005. The role of police is central in either starting investigations or deciding dismissals of cases and possible accusations. There is a clear distinction between suspected, accused, and sentenced cases. As shown in Table 3, the number of suspected cases is not high. It is assumed that the number of accused or sentenced cases is even much lower, because considerations of charges lead to very few trial processes or court decisions.

In recent years, one of the most well-known bribery cases in Finland dealt with external election finance. The case began in 2006, and its proceedings are not completed as it is now in the court of appeal. The case involves political corruption as an association was established for campaign finance purposes during local and national elections. It was later revealed

Table 3. Suspected Bribery Cases in Finland, 2005–2011.

Type of Bribery Cases	2005	2006	2007	2008	2009	2010	2011[a]
Bribery in business	0	5	3	1	3	5	10
Acceptance of a bribe in business	0	2	1	1	4	4	16
Giving of bribes	18	9	4	8	8	14	4
Aggravated giving of bribes	0	0	4	0	2	0	2
Acceptance of a bribe	13	6	5	1	6	17	3
Bribery violation	6	1	2	14	1	2	0
Aggravated acceptance of a bribe	0	1	1	0	0	0	2
Electoral bribery	0	0	0	1	0	0	0
Giving of bribes to a Member of Parliament	0	0	0	0	0	1	0
Acceptance of a bribe as a Member of Parliament	0	0	0	0	0	0	0
Total	37	24	20	26	24	43	37

Source: Leppänen & Muttilainen (2012, p. 27).
[a]Statistics are not final.

that the basic purpose of the association was to influence the political composition of the coming Finnish government, including the businessmen's
own interests in regional and local land use and construction.

The basic issue was money and powerful political positions. The group
of businessmen channeled a significant amount of money to "suitable" candidates in the elections. Large donations were given by the group of businessmen to public office holders. The businessmen and the office holders
were accused on the basis of bribery and abuse of public office. It was evident that mutual gratitude and reciprocity were expected among the businessmen. During the trial process, gifts, donations, and other financial
benefits were suspected as bribes. In the trial process of the local court,
they were found guilty and sentenced to conditional and unconditional
imprisonment from less than a year to more than four years. The court of
appeal rejected the local court's decision concerning the leading politician
or office holder, and reduced the punishment of the two businessmen.

CONCLUSION

This chapter has focused on the control of corruption in Finland by
describing some basic aspects of the corruption problem and the various
control measures against corruption as well as evaluating the effectiveness
of these measures. Finland's control system still needs redefining and
reform because of the three emerging challenges of corruption control.

Because of the low level of perceived corruption of Finland, one conclu-
sion is that the control has been in many respects successful so far. No
urgent need exists to draw more anti-corruption legislation or to establish
an administrative body such as an anti-corruption agency. However, in the
Finnish system, more emphasis is laid on public authorities and less on civil
society and citizens. Is there any controlling role for citizens to support
democratic government and highly reputable companies? Some institutions
and organizations provide whistle-blowing channels for citizens. These
channels improve the control of corruption in society. Still more efforts are
needed for activating civil society fighting integrity violations. For a low
corruption country, an important challenge in the future is how to get
issues relating to corruption to be an essential part of the political agenda.

Values of good governance – trust, equality, fairness – control integrity
violations and corruption intentionally, but indirectly. Openness seems to
be the cure for all diseases. The greater the transparency, the more effective

are the control and combating of corruption. Transparency mechanisms work as a control instrument such as free availability of public information, clarity in bookkeeping of organizations, and register of conflict of interests and lobbying. Supposing that risk areas and situations are traced, the possible anti-corruption strategy should be targeted to the effectiveness of the actors of Finland's control system: one crucial question is how to prevent the creation of distorted networking in politics, business, and public administration. Serious problems, connected to structural corruption, are sometimes facing the Finnish society. Gratitude in networking turns sometimes to unhealthy reciprocity. The line between a gift and a bribe should be clarified and at least discussed openly in the organizations. Gratitude and favoritism in politics may lead to cronyism. Therefore, in the long run, trust and fairness in society are threatened if these problems are not resolved.

The Finnish system has relied on values and the discretion of politicians, businessmen, and public servants. Ethical codes are mainly reserved for different professional fields, but not for politics, administration, or the public service in general. Value- and rule-based codes are needed for public service, local authorities, and politicians (elected MPs and local councils). This is in line with the recommendations of the recent GRECO report (2013) on corruption prevention in Finland. As Finland is an open society and a small economy, corruption has been controlled by different anti-corruption measures, as discussed in this chapter. However, for Finland to continue with its efficient and strong control functions among all sectors of society, further development of ethics and promotion of good governance are also needed.

REFERENCES

Andersson, S., & Bergman, T. (2009). Controlling corruption in the public sector. *Scandinavian Political Studies*, *32*(1), 45–70.

Caiden, G. E. (2001a). Dealing with administrative corruption. In T. L. Cooper (Ed.), *Handbook of administrative ethics* (pp. 429–455). New York, NY: Marcel Dekker.

Caiden, G. E. (2001b). Corruption and governance. In G. E. Caiden, O. P. Dwivedi, & J. G. Jabbra (Eds.), *Where corruption lives* (pp. 15–37). Bloomfield, CT: Kumarian Press.

Camaj, L. (2013). The media's role in fighting corruption: Media effects on governmental accountability. *International Journal of Press and Politics*, *18*(1), 21–42.

Chancellor of Justice. (2013). *The Office of the Chancellor of Justice*. Helsinki. Retrieved from http//www.okv.fi/en/. Accessed on May 16, 2013.

de Graaf, G., & Huberts, L. W. J. C. (2008). Portraying the nature of corruption using an explorative case study design. *Public Administration Review*, *68*(4), 640–653.

Galtung, F. (2006). Measuring the immeasurable: Boundaries and functions of (macro) corruption indices. In C. Sampford, A. Shacklock, C. Connors, & F. Galtung (Eds.), *Measuring corruption* (pp. 101–130). Aldershot: Ashgate.

GRECO (2013). Corruption prevention in respect of members of parliament, judges and prosecutors. *Evaluation report: Finland.* Strasbourg: Council of Europe, Group of states against corruption.

Heidenheimer, A. J., & Johnston, M. (Eds.) (2002). *Political corruption: Concepts and contexts* (3rd ed.). New Brunswick, NJ: Transaction Publishers.

Hood, C. (2000). *The art of the state: Culture, rhetoric and public management.* Oxford: Oxford University Press.

Huberts, L., Lasthuizen, K., & Peeters, C. (2006). Measuring corruption: Exploring the iceberg. In C. Sampford, A. Shacklock, C. Connors, & F. Galtung, (Eds.), *Measuring corruption* (pp. 265–293). Aldershot: Ashgate.

Ikola-Norrbacka, R., Salminen, A., & Viinamäki, O.-P. (2010). Promoting, preventing and watchdogging: Reinforcing citizens' role in the control of corruption. In A. Saminen (Ed.), *Ethical governance. A citizen perspective* (pp. 76–90). Vaasa: Research Papers 294, Public Management 39, University of Vaasa.

Johnston, M. (1999). A brief history of anti-corruption agencies. In A. Schedler, L. Diamond, & M. F. Plattner (Eds.), *The self-restraining state: Power and accountability in new democracies* (pp. 217–226). Boulder, CO: Lynne Rienner Publishers.

Langseth, P. (2006). Measuring corruption. In C. Sampford, A. Shacklock, C. Connors, & F. Galtung (Eds.), *Measuring corruption* (pp. 7–44). Aldershot: Ashgate.

Leppänen, A., & Muttilainen, V. (2012). *Poliisin tietoon tullut korruptiorikollisuus Suomessa 2007-2010 (Corruption crimes in Finland between 2007–2010 according to the police reports).* Tampere: Tampere University Press.

Ministry for Foreign Affairs, Finland. (2012). *Anti-corruption handbook for development practitioners.* Helsinki: Erweko Company.

National Audit Office. (2013). *Finland.* Retrieved from http://www.vtv.fi/en. Accessed on May 16, 2013.

Ombudsman. (2013). *The parliamentary Ombudsman.* Finland. Retrieved from http://www.oikeusasiamies.fi/Resource.phx/eoa/english/index.htx. Accessed on May 16, 2013.

Peurala, J. (2011). Assessing the corruption prevention measures and the bribery criminalization in the Finnish anti-corruption framework. *European Journal of Crime, Criminal Law and Criminal Justice, 19*(4), 319–362.

Quah, J. S. T. (1999). Comparing anti-corruption measures in Asian countries: Lessons to be learnt. *Asian Review of Public Administration, 11*(2), 71–90.

Salminen, A. (Ed.). (2010). *Ethical governance: A citizen perspective.* Vaasa: Research Papers 294, Public Management 39, University of Vaasa.

Salminen, A., & Ikola-Norrbacka, R. (2011). Trust, good governance and unethical actions in Finnish public administration. *International Journal of Public Sector Management, 23*(7), 647–668.

Salminen, A., & Mäntysalo, V. (2012). Old-boys' networks and administrative corruption – case of external election finance in Finland. Presented at the European Group of Public Administration Annual Conference in Bergen. Study Group: Ethics and Integrity of Governance, September 5–9, 11 pages. Retrieved from http://www.egpa2012.com

Salminen, A., & Mäntysalo, V. (2013). Exploring the public service ethos: The ethical profiles of regional and local managers in Finnish public administration. *Public Integrity, 15*(2), 167–185.

Salminen, A., Pitkänen, L., & Heiskanen, L. (2013). Codes as an instrument of regulation: A local government challenge. Presented at the XVII IRSPM Conference in Prague. Panel: Government Corruption and Global Crisis, April 10–12, 15 pages.

Salminen, A., Viinamäki, O.-P., & Ikola-Norrbacka, R. (2007). The control of corruption in Finland. *Revista Administratie si Management Public* (Administration and Public Management Review), *9*, 81–95.

Schultz, D. (2010). Ethics regulation across professions: The problem of gifting. *Public Integrity*, *12*(2), 161–172.

Sitkin, S. B., Cardinal, L. B., & Bijlma-Frankema, K. M. (Eds.) (2010). *Organizational control: Cambridge companion to management*. Cambridge: Cambridge University Press.

Tallberg, T. (2009). *Networks, organizations and men: Concepts and interrelations*. Helsinki: Swedish School of Economy and Business Administration.

Tiihonen, P. (2003). Good governance and corruption in Finland. In S. Tiihonen (Ed.), *The history of corruption in central government* (pp. 99–118). Amsterdam: IOS Press.

Transparency Suomi. (2012). *National integrity assessment: Finland*. Helsinki: Transparency International.

van Hulten, M. (2007). *Ten years of corruption (perceptions) indices: Methods – results – what next? An analysis*. Berlin: Transparency International.

CHAPTER 4

ENGAGING THE PUBLIC: HONG KONG'S INDEPENDENT COMMISSION AGAINST CORRUPTION'S COMMUNITY RELATIONS STRATEGY

Ian Scott

ABSTRACT

The implicit assumption underlying the work of most anti-corruption agencies (ACAs) is that they need to change public attitudes toward corruption to ensure a cleaner future. The means of achieving this objective usually rest on sanctions, prevention, and sermons. Changing attitudes is seen to be largely a matter of prosecuting the corrupt, putting preventive measures in place, emphasizing the negative social and criminal consequences of corruption, and exhorting the public to achieve higher moral standards. Engaging the public is rarely undertaken directly. If it were, it would entail a community relations approach based on face-to-face, decentralized interaction between the ACA and the public. In principle, this approach might have three significant advantages. First, it could enable the anti-corruption message to be communicated more directly

Different Paths to Curbing Corruption: Lessons from Denmark, Finland, Hong Kong, New Zealand and Singapore
Research in Public Policy Analysis and Management, Volume 23, 79–108
ISSN: 0732-1317/doi:10.1108/S0732-1317(2013)0000023004

and, possibly, more effectively. Second, it might assist the ACA in identi-
fying groups within the community which have developed, or are develop-
ing, attitudes which are potentially antithetical to its objectives. Third, it
could serve as a springboard for local anti-corruption initiatives which
might help to embed desired practices in the community or groups within
it. In this chapter, we examine the extent to which one of the few
agencies to adopt a full-blown community relations strategy —
Hong Kong's Independent Commission Against Corruption (ICAC) —
has been able to achieve those benefits.

INTRODUCTION

Anti-corruption agencies (ACAs) and scholars alike agree that successful
corruption prevention policies depend on securing active public support
(Grabosky, 1990; Independent Commission Against Corruption (ICAC),
2012, p. 62; Thanudo, 2013; UNODC, 2012). Yet the extent to which this
commitment has been positively realized in practice through specifically
directed decentralized community relations policies or consistent agency
interaction with civil society organizations (CSOs) has been surprisingly
limited. It is true that ACAs often appeal to the public to refrain from
corruption, to warn of its consequences and the dangers of allowing it to
go unchecked, to encourage people to report corrupt behavior, and sometimes even to try to construct partnerships with CSOs. In principle, they
usually recognize that community participation may help to stimulate
social change and reinforce positive values, ensure that there is congruence
with present or future desired public norms, and provide better longer-term
corruption prevention benefits than relying solely on sanctions and punishment (OECD, 2003). But turning the aspiration to engage with the public
into a coherent, sustained community relations strategy has often proved
to be more difficult. Resources are often limited and civic engagement is
labor-intensive. Enthusiasm for building links with civil society may falter
in the light of public cynicism over the lack of progress in controlling
corruption. There may be political demands for quick results. Strongly
entrenched community norms supporting corrupt and unethical practices
may make engagement problematic. And there may be commitment to
"one size fits all" programs and a centralized approach to corruption
control (Gong, 2011; Gorta, 2003; OECD, 2003; Osse, 1997; Preston, 1994;

Smilov, 2009, p. 86). In consequence, for all or some of these reasons, ACAs tend to follow top-down strategies in which engaging the public becomes something of a poor relation behind the more immediate and pressing goals of catching and prosecuting corrupt offenders and introducing corruption prevention measures in public and private institutions.

A community relations anti-corruption strategy does not simply involve publicity through the mass media warning of the evils of corruption; it also involves a more direct relationship with the public through the creation of local agency offices and the establishment of permanent relationships with CSOs and local political and bureaucratic institutions. The advantages of such a strategy may be threefold. First, if a partially decentralized administrative system is introduced, some of the fundamental tasks of the ACA could be more easily achieved. Ensuring that corrupt acts are reported, for example, is an essential consideration for all ACAs. If it is possible to report in person to a branch office of an ACA, more favorable conditions are in place to lodge complaints conveniently than if the process is centralized and remote. Similarly, if centrally based officials only visit the community sporadically, liaison with CSOs and with local level institutions, both political and bureaucratic, is less likely to be less continuous and immediate. If the ACA has a local level presence, there is also less likelihood of local attitudes developing which are contrary to its aims. It might be argued that strong CSOs fulfill the task of ensuring that there is a vigilant citizenry ready to take action against corruption. But CSOs do not always have anti-corruption activities as their primary goal. In addition, social attitudes toward corruption and the composition of the community itself may change quite rapidly and local institutions may develop practices which are less easily detected by a centralized body. In short, a partially decentralized ACA has the positive benefits of enabling important functions to be carried out more extensively and successfully and of maintaining a watching brief over attitudes toward corruption in local level institutions and CSOs.

A second, and related, advantage of a community relations policy is that it may enable the ACA to become aware of any incompatibility between the message which it wishes to send to the public and prevailing community attitudes and perceptions toward corruption. There is overwhelming evidence that the anti-corruption values formally proclaimed by the centralized ACAs are not always those to which local communities, or even the government itself in many cases, actually subscribe (Bracking, 2007; Co, 2007; Gong, 2012; Truex, 2011). If these attitudes are socially embedded, the prospects for reducing corruption by exhortation alone are slim.

Engaging the public at this level can take two forms. It may relate to a geographically defined community in which the ACA has a presence or it may relate to specific socioeconomic groups, such as, for example, youth, the elderly, or lower income earners, who have significantly different attitudes toward corruption compared to other groups. In either case, there is the prospect of innovative policy-making based on the evidence of different attitudes toward corruption and the consequent refinement of a "one size fits all" approach. Scholars have increasingly identified this "bottom-up" approach as a way forward in bringing about social change, combating entrenched attitudes, and tailoring the anti-corruption message to the needs of specific groups (Gatti, Paternostro, & Rigolini, 2003; Rose-Ackerman & Truex, 2012; Truex, 2011; Zaloznaya, 2012). In essence, the approach rests on a community relations strategy in which the ACA has a well-developed sense of local social attitudes and which enables it to differentiate between the needs, levels of tolerance, and perceptions of corruption of various socioeconomic groups.

A third advantage of a community relations approach is that it may support local initiatives to combat corruption. It is likely that in decentralized political systems local anti-corruption initiatives will develop with or without a community relations strategy (Gong, 2012; Li, 2001). ACAs may be aided in their work by these initiatives especially if they reflect important local concerns (Grabosky, 1990). In some cases, however, local action may prove counterproductive or ineffective. The presence of a local office of an ACA may help to provide guidance or may strengthen the chances of a successful outcome. It is also possible that local initiatives may have wider relevance and can be usefully transplanted to other local contexts. More generally, this kind of interaction between the ACA and the community should ensure that the anti-corruption strategy as a whole remains coherent and that local initiatives are not inconsistent with wider goals.

In this chapter, Hong Kong's ICAC's community relations strategy is assessed against these three evaluative criteria: whether the strategy assists in the achievement of the ICAC's central aims; whether it supports the development of evidence-based policy-making to target specific groups; and whether it serves to encourage local anti-corruption initiatives. The ICAC has been characterized as a "universalistic" ACA because of its three-pronged approach to corruption: investigation, prevention, and education (Heilbrunn, 2004) and it has long been regarded as the standard against which other ACAs should be measured (Batory, 2012). Much attention has been devoted to its successes in turning around a corrupt public service, in devising corruption prevention measures, and in maintaining a zero tolerance approach toward corruption (Manion, 2004; Meagher, 2005; Quah, 2011; Scott, 2011, 2013). With the exception of David Clark's (1987) pioneering article, much less attention has been devoted to the community relations aspects of the ICAC's work than to its more spectacular successes. An assessment of the ICAC's community relations strategy is presented in this chapter against the backdrop of some of the results of the independent annual survey and of a pilot study of social attitudes toward corruption in two of Hong Kong's poorest communities, Tin Shui Wai and Sham Shui Po.

THE COMMUNITY RELATIONS STRATEGY AND THE ANTI-CORRUPTION MESSAGE

In this section, we explore the work of the ICAC's Community Relations Department (CRD) in its efforts to convey an anti-corruption message at the local level. The ICAC's later success tends to mask the very real difficulties which it faced during its early years. The CRD, in particular, was confronted with problems of funding, with a police mutiny and subsequent amnesty which nearly undermined its entire strategy, and entrenched social attitudes and business practices which offered opportunities for corruption. CSOs and government departments were sometimes suspicious of its work and this, in turn, affected its involvement with the community. To overcome these difficulties required sustaining a level of commitment among its officers in the field and a belief that interaction with the public was indispensable if the objectives of the entire organization were to be achieved.

When the colonial Governor, Sir Murray MacLehose, announced the creation of the ICAC as an independent investigatory body in October 1973, there was no mention of a CRD as such. The ICAC was to comprise two departments, an operations department and a "…civil unit whose main task will lie in educating the public as to the evils of corruption…. It will also critically examine administrative procedures which lend themselves to corrupt practices" (Legislative Council, 1973, p. 18). By January 1974, it had been decided that the functions of prevention and community relations would be the responsibility of separate departments. However, the CRD did not formally begin work until the beginning of 1975 when it had an establishment of 28. By that stage, the structure of the ICAC, which has remained in place since that time, comprised the Operations Department

(OD), the CRD, the Corruption Prevention Department (CPD), and an administrative support branch.

The CRD was then organized into two divisions which reflected its responsibilities under the ICAC Ordinance (Cap 204) to "educate the public against the evils of corruption" and "to enlist and foster public support in combating corruption" (ICAC Ordinance, 2003, S. 12 (g) and 12 (h)). The Media and Education Division (initially called Information, Support, and Research) was to be responsible for publicity and relations with the press while the Liaison Division took on the task of working with the community. A Citizens' Advisory Committee, composed of well-known community figures, was appointed by the Governor to make suggestions on the objectives and direction of the CRD. The Committee in turn set up three subcommittees to advise on relations with the mass media, public education, and community liaison. The CRD's organization chart in 2011 is shown in Fig. 1.

Community liaison work was primarily to be directed from eight sub-offices (later called regional offices and reduced to seven in number) that were to be established in high density areas throughout Hong Kong. The sub-offices were to have the appearance of a shop-front to encourage people to make complaints and to obtain information. They were to be open for 14 hours every day including Sundays and were to be managed by a Grade 1 Senior ICAC Officer. The first sub-office was opened in July 1975 but progress was stalled by an economic downturn and it was not immediately possible to open all the remaining sub-offices. For funding purposes, the Hong Kong government, which was renowned for fiscal austerity at the best of times and tended to make savage cuts in difficult economic circumstances, treated the ICAC like any other government department. The CRD had to make difficult choices and chose to give priority to its mass media campaigns. Consequently, there were insufficient funds to open all the regional offices until 1983 (Ma, 1988, p. 35). The Finance Committee of the Legislative Council also raised objections to the appointment of a Grade 1 officer to run the sub-offices. For three years, the Finance Committee insisted that the appointment should be at Grade II upper level and it was not until May 1977 that the CRD was finally able to convince the Finance Committee to make appointments at the higher level (ICAC, 1977, pp. 35–36, 1978, p. 30). Subsequently, following its successes and increasing public support for its work, the ICAC was less vulnerable to funding cuts. In the 2000s, for example, when government departments were being significantly downsized, the ICAC establishment was retained at approximately its existing level (see Fig. 2).

Fig. 1. Community Relations Department's Organization Chart. *Source*: ICAC (2012).

There were also initial problems in recruiting senior- and middle-level personnel to the CRD. The Director reported that he was pleased with the "predominantly young, though highly intelligent and very enthusiastic" field staff who had been recruited, but they lacked experience and needed to be trained (ICAC, 1977, p. 35). The most dramatic increase in the strength in the CRD occurred in 1977 and 1978 when new sub-offices were

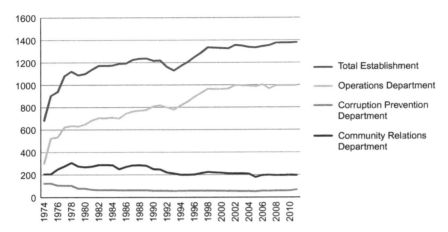

Fig. 2. ICAC Establishment, 1974–2011. *Source*: ICAC (1975–2011).

being opened. It is possible that problems of reduced community support following an amnesty for the junior police officers who had marched on the ICAC central offices in November 1977 also persuaded the ICAC and the government that more posts were needed in the field. In 1978, the CRD establishment was 305 (although only 235 posts were filled) and constituted over 27 percent of the entire ICAC establishment (ICAC, 1979; see also Fig. 2). Community liaison staff alone continued to number well over 200 until well into the 1990s. The departmental establishment has subsequently declined, however, and has remained below 200 since 2003 (ICAC, 2004, p. 28). In 2011, its strength was 177 (ICAC, 2012, p. 22). The decline in establishment is probably a reflection of a changing emphasis in the community relations strategy from a focus on personal contact in the field to a greater concern with conveying the same anti-corruption message to the public as a whole rather than tailoring it for specific groups. There has also been a significant drop in the number of corruption complaints lodged in the regional offices from 36 percent of all complaints in 1999 to 17 percent of all complaints in 2011, primarily because all telephone complaints have now been diverted from regional offices to a centralized report center (ICAC, 2000, 2012). Finally, there is now a feeling that local communities are generally well aware of what does and does not constitute corruption and that the task is one of maintenance rather than the proactive approach of earlier days.

That was certainly not the case in 1975 when the CRD found itself dealing with deeply ingrained attitudes in a society in which corruption was a way of life. Its Director graphically described the situation in the 1970s as follows:

> We needed to pay bribes practically from cradle to grave. Hopeful mothers had to bribe the hospital attendants to give them a glass of water, anxious fire victims needed to "beg" the firefighters to save their life and home with bribes, candidates of driving tests could literally buy the driving licenses, putting the lives of other road users at high risk. Illegal kickbacks were necessary lubricants for oiling the wheels of business. Police officers, including those responsible for investigating corruption offenses at that time, condoned all sorts of illegal activities. (ICAC, 2008)

The CRD's approach to these problems focused sequentially on awareness, penetration, and involvement. Awareness related to the knowledge of the ICAC's activities. Thanks to the scandalous circumstances which had led to its creation (see Quah, 2011, pp. 252–253), there was widespread awareness of the ICAC's role; a survey in 1977, and every subsequent survey, found that almost everyone in Hong Kong had heard of the ICAC. Awareness was further enhanced by the work of the Media and Education Division, which was soon running a television series, "The Quiet Revolution," carrying a strong anti-corruption message. One of the Division's first television advertisements of a poor woman with a baby on her back pausing outside an ICAC sub-office, wondering whether she should report corruption, achieved iconic status.

The effects of the media campaign and public enthusiasm for stamping out corruption buoyed support for the field workers. The sub-offices became an important source of obtaining complaints about corruption and served also as a base for liaison with community organizations. The number of corruption complaints in 1974 and 1975 was over 3,000, dropping slightly in 1976 to 2,433. The ICAC regarded three aspects of the complaint process as particularly encouraging. First, there was a gradual rise in the number of the people who were willing to make complaints in person. In 1974, only 35 percent had been prepared to give their names. Anonymity sometimes made it difficult to pursue cases and in June 1975, the CRD sought to counter the reluctance of complainants to identify themselves by releasing two television clips, which commended those who left their names and addresses (ICAC, 1976). By 1977, the number of complainants who were willing to identify themselves had risen to over 50 percent. During 1975–1999, on average approximately 60 percent of the complainants were willing to make their complaint in person (Wong, 1999). Second, between 31 and 38 percent of all complaints made to the ICAC between 1977 and

1987 were made to the regional offices which were seen as an indication that field officers had the trust of the local community (Ma, 1988, p. 40). An ICAC officer, who served in a regional office at the time, recalls that some complainants who came in the front door asked to leave by the back door. The regional offices did in fact encouraged complainants to leave their names but they also respected their wish to remain anonymous. The duty officer was deliberately situated closest to the door so that only he or she would know the identity of the complainant (Ma, 1988, p. 39). Third, many complaints received, reaching a high of nearly 75 percent of all complaints in 1980, were non-corruption complaints even though some of the complainants knew full well that the ICAC's brief did not stretch to those issues (Ma, 1988, p. 19). The ICAC regarded this as sign of public confidence and, together with the increasing number of complainants who were willing to be named, as evidence that the community was willing to use the regional office as a means of expressing grievances or seeking clarification on government regulations or policies. The regional offices forwarded non-corruption complaints to government departments or appropriate statutory bodies to deal with them.

Although the first few years of the CRD produced encouraging public responses both to its media campaigns and to its community liaison programs, its efforts suffered a major setback as a result of the police mutiny and subsequent partial amnesty in November 1977. By 1977, the ICAC had already arrested and convicted several hundred corrupt policemen and the numbers seemed to be rising. In the first three weeks of October 1977, 140 policemen were arrested (Lethbridge, 1985, p. 140). Junior police officers began organizing meetings calling for the cessation of the ICAC's work. On October 28, 1977, several thousand policemen held a meeting on Hong Kong Island and marched to the office of the Commissioner of Police, after which a smaller group of between 40 and 100 broke off and stormed the ICAC headquarters. Governor MacLehose was faced with a difficult situation which he eventually resolved by stipulating that the ICAC would not henceforth act in relation to offenses committed before January 1, 1977 except in respect to officers who had been dismissed from the Police Force, persons against whom warrants had been issued, or persons outside Hong Kong (Legislative Council, 1977, p. 157).

Although the policemen who had taken part in the assault on the ICAC headquarters were subsequently dismissed, the effect on the ICAC and, in particular, on the CRD was almost immediate. The amnesty was a serious blow to the ICAC's credibility and resulted in a sharp fall in the number of corruption complaints received by the organization. Corruption complaints fell from 2,433 in 1976 to 1,700 in 1977 to 1,234 in 1978 (ICAC, 1977–1979). Interestingly, although the ICAC experienced a rapid decline in the total number of corruption complaints, the actual number of complaints, both corruption and non-corruption, lodged in regional offices rose slightly between 1977 and 1978. This may have been because the CRD was opening more offices and/or because the regional offices were beginning to be perceived as wider complaint-handling bodies. Nonetheless, the CRD was faced with the task of winning back public confidence and embarked on a highly labor-intensive campaign, which consisted of going from housing block to housing block, door-by-door, and even boat-to-boat in the case of boat-dwellers, to persuade the public that the ICAC was still in business. Gradually, these efforts paid off. In 1979 and 1980, corruption complaints began to rise from 1,665 complaints in 1979 to 1,772 in 1980 (ICAC, 1980–1981). However, the increase in non-corruption complaints was even more striking. In 1980, of a total of 7,064 complaints, 5,292 (74.9 percent) were non-corruption complaints, suggesting that the ICAC was filling a gap as a grievance-handling organization even if there was still some uncertainty about whether it could fill a role as an effective agency for controlling corruption.

The CRD recognized early on that awareness of the ICAC and willingness to report corruption could only be sustained by changing embedded attitudes. "Penetration," the second step in the community relations strategy, involved winning public support to fight corruption but also provided some evidence that the CRD's activities were having some effect on behavior. The regional offices had an important role to play in this regard but because the activities were so labor-intensive and required face-to-face contact much reliance was also placed on the mass media. The CRD prides itself on the fact that it was the first public organization in Hong Kong to launch television commercials and to produce television dramas and animation series (Wong, 1999). The dramas, which were based on real cases, proved popular not only in Hong Kong but in mainland China.

The efforts of the regional offices and the mass media campaign were backed by a Community Research Unit, which came under the administrative support branch. In 1977, 1978, and 1980, the Community Research Unit conducted mass surveys to gauge corruption perceptions. Some of the findings of those surveys showed the extent to which attitudes were embedded. For example, even though the ICAC had been in existence for three years, many respondents did not view giving "tea money" to government employees as corruption; nearly half thought that "under the table" kickbacks were normal business practice; and 46 percent believed that there was corruption in every Hong Kong government department (Leung, 1981, pp. 9–10). The "tea money" issue was of particular concern because it reflected the long-standing practice of paying for public services on top of any required charges. The Prevention of Bribery Ordinance (POBO), which is the principal anti-corruption legislation in Hong Kong, defines corruption as accepting an advantage. One of the ICAC's priorities was to try to ensure a clean government in which services were provided without any additional charges being levied. If the practice of paying "tea money" were to continue and to be supported in the community, the prospects of a future clean government were significantly reduced. Multiple methods were used to address the problem, including mass media campaigns and public education, liaison work and discussions with specific groups, targeting youth and using them to convey the message that tipping was illegal to their parents, and some experimental research. By 1986, when mass surveys were again undertaken, there was evidence that change was taking place. In 1977, only 32 percent of the respondents knew that tipping public sector employees was illegal; by 1986, 72 percent knew that it was illegal (McDonald,1994, p. 28).

It was also clear that perceptions of corruption in government more generally were changing and that awareness of the work of the ICAC had increased. In 1977, 38.3 percent of respondents believed that there was widespread corruption in government; by 1984, this had dropped to 5.8 percent (ICAC, 1984, paras 56–57). Knowledge of the ICAC had also increased. By 1984, 95 percent of respondents knew its name and what it did; 82 percent claimed to know its hotline number; 75 percent could name one of its regional offices; 46.7 percent said that they knew what the CRD did (ICAC, 1984, paras 90, 99–100, 106–107).

"Involvement," the third step in the community relations strategy, has gradually assumed more importance with the number of civil society, business, and government organizations working with the ICAC increasing rapidly over the years. The CRD realized from the outset that it needed to cultivate good relationships with these organizations if it were to pass on its message to their members. In the first four months of its existence, for example, it held 65 meetings with a broad cross-section of the society ranging from students to businessmen and rural leaders to fishermen and hawkers (ICAC, 1975). From this modest beginning, its partnership with other organizations has expanded exponentially over the years. By 1980, the CRD was already reporting contact with some 9,794 organizations (ICAC, 1981, p. 54). By 2010, the annual report recorded that, in the business sector alone, the CRD was leveraging on a network of some

60 chambers of commerce and trade associations to pass on its message to their 26,000 member companies (ICAC, 2011, p. 61). Similar efforts have been made to work with youth organizations and with the universities in devising various anti-corruption programs and with the many nongovernmental organizations (NGOs) assisting new migrants. This blanket coverage of society has extended to the point where the CRD is in contact, either directly or through partner organizations, with many hundreds of thousands of people per year.

As Table 1 shows, the independent annual surveys, which the ICAC commissions, have consistently shown widespread public support for its work, a belief that its actions are effective, an increasing willingness to report corruption in person, and an appreciation that corruption may affect the level of economic development. The ICAC has also assumed a position within the political system as the guarantor of clean government

Table 1. ICAC Annual Survey Responses: Selected Questions, 1997−2011.

Question	Answer	Range
How common is corruption in Hong Kong?[a]	Not common or very uncommon	43.7−71.3%[b]
How tolerant are you of corruption?	Totally intolerant	In government (2001−2009): 64.4−73.7% In business (2001−2009): 46.0−57.4%
Have you or your relatives or friends come across corruption in the past 12 months?	No	91.0−98.5%
Are you willing to report corruption?[c]	Yes	64.7−81.3%
How effective is the ICAC's work?[d]	Very effective or quite effective	60.2−87.8%[e]
Does the ICAC deserve your support?	Yes	97.1−99.4%
How important is keeping Hong Kong corruption-free to the overall development of Hong Kong?	Very important or quite important	96.3−99.2%[f]

Source: ICAC (1998−2012).
[a]A further 0.2−12.9% said that they did not know.
[b]The percentage is the subtotal of "Not common" and "Very uncommon."
[c]A further 12.4−27.3% said that it "depends on the circumstances."
[d]The percentage is the subtotal of "Very effective" and "Quite effective."
[e]A further 0.3−9.0% said that they did not know.
[f]The percentage is the subtotal of "Very important" and "Quite important." This question was only asked in 2010 and 2011.

and as an institution which the public can trust. One survey found that it was the most trusted of all Hong Kong political and governmental institutions (Chan & Chan, 2006). This finding cannot be attributed solely to the work of the CRD because trust almost certainly also derives from the OD's successful prosecution of the corrupt and the CPD's efforts to ensure that Hong Kong government practices do not present opportunities for corruption. The CRD, however, has been instrumental in ensuring that the perceptions of corruption have changed and that the public is no doubt that the ICAC will not tolerate corruption.

"BOTTOM-UP" APPROACHES TO CORRUPTION PREVENTION

In recent years, scholars have become increasingly interested in the prospect that an understanding of the corruption perceptions of differentiated socioeconomic groups might lead to a more focused evidence-based approach to corruption prevention (Gong & Wang, 2012; Rose-Ackerman & Truex, 2012; Truex, 2011; Zaloznaya, 2012). The approach is founded on the premise that socioeconomic groups might have embedded perceptions about corruption which are contrary to, and may override, government or agency's values and desired objectives. To address this kind of problem requires community engagement: the existence of differentiated views on corruption among various social groups or in particular communities in itself suggests that the central anti-corruption message has either not been communicated effectively or has been ignored. But changing attitudes which might be embedded in a culture and in long-standing practice is clearly no easy matter. What might such a successful strategy entail?

The ICAC's experience in the first few years of its existence is instructive. It had to deal with two questions which are central to a successful corruption prevention strategy from a "bottom-up" perspective: How do we change community perceptions about corruption? And how do we know when perceptions have in fact changed? A typical liaison strategy of the late 1970s and early 1980s, which was devised for interaction between the CRD officers and specific groups, involved a number of related components. First, and most important for the purposes of this analysis, liaison programs aimed at "changing the public's acceptance of corruption as a normal way of life by creating an awareness that corruption can lead to injustice, social instability, extortion, inflation and that everyone in the society are [*sic*] just as likely to share its bad effects directly or indirectly" (Leung, 1981, p. 21). Second, the aim was to promote confidence in the ICAC. Third, the officers were expected to discuss the law. Fourth, they were to establish channels of communication to ensure that the participants knew how and where to report corruption and how to obtain further information (ICAC, Public Education Unit, 1980, reproduced in Leung, 1981, Appendix V).

In practice, the last three components of the strategy quickly fell away when the officers in the field discovered that most people did have confidence in the ICAC, that they knew about the law, and how and where to report corruption. Attempts to change attitudes toward corruption were based on the assumption that there was a need to appeal to both individual self-interest and a wider community good. For example, restaurant owners were not simply told that it was illegal to tip health inspectors but also that, if the health inspectors did not do their job properly, customers might fall sick and the restaurant would lose its license. In some cases, such as taxi and mini-bus drivers who were victims of extortion by corrupt policemen, the appeal to self-interest was clearly evident and the task became more focused on persuading the group that the ICAC would take action against the offenders. The appeal to the wider community good was based largely on the question: in what kind of society do you and your children wish to live? The negative effects of corruption on the standard of living, the economy, and the moral fabric of the society were strongly stressed (ICAC, Public Education Unit, 1980, reproduced in Leung, 1981, Appendix V).

Although the liaison work in the field was usually well received, the ICAC was not initially entirely convinced that its work was leading to changed attitudes toward corruption. The Community Research Unit consequently conducted a survey of youth which sought to test their attitudes both before and after exposure to the ICAC's message. The questionnaire consisted, inter alia, of detailed scenarios, asking, for example, whether it was acceptable to tip hospital staff, private sector employees, or civil servants. Although the survey generally found that attitudes changed positively after contact with the ICAC, some findings also suggested that there were areas where public attitudes were contrary to the message which the ICAC wanted to convey. There was a belief, for example, that corruption did promote efficiency and that it was acceptable to tip in the private sector even after the ICAC explained circumstances in which it would be regarded as corruption (Leung, 1981, pp. 43, 51). The research, which was experimental rather than conclusive, did suggest areas in which the ICAC could improve its efforts, providing a focus for publicity. The findings were also strengthened by the mass surveys in the 1980s which showed that attitudes had changed significantly over a relatively short period.

This initial intensive and highly disaggregated approach gradually changed to the maintenance of a more generalized, single community-wide anti-corruption message and an adaptation to the challenges of new forms of corruption extending well beyond the ICAC's original focus on bribery. By the mid-1980s, the mass surveys were indicating a much greater public awareness of the role of the ICAC and wider knowledge of the content of the POBO. The assumption was that the broader community was supportive of the ICAC's work and that it did not need specific attention and guidance through disaggregated socioeconomic groups. To the extent that the ICAC focused on particular sectors of the community, the groupings were larger − in particular, public servants, businesspeople and youth − and thematic messages, inasmuch as they supplemented the general message of zero tolerance of corruption, were aimed at those groups. That has not prevented the ICAC from launching new programs or to refocus on more disaggregated groups if it felt that there was a need. There were major new initiatives aimed at youth after 1996 when surveys showed that they were becoming more tolerant of corruption. New migrants have also been a continuing focus since migration from the mainland began to increase after 1997. In the paragraphs that follow, we consider the CRD's relationship with sectors of the community that have been its perennial source of concern: business, youth, and the public service and with the more recent attention to the corruption attitudes of new migrants.

Business

Although the CRD claimed that it received a warm response from many organizations, at the outset its reception from business was somewhat less than cordial. Businesspeople were apprehensive that the ICAC would begin to clamp down on some of the loose and potentially corrupt practices which had traditionally characterized commerce. In some cases, CRD officers were mistaken for OD investigators and treated with hostility; in others, they were told that there was nothing to talk about (ICAC, 2004, pp. 58, 108). An important initial issue was the payment of commissions by one firm to another for services rendered, which business regarded as necessary practice but which was prohibited after the ICAC's successful prosecution of a company in 1976. The Chinese Manufacturer's Association then lobbied the government to try to exempt the payment of commissions from prosecution under the POBO, but neither the government nor the ICAC were swayed (Manion, 2004, p. 45). As public sector corruption was gradually brought under control, the ICAC increasingly focused on the private sector. In 1988, for the first time, private sector corruption complaints rose to 1,153 exceeding those in the public sector and have continued to do so since then (ICAC, 1989). Private sector corruption issues also became more prominent as a result of some high profile cases. Between 1984 and 1994, for example, the ICAC dealt with private sector fraud cases to the value of US$1.25 billion including several collapsed banks (Kwok, 1995). It also conducted a long-running investigation into the demise of the Carrian company. Carrian was a multinational corporation which at one stage was the fifth largest company by capitalization in Hong Kong but which was liquidated, after cash flow problems, in October 1983. The Malaysian-based Bank Bumiputra Malaysia Berhad was estimated to have lost US$1 billion in the Carrian collapse, which at the time was the largest bank failure by value ever known (for details, see Milne, 1987). There was evidence of widespread fraud and criminal activities. The Bank Bumiputra's internal auditor, who was sent to investigate the case, was murdered and there followed some surprising legal decisions in the Hong Kong courts and lengthy attempts by the ICAC to extradite some of the suspects from Britain. The ICAC began the investigation in 1985 after a complaint was lodged under the POBO but the case was not finally concluded until 2000.

These high profile cases reinforced the importance of the contacts which the CRD had already began to establish in the industrial and commercial sector. By 1982, the CRD was already estimating that 45 percent of its liaison work was concerned with diverse private sector companies ranging from air freight, to real estate, to restaurants, and import/export (ICAC, 1983, p. 52). It began a program whose aim was to contact the small companies which make up 98 percent of Hong Kong's commercial sector. In the first year of the program more than 6,000 business organizations were contacted of whom 5,400 (90 percent) were approached for the first time (ICAC, 1984, p. 68). In the following year, the number increased to 9,000 of which 8,124 (90.3 percent) were first-time contacts (ICAC, 1985). The range of the CRD's activities was extensive, impressive, and targeted to have maximum impact. After the bank collapsed in the 1980s, for example, the CRD decided that it needed to put its message across to bank staff and gave talks to 25,000 of them over the course of a year. There was also increasing emphasis on contact with peak professional and commercial organizations, such as the Hong Kong General Chamber of Commerce, the Chinese

Manufacturer's Association, the Federation of Hong Kong Industries, the Society of Accountants, the Hong Kong Medical Association, and the Hong Kong Institution of Engineers. In 1995, liaison work with these professional and commercial organizations was given recognition within the CRD by the creation of the Hong Kong Ethics Development Center (HKEDC), which has the specific role of liaising with these bodies. The HKEDC has produced guides for good practice for specific businesses, such as bank managers, doctors, building contractors, engineer, and accountants, and advises companies on how they can comply with the law.

For the most part, in the 1980s and 1990s, the work of the CRD followed the predictable path of contact, talks focusing on what was prohibited under the POBO, distribution of written material designed specifically for the private sector – for example, a 1980s pamphlet which was entitled "When Money Business Becomes Monkey Business" – and follow-up liaison work which sometimes took the form of joint programs with the organization. With the opening up of China and much greater economic interaction between the mainland and Hong Kong cross-border corruption became an issue. Cross-border corruption complaints doubled between 1992 and 1996 although, as the ICAC Commissioner pointed out, they still amounted to only 5 percent of all complaints (Legislative Council, Panel on Security, 1996). The problem was not that of Chinese companies doing business in Hong Kong which could be prosecuted if they acted corruptly. Rather the difficulty was for Hong Kong companies doing business on the mainland. Those companies might behave with total propriety in Hong Kong but were often faced with circumstances in China where, if they did not act corruptly or at least unethically, they could not do business at all. The ICAC has, of course, no jurisdiction outside Hong Kong although a mutual case assistance scheme has been in force since 1988 (ICAC, 2011, p. 16). The CRD did set up a liaison unit with its mainland counterpart on nonoperational matters after the resumption of Chinese sovereignty in 1997, but the problem remains.

Youth

The CRD's concern with moral education and attitudes of youth toward corruption goes back to its inception in 1975. A Public Education Unit (PEU) was established within the CRD in that year but because of funding problems remained in "embryonic" form for several years afterwards. The intent, which was eventually realized, was that the PEU should work with the Education Department to produce teaching kits on moral education and should seek to influence attitudes toward corruption in the school environment (Clark, 1987; ICAC, 1976, p. 37). The CRD's efforts in this respect expanded very considerably in the 1980s. By 1984, it was developing teaching aids and films for students at various levels and testing them before their general release. Camps were held for young people who had left school and 250 young people were trained for voluntary work (ICAC, 1985, p. 58). A decade later, the CRD launched the program, *Onward to 21*, a career guidance package to prepare students for their first job which was delivered to 83,446 students in 1994 (ICAC, 1995, p. 43).

There was continuing concern, however, that the message to youth was not being as well received as the CRD expected. Two surveys, one conducted in 1996 by the CRD, the other by the Hong Kong Federation of Youth Groups, caused alarm bells to ring because it showed that youths were developing "comparatively tolerant" attitudes toward corruption (ICAC, 1997, p. 50). The Hong Kong Federation of Youth Groups survey found that nearly 20 percent of their respondents agreed with the statement "as long as it is not immoral, one can use any means, legal or illegal, to make money." The survey results also showed that the younger the respondents, the more likely they were to be tolerant of corruption and that there was a greater tolerance among all respondents of corruption in business than in the public sector (Hong Kong Federation of Youth Groups, 1997). Coupled with concerns about cross-border issues and the widespread perception that corruption would again become rampant after 1997, the CRD felt that new initiatives were needed. It reviewed its strategy on moral education and focused much of its intention in 1998, together with partner organizations, in contacting some 500,000 youths (ICAC, 1998, p. 53). The methods adopted were innovative and made good use of new technological advances and the CRD's considerable capacity and experience in the use of mass media. The CRD organized concerts, radio programs, and dramas and distributed compact discs with songs promoting the anti-corruption message. A cartoon series for young children, Gee-dor-dor (the "flying rabbit"), proved very popular, resulting in sequels and an accompanying parenting booklet. In 2000, the CRD also launched a web site for teenagers, "Teensland," which within three years had received 26 million hits with an average stay of 18 minutes. In 2010, the Education and the Mass Communication sections were replaced by a Youth and Moral Education Office.

Youth remains a primary focus of the CRD. Its methods, however, have changed. The talks to school children and university students have been replaced by more interactive programs utilizing computers and the social media (ICAC Director, Community Relations, 2013). In the universities, there is a program for ICAC "ambassadors" who participate in events organized by the CRD and who are supposed to organize their own functions to spread the word among their fellow students. There is, however, some evidence that youth in Hong Kong, while they are strongly opposed to corruption defined as bribery, are less inclined to be proactive in resolving corruption problems, preferring to leave anti-corruption efforts to the ICAC (Gong, Wang, & Ren, 2013).

The Public Service

The public service, and particularly corruption in the Police Force, was the initial focus of much of the ICAC's activities. It was successful in cleaning up the Hong Kong public service relatively quickly and prosecutions for corruption dropped sharply. From the early 1980s until the mid-1990s, the ICAC maintained its vigilance using previously employed methods but did not introduce any major new initiatives. With the imminent change of sovereignty, however, there was an increase in cross-border corruption and the perception that it would increase after 1997. There was also a case of unethical behavior by a very senior civil servant which caused public concern (Scott & Leung, 2012). After 1997, on the initiative of the Chief Secretary for Administration, efforts were made to enhance integrity and to try to deal with ethical issues, conflicts of interest, and new forms of corruption in the public sector that went beyond the traditional focus on corruption as bribery. One of the outcomes of this policy was the appointment in 2006 of Ethics Officers, very senior government officials, in every bureau and department. The program which is run by the ICAC and the Civil Service Bureau aims at maintaining traditional rule-based checks on corruption but supplementing this with a greater emphasis on value-based elements particularly relating to conflicts of interest and professional behavior (Brewer, Leung, & Scott, 2010).

The integrity management program illustrates the differences between a generic and a tailored anti-corruption message. Just under half of the strength of the Hong Kong civil service is composed of about 55 small departments and bureaus with staff of less than 4,000. Because these departments are not sufficiently large to warrant their own training facilities, they are reliant on the ICAC and the Civil Service Bureau for training materials. This tends to give their programs for those departments a generic flavor although they have been modified in some instances by the secondment of centrally based training staff to the departments. In large departments, which have their own training capacity, it is possible to tailor the integrity management program to the needs of the department. For over a decade, for example, the Police Force have had in place a successful program called "Living the Values" which highlights annually one of its core values and seeks to enhance that value through focus groups, seminars, and competitions.

New Migrants

By the beginning of 2013, about 10 percent of Hong Kong's population, some 762,000 people, was composed of Chinese mainland migrants who had arrived after 1997 (Legislative Council, 2013, p. 7500). About 97 percent of the migrants came to Hong Kong under the family reunification scheme, usually spouses joining their partners or children joining their parents (Legislative Council, 2013, p. 7501). For the most part, they were poor, uneducated compared with their Hong Kong counterparts, and often spoke neither Cantonese nor English (Siu, 2009). They tended to gravitate toward the least prosperous areas of Hong Kong such as Tin Shui Wai and Sham Shui Po. There is a widely held perception in Hong Kong, which is supported by strong evidence (Gong & Wang, 2012), that attitudes toward corruption in Hong Kong are very different from those in mainland China. The ICAC and, to some extent, the public have consequently been concerned that the new migrants might be more tolerant of corruption than Hong Kong citizens.

In dealing with this potential problem, there has been a heavy, although not exclusive, reliance on NGOs. In the past, the ICAC gave talks to migrants before they came to Hong Kong but this program has now been contracted out to an NGO, International Social Services, which also provides more general information to the migrants on living in Hong Kong and follow-up information once they arrive (ICAC Director, Community Relations, 2013). The program is provided free and incorporates information on Hong Kong's anti-corruption laws based on material compiled by the ICAC which is distributed as a compact disc to all NGOs dealing with new migrants. An anti-corruption video, featuring a prominent actress and singer, is also played when new migrants line up for their identity cards. The ICAC has itself been proactive in organizing programs for new migrants. In Tin Shui Wai, the regional office discovered that a priority for many new migrants was to learn English. It then organized its own English course, drawing on examples from the anti-corruption laws and the ICAC's experience and practices.

We were interested to see whether these various measures had any significant impact on the attitudes and perceptions of corruption of new migrants. In 2012, we undertook a pilot study of 207 people in Tin Shui Wai and Sham Shui Po to see, inter alia, whether we could discern any differences between the new migrants and Hong Kong citizens. The respondents were offered various scenarios in which they were asked whether they regarded a particular action as corrupt and were also asked about their attitudes toward corruption.[1]

There were no significant differences between the new migrants and Hong Kong citizens on such matters as whether it was permissible for a government official to accept "tea money," for a businessman who paid a commission to obtain a license quickly, for a government official to help relatives to obtain admission for a child to a school, or for a senior government official to accept free accommodation from businessmen. All were regarded as acting corruptly. However, if a distinction is drawn between those new migrants who had been in Hong Kong for less than four years and those who had four to seven years' residence, then some slight differences do emerge. Those with less than four years' residence were more likely to believe that it was not corrupt for a government official to use a government vehicle to transport his family, to take up employment with a company with which he had been dealing as a government official, or failing to report financial interests. But in this respect they were not too dissimilar from other Hong Kong residents of Tin Shui Wai and Sham Shui Po. If we compare the attitudes of those new migrants with four to seven years' residence with Hong Kong residents, they tend to be slightly less tolerant of corruption. The most significant difference between the new migrants and the Hong Kong citizens was that the new migrants were more likely to believe that corruption in human society was unavoidable whereas, by implication, Hong Kong citizens believed that it could be controlled.

These findings have to be treated with caution pending a more comprehensive study. They do suggest, however, that the anti-corruption message for the new migrants has been reinforced since they arrived in Hong Kong, perhaps through exposure to the activities of the NGOs and the generic message of the ICAC. It is not surprising that new migrants should carry with them memories of their experience in China where, for example, it is permissible for officials to use government vehicles to transport their families. These memories may fade over time in the face of what are

regarded as unacceptable practices in Hong Kong, a message that is conti-
nually reinforced by the ICAC.

In assessing the extent to which the ICAC has been able to identify and
act upon different perceptions and attitudes toward corruption among disaggregated socioeconomic groups, there is clearly a distinction between its
focus on such groups in the early years and its rather less interactive
approach after the mid-1980s. Its belief that attitudes toward corruption
were more stable and that there was less need for direct involvement was
evidently important in shaping a less intensive approach after the results of
the mass surveys of the 1980s showed both support for the ICAC and an
increasingly less public tolerance of corruption. One indication of this shift
in approach was the dissolution of the Community Research Unit in 1992
when it was felt that it was no longer necessary to have an independent
research capacity within the ICAC. From that time forward almost all
research has been outsourced with the independent annual survey providing the principal indicators of attitudes toward corruption and of support
for the ICAC. While there are no doubt advantages to outsourcing
research, the response time to changing situations particularly at the local
level and in unacceptable business practices is likely to be slower than if
there were an in-house research capacity such as that which the
Community Research Unit provided. In 2009, the ICAC set up a Center of
Anti-Corruption Studies which, although it currently outsources almost all
its research, does have the potential to expand into a body which carries
out research for the ICAC as a whole. Although the ICAC can be well-
satisfied with the reception which its message has received in the community, there is still room for focused research which will enable it to tailor its
policies and publicity specifically, if necessary, rather than only generically.

LOCAL INITIATIVES AND EMBEDDED ANTI-CORRUPTION ATTITUDES

One of the potential advantages of engaging the public directly is that
ACAs may be able to encourage local initiatives to combat corruption.
This stretches far beyond persuading the public to report corruption. It
involves proactive measures to formulate strategies and create social networks and civic organizations to reveal and propose solutions to corruption at the local level and to take on "ownership" of the problem. This is
particularly important in large jurisdictions where central agencies can

hardly be expected to monitor the multiplicity of practices and transactions that occur in local government and in private firms operating at the local level. They need the "eyes and ears" of local anti-corruption bodies not only to alert them to problems but to take preventive measures in local government to ensure that such problems do not occur again. Even in a small jurisdiction such as Hong Kong, some of the corruption that occurs is locally based in electoral fraud in district council elections, building management, misuse of district council funds, and in conflicts of interest between members of the councils and companies tendering for contracts. What has the community relations strategy done to help promote local initiatives and to embed anti-corruption attitudes in organizational form at the local level?

The ICAC has a monopoly over community education and publicity on corruption in Hong Kong. Although it has successfully established partnerships with many organizations, it monitors their work closely and ensures that the ICAC's line on corruption is being pursued. It has not been particularly proactive in encouraging citizens' groups at the local level to form their own networks and organizations and it has been lukewarm to the establishment of anti-corruption NGOs in Hong Kong. There appear to be two main reasons why, despite a strategy of engaging the public, this has not led to the creation of local anti-corruption civic organizations or NGOs with an anti-corruption focus. The first is that, as one ICAC officer remarked, the ICAC is "a victim of its own success." In their research comparing the attitudes of youth toward corruption in China and Hong Kong, Gong et al. (2013) show that Hong Kong youth tend to believe that they can leave corruption matters to the ICAC. Chinese youth, by comparison, tend to believe that they have little option but to take corruption issues into their own hands. Gong (2012) has shown that many local anti-corruption initiatives flourish in China. Many of those that she describes, perhaps most, are ineffectual and sometimes muddle-headed but they do represent a community response to the problem. In Hong Kong, it is usually a matter of leaving corruption issues to the ICAC.

A second possible reason why the ICAC has not been particularly encouraging toward local initiatives or the establishment of anti-corruption NGOs is that it may believe that it needs to guard the purity of its message to the public and its hard-won position in their esteem. The message has always been, and continues to be, one of zero tolerance for corruption. The possibility that this message may be qualified, distorted, or may cast doubt on the ICAC's own work is of concern if local anti-corruption initiatives, such as those Gong (2012) describes in China, were to spring up in

Hong Kong. Bureaucratic politics may also play a role. The ICAC may need to maintain its distance from local government, societal groups, and other government departments to ensure that it continues to be independent and that it is not drawn into controversies which may affect its public image.

Perhaps as a consequence of these concerns, interaction between the ICAC regional officers and local district councils tend to follow similar paths. Every year the regional officer will present a work plan to the district council which in essence is common to regional offices across Hong Kong. Notionally, the plan is for discussion but it is rare for the ICAC to be faced with challenges to what it intends to do and it is difficult for councilors to come up with any alternative ways of dealing with corruption because the ICAC's approach tends to be comprehensive. The ICAC regional office's 2013–2014 work plan for the Wong Tai Sin and Sai Kung District, for example, aimed at contacting 78,000 people, conducting 750 corruption prevention activities, and organizing 25 publicity programs (ICAC Regional Office, Kowloon East and Sai Kung, 2013). The District Councils provide about 50 percent of the funding for these activities in each of the ICAC regions. Below the District Council level, there is also interaction between the ICAC officers and area committees which are local organizations composed of the district councilors and other representatives in the subdistricts. The events organized by these committees are used by the ICAC as a vehicle for disseminating its own promotional materials (ICAC Regional Officer, Kowloon West, 2013).

Initiatives taken by the regional offices are decided centrally by the ICAC in communications between the directorate and the regional officers although there are variations in the percentage of resources that each region may devote to a particular topic. In 2013/2014, the featured areas consisted of: a holistic approach to promoting probity; strengthening moral education for young people; promoting business and professional ethics and sound governance; sustained efforts to promote clean building management; and consolidating a probity culture in the public sector (ICAC Regional Office, Hong Kong West/Islands, 2013). Of these objectives, the only one which expresses a strongly felt district level concern is that of building management. About 40 percent of private sector corruption complaints are concerned with issues relating to the management of Hong Kong's numerous apartment blocks (ICAC Regional Officer, Kowloon West, 2013). While some of these complaints are justifiable, many stem from poor communication within the owners' corporations or incompetence. The ICAC investigates the complaints but declines to oversee the operation of the owners' corporations, despite invitations from some corporations to monitor the process and some enthusiasm for more active involvement from councilors. It has, however, produced several prevention toolkits and training videos on good management practices and, for a time, there was also a section in the CRD specifically devoted to building management.

We may conclude that, although the ICAC does engage with the public at the district level and below, its strategies are still centrally determined and do not owe much to local level initiatives. There are advantages to its top-down strategy in the consistency of its message and the emphasis on particular areas of concern which are conveyed throughout Hong Kong. But there are also questions about the extent to which anti-corruption attitudes are embedded in the community. Expressing support for the ICAC and zero tolerance for corruption are certainly high (see Table 1) but they do not translate into proactive initiatives to deal with corruption at the district level. The assumption is that the ICAC will deal with any transgressions. For the present, that is probably a valid assumption but it may also mean that if the ICAC's position weakens – if its monopoly over the control of corruption is challenged, for example, or if the high levels of public confidence in its performance erode – then there is little by way of home-grown, local anti-corruption organizations or networks to take up the slack.

CONCLUSION

There is no doubt that a strategy of engaging the public has been one of the cornerstones of the ICAC's success. Public support has been central to its operations and to the creation of a community in which corruption is regarded as unacceptable. The CRD's activities in the 1970s were based on face-to-face contact and an excellent public relations campaign. Their young and idealistic officers in the field were driven by a mission to tell the public why corruption was so insidiously bad for the society and the economy, how they could report it, and how the corrupt offenders would be prosecuted. This mission was achieved remarkably quickly. Within a decade, the ICAC was satisfied that support for its work was widespread and that the public was far less tolerant of corruption than it had been. It was then able to reduce its intensive efforts in the field and to maintain more of a watching brief over the society.

There are lessons to be learned from this experience. First, face-to-face engagement, as the work of the Community Research Unit showed, has been critical in changing attitudes. Explanations rather than simple exhortations seem to have been important in this respect. Face-to-face contact provided the opportunity not simply to argue for the community interest but also to show that self-interest could be enhanced with effective controls over corruption. Second, the focus on particular groups enabled the CRD to target its message to the specific problems. Addressing the problems which occurred in the workplace rather than offering only generic advice, devising a concrete plan of action, and meeting the groups on the job or in their homes provided an immediacy which could not have easily been obtained by other forms of communication. Third, although the intensive campaigns of the early years of the ICAC were very effective, it is questionable whether they could or should have been sustained in the light of both resource constraints and the possibility that "message fatigue" would eventually set in. The ICAC has to be careful, however, that it does not lose the capacity to identify rapidly changing practices and inimical attitudes toward corruption within specific groups. Fourth, the CRD has worked well to replace its reduced presence in the field with extensive partnerships with organizations throughout the community who spread its message to their members. The caveat is that the ICAC has not been particularly supportive of anti-corruption activities that fall outside its orbit, possibly a reflection of its self-belief that its work is effective but possibly also perhaps because it fears that the local anti-corruption bodies or international NGOs might hinder or duplicate its own programs.

Overall, in terms of the three potential benefits that a community relations strategy might have, the ICAC's experience does demonstrate that it is an effective way to communicate an anti-corruption strategy and to win support for it. It has also shown the value of an approach to corruption which focuses on disaggregated socioeconomic groups. But there is little evidence to suggest that the approach has served to foster local initiatives or to lead to the creation of other anti-corruption bodies or networks. The ICAC remains the dominant force fighting corruption in Hong Kong and most of its citizens seem content to allow it to remain so.

NOTE

1. The study was a survey designed in association with Ting Gong and Shiru Wang of the Department of Public Policy at the City University of Hong Kong and conducted for us by the Social Science Research Center at the University of Hong Kong under the direction of John Bacon-Shone. I gratefully acknowledge the

support of these colleagues, the Department of Public Policy at City University and the research support of Winnie Tian and Deng Lijun.

REFERENCES

Batory, A. (2012). The difficult life of anti-corruption agencies. *Governance, 25*(4), 639–660.

Bracking, S. (2007). Political development and corruption: Why 'right here, right now!'. In S. Bracking (Ed.), *Corruption and development: The anti-corruption campaigns* (pp. 3–27). Basingstoke: Palgrave Macmillan. Chap. 1.

Brewer, B., Leung, J. Y. H., & Scott, I. (2010). *A preliminary report on the survey of ethics officers and assistant ethics officers.* Hong Kong: City University of Hong Kong.

Chan, J., & Chan, E. (2006). Perceptions of universal suffrage and functional representation in Hong Kong: A confused public? *Asian Survey, 46*(2), 257–274.

Clark, D. (1987). A community relations approach to corruption: The case of Hong Kong. *Corruption and Reform, 2*(3), 235–257.

Co, E. E. A. (2007). Challenges to the Philippine culture of corruption. In S. Bracking (Ed.), *Corruption and development: The anti-corruption campaigns* (pp. 121–137). Basingstoke: Palgrave Macmillan. Chap. 6.

Gatti, R., Paternostro, S., & Rigolini, J. (2003, August). *Individual attitudes towards corruption: Do social effects matter?* World Bank Research Working Paper No. 3122, Washington, DC.

Gong, T. (2011). An "institutional turn" in integrity management in China. *International Review of Administrative Sciences, 77*(4), 671–686.

Gong, T. (2012, April). *Integrity management: Local experiments and variations in the Pearl River Delta.* Mimeo, Hong Kong.

Gong, T., & Wang, S. (2012). Indications and implications of zero tolerance of corruption: The case of Hong Kong. *Social Indicators Research* (DOI 10.1007/s11205-012-0071-3).

Gong, T., Wang, S., & Ren, J. (2013). Perception-driven attitudes towards corruption: A comparative study of university students in mainland China and Hong Kong. Paper presented at the workshop on "Integrity Management: Theory and Practice," City University of Hong Kong, March 11.

Gorta, A. (2003). The NSW independent commission against corruption's experience in minimizing corruption. *Asian Journal of Political Science, 11*(1), 1–21.

Grabosky, P. N. (1990). Citizen co-production and corruption control. *Corruption and Reform, 5*(2), 125–151.

Heilbrunn, J. R. (2004). *Anti-corruption commissions: Panacea or real medicine to fight corruption?* Washington, DC: World Bank.

Hong Kong Federation of Youth Groups (1997). *Youth opinion polls: No. 41: Young people's outlook on life.* Hong Kong: Hong Kong Federation of Youth Groups.

ICAC. (1974–2011). *Annual reports.* Hong Kong: Various publishers. Retrieved from www.icac.org.hk

ICAC. (1975, June 4). *ICAC Bulletin 008.* Mimeo, Hong Kong.

ICAC. (1984). *Mass survey.* Hong Kong: Community Relations Department.

ICAC. (1998–2012). *Annual surveys 1997–2011.* Hong Kong: Community Relations Department.

ICAC. (2003). *Independent Commission Against Corruption Ordinance*, Cap 204. Hong Kong. Retrieved from www.gov.hk

ICAC. (2004). *Partnering for probity*. Mimeo, Hong Kong.

ICAC. (2008). Speech of the Director of Community Relations, ICAC at the opening ceremony of the 6th Postgraduate Certificate Course in Corruption Studies, November 4.

ICAC Director, Community Relations, ICAC. (2013). *Interview*, April 24.

ICAC Regional Office, Hong Kong West/Islands. (2013). *Work Plan 2013/14*. C&W CLSAC Paper No.15/2013, April 10.

ICAC Regional Office, Kowloon East and Sai Kung. (2013). *Work Plan 2013/14*. WTSDC Paper 43/2013, May 14.

ICAC, Regional Officer, Kowloon West. (2013). *Interview*, May 27.

Kwok, T. M. K. (1995). Corruption related fraud in the financial sector. Paper presented at the Financial Fraud Seminar, Shanghai. Retrieved from http://www.kwok-manw.com/Speeches/Corruption-Related_Fraud.html

Legislative Council. (1973, October 17). *Official record of proceedings*. Hong Kong. Retrieved from www.gov.hk

Legislative Council. (1977, November 7). *Official record of proceedings*. Hong Kong. Retrieved from www.gov.hk

Legislative Council. (2013, March 20). *Official record of proceedings*. Hong Kong. Retrieved from www.gov.hk

Legislative Council, Panel on Security. (1996, October 7). *Minutes*. L.C. Paper No. CB (2) 329/96-97. Hong Kong. Retrieved from www.gov.hk

Lethbridge, H. J. (1985). *Hard graft in Hong Kong*. Hong Kong: Oxford University Press.

Leung, S. Y. K. (1981). *Public education as a means of combatting corruption: An exploratory study*. M.Soc.Sc. dissertation, University of Hong Kong.

Li, L. (2001). Support for anti-corruption campaigns in rural China. *Journal of Contemporary China*, *10*(29), 573−568.

Ma, M. S. P. (1988). *A study of the ICAC's role in handling non-corruption complaints*. M.Soc. Sc. dissertation, University of Hong Kong.

Manion, M. (2004). *Corruption by design: Building clean government in China and Hong Kong*. Cambridge, MA: Harvard University Press.

McDonald, G.M. (1994). Value modification strategies on a national scale: The activities of the independent commission against corruption. In W. M. Hoffman, J. B. Kamm, R. E. Frederick, & E. S. Petry (Eds.), *Emerging global business ethics* (pp. 14−35). London: Quorum. Chap. 2.

Meagher, P. (2005). Anti-corruption agencies: Rhetoric versus reality. *Journal of Policy Reform*, *8*(1), 69−103.

Milne, R. S. (1987). Levels of corruption in Malaysia: A comment on the case of Bumiputra Malaysia finance. *Asian Journal of Public Administration*, *9*(1), 56−73.

OECD (Organisation for Economic Co-operation and Development). (2003). *Managing conflict of interest in the public service: OECD guidelines and country experiences* (prepared by J. Bertok). Paris.

Osse, A. (1997). Corruption prevention: A course for police officers fighting corruption. *Crime, Law and Social Change*, *28*(1), 950−964.

Preston, N. (1994). *Ethics for the public sector*. Annandale: Federation Press.

Quah, J.S.T. (2011). *Curbing corruption in Asian countries: An impossible dream?* (pp. 237−268). Bingley: Emerald Group Publishing. Chap. 7, Hong Kong.

Rose-Ackerman, S., & Truex, R. (2012). *Corruption and policy reform.* Working paper prepared for the Copenhagen Consensus project, February 17.

Scott, I. (2011). The Hong Kong ICAC's approach to corruption control. In A. Graycar & R. G. Smith (Eds.), *Handbook of global research and practice in corruption* (pp. 401–415). Cheltenham: Edward Elgar. Chap. 25.

Scott, I. (2013). Institutional design and corruption prevention in Hong Kong. *Journal of Contemporary China, 22*(79), 77–92.

Scott, I., & Leung, J. Y. H. (2012). Integrity management in post-1997 Hong Kong: Challenges for a rule-based system. *Crime, Law and Social Change, 58*(1), 39–52.

Siu, H. F. (2009). "Hong Kongers" and "new immigrants." *Hong Kong Journal,* Summer.

Smilov, D. (2009). Anti-corruption bodies as discourse-controlling instruments: Experiences from south-east Europe. In L. de Sousa, P. Larmour, & B. Hindess (Eds.), *Government, NGOs and anti-corruption: The new integrity warriors* (pp. 85–101). London: Routledge. Chap. 6.

Thanudo, N. S. (2013). Reassessing the impact of civil society: Nonprofit sector, press freedom and corruption. *Governance, 26*(1), 63–89.

Truex, R. (2011). Corruption, attitudes and education: Survey evidence from Nepal. *World Development, 39,* 1133–1142.

UNODC (United Nations Office on Drugs and Crime). (2012). The Jakarta Statement on Principles of Anti-Corruption Agencies. Retrieved from http://www.unodc.org/southeastasi aandpacific/en/2012/12/corruption-kpkl/story.html

Wong, F. (1999). Community and public education: The Hong Kong experience. Paper presented at the 9th International Anti-Corruption Conference, Durban, South Africa, October 15.

Zaloznaya, M. (2012). Organizational cultures as agents of differential association: Explaining variations in bribery practices in Ukrainian universities. *Crime, Law and Social Change, 58*(3), 295–320.

CHAPTER 5

CLEAN AND GREEN WITH DEEPENING SHADOWS? A NON-COMPLACENT VIEW OF CORRUPTION IN NEW ZEALAND

Robert Gregory and Daniel Zirker

ABSTRACT

New Zealand has long been regarded as a country with little or no governmental corruption. In recent times it has been ranked consistently as one of the five least corrupt countries in the world, on Transparency International's (TI) Corruption Perceptions Index (CPI). In 2009 and 2011 it was ranked as the single most corruption-free country on the CPI, and in 2012 it shared first place with Denmark and Finland. This chapter examines the reasons why historically New Zealand has been largely free of governmental corruption, using widely accepted definitions of what constitutes corrupt behavior. It goes on to argue that, at least by its own normal standards, the country might now be more susceptible to corruption, for a variety of reasons, in both the public and private sectors, and that more political and administrative attention may need to be paid to this issue. This chapter discusses New Zealand's surprising tardiness in ratifying the United Nations Convention against Corruption,

Different Paths to Curbing Corruption: Lessons from Denmark, Finland, Hong Kong, New Zealand and Singapore
Research in Public Policy Analysis and Management, Volume 23, 109–136
ISSN: 0732-1317/doi:10.1108/S0732-1317(2013)0000023005

an apparent reluctance that leaves the country sitting alongside other non-ratifying countries which have endemic levels of corruption in all its forms. In this context, this chapter also notes some international dissatisfaction with New Zealand's anti-money laundering legislation, enacted in 2009.

INTRODUCTION

New Zealand has a long-standing reputation as a country in which there is little or no corruption in either government or in the business sector. A seldom asked question is: why is this so? In fact, the reasons as to why any country has high or low levels of perceived corruption are seldom self-evident, and usually beg closer examination. There are several main factors, discussed below, which provide an answer to this question in New Zealand's case. However, circumstances change, and there is no guarantee that either corruption generally or governmental corruption specifically will not become significant problems in New Zealand. There are some signs, which are examined in this chapter, which suggest that while relative to other countries New Zealand continues to enjoy very low levels of corruption, nevertheless there is no room for national complacency on this issue, certainly not if concern is gauged against the country's own high standards. The country's strong international reputation in this regard, which in itself is an important national asset, could be subjected to significantly closer scrutiny in the years ahead.

NEW ZEALAND'S PERFORMANCE ON THE CPI

New Zealand has long been rated by Transparency International's (TI) Corruption Perceptions Index (CPI) as one of the six least corrupt countries in the world. It was rated as first, or joint first (i.e., perceived as the least corrupt or equally least corrupt country in the world), in 2006, 2007, 2008, 2009, and 2010, sitting alone atop the rankings in 2009 and 2011, and sharing the top position again with Denmark and Finland in 2012. New Zealand's image as a country in which there is very little, if any, corruption in either government or business is all the more impressive because of the country's bicultural and multicultural character, as charges and countercharges of corruption are thought to be more common in multicultural settings.[1] Larmour (2006) has argued that ideas about "culture" are often used to explain, or excuse, corruption. The CPI largely avoids rapid shifts in rankings, and may even carry with it a propensity to serve as a self-fulfilling factor. And one of the founding members of Transparency International has argued that the CPI, following the advent in 2003 of the United Nations Convention against Corruption (UNCAC), should no longer be published in its present form because it tends to undermine the efforts of reformers (Galtung, 2006). Nevertheless, Iceland, which ranked joint first in 2006 (with Finland and New Zealand) but later experienced a national banking collapse, had dropped to 13th position by 2011 (rising to 11th position in 2012), thus demonstrating that prevailing perceptions of a country's national integrity and honesty can indeed change quite rapidly (Zirker, Gregory, & Scrimgeour, 2012).

REASONS FOR NEW ZEALAND'S CORRUPTION-FREE RECORD

Among the most difficult research questions which arise out of the CPI are those which seek to explain why some countries differ in their levels of governmental and societal corruption. At one level, such answers are not far to seek, on the face of it at least, if researchers want to know why, for example, Denmark or New Zealand experience much lower levels of corruption than, say, Vietnam or the Philippines, or Mongolia, or Somalia. Conventional responses in such cases would probably refer to data such as that provided by the World Bank's Worldwide Governance Indicators (WGI), which focus on six factors: political stability and the absence of violence, government effectiveness, the rule of law, regulatory quality, voice and accountability, and the control of corruption. At the risk of being somewhat tautological, the control of corruption dimension suggests that corruption is low because it is well controlled. Such a focus on the control of corruption is of crucial importance, and much of the comparative literature on corruption argues the importance of institutionalized principal-agent relations, notably a well-resourced, independent, and impartial anti-corruption agency driven by high levels of political will, the rule of law, a similarly independent and impartial judiciary, and so on, in the successful containment of corruption (Quah, 2003, 2010, 2011). However, these principal-agent interpretations, as important as they are, often do not tell the full story. In focusing largely on political dimensions they tend to overlook the more dynamic historical, cultural, and social factors which often are at least as, if not more, important in understanding why some countries have lower levels of corruption than others. In fact, each country has its own particular narrative. A good example of such a narrative is the following, offered as a partial explanation of the rise in corruption in Spain around the mid-2000s:

> ... in the years following Franco's death (1975) up to the early 1990s, the focus of the builders of the new local and regional politico-administrative structures − that is to say, mainly the Socialists − was on weakening the administrative controls on local governments inherited from the dictatorship .... The building of a public administration for the new democracy was largely neglected. This shortcoming was accompanied by an outsized interpretation by the Constitutional Court and others of the newly acquired municipal autonomy bestowed uniformly on all municipalities by the 1978 constitution ... . These two elements (large autonomy and weak control) led to a very weak checks and balances system ... and to the assumption that at the local and regional government levels, a politician winning an election had carte blanche, an unrestricted power to do as he saw fit. (Cardona, 2013, p. 95)

For the purposes of comparison, it is not difficult to provide, for example, a plausible explanation as to why Somalia has much more corruption than Denmark, an explanation that will owe much more to historical and cultural factors than to principal-agent differences. Conversely, historical and cultural factors are likely to be less important than principal-agent approaches in explaining why two countries, Denmark and New Zealand, are consistently ranked on the CPI as being largely corruption-free. In comparisons like this, cultural and historical factors seem less important than the fact that both countries are highly rated on the WGI.

In such cases comparative investigation into cultural and historical elements seems irrelevant. But is it? What about, for example, Australia and New Zealand, two countries with similar cultures and heritages (the "ANZAC" tradition), and both Westminster-styled parliamentary democracies, but which have continued to display consistently different rankings on the CPI, with New Zealand always significantly higher than Australia?[2] In the 13 years from 2000 to 2012, New Zealand's lowest position on the CPI was third or joint third position, while from 2006 to 2012 it was either first or joint first position. On the other hand, Australia's lowest ranking was 13th position in 2000, and its highest ranking was joint seventh position in 2012. New Zealand's average CPI score during this period was 9.42, while Australia's was 8.65 − a substantial difference in perceived levels of corruption within these two countries with such similar backgrounds. How can this difference be explained?

Some obvious factors immediately suggest themselves as plausible explanations: for example, early European Australia was to a large extent a penal colony, whereas New Zealand was a British settler society; and Australian political culture never embraced egalitarian ideals, as did New Zealand's – whereas Australia, perhaps because of resentment of the English, developed its self-image along individualist and competitive American lines. By contrast, New Zealanders generally looked fondly on Britain as "home," and were one of the first countries to develop a welfare state. Moreover, as a federal system, Australia experienced political corruption reminiscent of American "Tammany Hall" politics, especially in New South Wales and Victoria in the earlier half of the 20th century (see Griffin, 1990, 2004). While this form of politics was not completely absent in New Zealand, it was much less common. However, while it might seem plausible – on the face of it – to suggest that Australia's 19th century history as a British penal colony gave rise to non-compliance norms and values (presumably because a higher propensity for unlawful behavior has been passed down through Australian generations), it would be drawing a very long bow to conclude that this helps to explain why there have been higher *overall* levels of corruption, or at least the perceptions thereof, in Australia than in New Zealand. Ironically, the central figure in New Zealand's early colonization – the Director of the New Zealand Company, Edward Gibbon Wakefield – had in 1827 himself been sentenced to three years in London's Newgate prison on abduction charges (Temple, 2002).

We will provide some reasons as to why New Zealand, in its own terms, has enjoyed for so long a reputation for having very low levels of corruption, especially in government. There are two interrelated issues: New Zealand's *reputation* as being a country with very low levels of corruption, on the one hand, and the reality of corruption in New Zealand, on the other. Clearly, most of the available evidence suggests that the reputation quite closely matches the reality: there are unlikely to be expanding black seams of governmental venality occluded behind the country's "clean and green" and corruption-free image. Accepting that proposition then, we find that any explanation of why this is the case must take the form of some story, a narrative that blends historical, social, political, and cultural dimensions into a reasonably coherent and plausible explanation. The alternative – a rigorous scientific collation and interpretation of hard data, producing a conclusive result – is almost certainly beyond practical reach.

Perhaps the most important factor has been New Zealand's strong egalitarian ethos that underwrote one of the world's first welfare states (King, 2003; Lipson, 1948; Sutch, 1969).[3] Most early New Zealand settlers came in the mid-19th century from Britain, in which they themselves were oppressed by class divisions. Although privilege did emerge, largely in the form of "squatters" who acquired large land-holdings, the emergent political culture was resistant to such acquisition, and by the turn of the 20th century, it had broken down. As Fischer (2012) has demonstrated in his comprehensive historical comparison between New Zealand and the United States, New Zealanders have traditionally been far more committed to fairness rather than freedom, while in America the converse has generally been true. In fact, by 1930 the news media in America tended to characterize New Zealand's carefully regulated emphasis on fairness in society as an outrageous denial of freedom, even the hallmark of an emerging Fascist state. In an article by a "special correspondent," entitled "Life in New Zealand Now Ruled by Decree; Even Chicken-Raising is Regulated by State," *The New York Times* reported that:

> The nooks and corners that [New Zealand] has explored in its Fascist rule may be seen from the fact that it has forbidden the building of any more movie theatres without permission, on the ground that there are already more than enough, has refused to issue any more leases to coal operators to mine on State lands because of over-production of coal, and has even determined to register and control all persons who own ten hens or more and sell eggs. ... Slowly this democracy is turning into a Fascist State. When it completes the cycle it will do so with a thoroughness which will fill the Black Shirts with envy. (December 11, 1930, E4)

As two commentators later said about the New Zealand government's economic stabilization program, during the Second World War, "the government was engaged in an elaborate piece of social engineering. Ministers were attempting to construct a wartime economy that would treat all sections as fairly as possible" (Bassett & King, 2000, p. 201). Another observer has described the country's egalitarian ethos as "a society of fair shares" (Roberts, 1978, p. 73).

Nevertheless, any relationship between egalitarianism — especially as "fairness" — and corruption itself awaits adequate explanation (Gregory, 2003). Relatively low levels of government corruption are also seen in jurisdictions like Singapore and Hong Kong, which are by no means egalitarian, and in New Zealand itself, where income inequality increased dramatically after the economic reforms of the late 1980s and early 1990s, the country still ranks at the top of the CPI. On the other hand, Denmark, Norway, and Sweden, all at or near the top of the CPI, are countries with historically strong egalitarian cultures, and all today have Gini coefficient scores much lower than New Zealand's, as has Australia. All these countries (including Hong Kong and Singapore) score well on the WGI, however, confirming that lower levels of corruption are a function of factors other than just egalitarianism. In his commentary on an analysis of a recent increase in corruption in Spain, Cardona (2013, p. 95) wrote: "I could not agree more with the concluding remarks of the article: 'institutional designs and procedures that promote accountability and transparency in government, to the extent that they prevent corruption, may help diminish disaffection and promote compliance with laws and social norms.' For the sake of completeness, I would only add that if policies also promote equality, the propensity to seek corrupt deals dwindles." Again though, the question is — why? It might be because egalitarianism per se, that is, income equality, does not keep corruption at minimal levels, but that egalitarianism itself reflects a social ethos which places a relatively low emphasis on acquisitive and competitive values, especially those which define social status overwhelmingly as a function of wealth.

Another important and allied factor in New Zealand was the strong Calvinist culture that the country's British settlers brought with them, especially from Scotland, and which endured at least until the middle of the 20th century. Values of thrift, hard work, and social cohesion were central to the country's development as "God's Own Country" (or "Godzone," as it is more cynically referred to today), a relatively prosperous, modern mixed economy, a welfare state built on land-based primary industry. Throughout most of the 20th century, until the loss of primary markets, and the oil shocks in the 1970s, New Zealand's economic policies were deeply interwoven with its egalitarian social structure. These policies embodied the key objectives of full employment, financial stability, favorable terms of trade, and high productivity.

Furthermore, New Zealand is a small country in terms of population as it has a land area of 270,534 sq. km (Economist, 2012, p. 186). Its population in 2011 was 4.6 million (Schwab, 2012, p. 383). As an island nation in the South Pacific, it has also been largely "quarantined" from international influences that might otherwise have threatened to strain its social fabric. At least until Maori migration from rural to urban areas from the 1950s onwards, the rapid rise in Pacific Island immigration from about the same time, and the rapid increase in Asian immigrants from the 1980s, the country was dominated by European New Zealanders, fostering at least the illusion of a homogeneous culture and society.

Especially during the decades when New Zealand was even less populous than it is today, urban and provincial communities enjoyed high levels of social capital, reciprocal bonds of collective cooperation, and high levels of interpersonal trust. Thorstein Veblen's "conspicuous consumption" was in these times scarcely apparent in New Zealand, not because high levels of individual and family wealth did not exist, but because strong social norms and expectations ensured that it was seldom flaunted. Social "respectability" was highly valued and most people were wary about engaging in any form of behavior which, if exposed to public scrutiny, would result in a loss of individual or family reputation. In many ways, therefore, the social and political climate in New Zealand was for a long time highly conformist, indeed in many ways stifling; but at the same time it was not an environment encouraging of those with corrupt intent. In short, New Zealand was largely a country of innocence, straight-laced, rather naïve and unsophisticated, and with virtually no organized crime built around prostitution, gambling, or boot-legging. Even low-level tipping was not socially acceptable. The New Zealand Police (formerly called the New Zealand Police Force) was itself almost entirely devoid of the sort of corruption commonly associated with police behavior in other countries, including Australia (Holmes, 2010).

Unlike Australia, New Zealand has had a unitary system of government since its fledgling provincial governments were abolished in 1876. Like Australia, however, its head of state is the British monarch, and both countries inherited the Westminster model of Parliamentary democracy, though each has developed its own parochial version of that system (Weller, Wanna, & Patapan, 2005). New Zealand was a full-fledged member of the "Old Commonwealth" − along with Britain, Canada, and Australia, countries not known for having significant levels of governmental corruption. (South Africa may be regarded as the exception in this regard, among the "Old Commonwealth" countries.) New Zealand did not acquire formal constitutional independence from Britain until 1947, but in the preceding decades had achieved a great deal of de facto independence.

In this era of nation-building, the passage through Parliament of the Public Service Act of 1912 (coming into force the following year) was a seminal and foundational event. The Act, consistent with developments in other parts of the English-speaking world, established a unified, professional, merit-based public service career system, one that was centrally controlled, and that endured until the radical state sector reforms of the 1980s and 1990s. The Act put a stop to the rampant political patronage that had hitherto characterized public service employment in the preceding decades. It laid the foundation for the emergence of a strong public service ethos, which became instilled in employees from the time of their initial recruitment after leaving school or university until their retirement from this essentially closed-shop career 30 or 40 years later. During this time, most employees saw themselves generically and collectively as "public servants," regardless of the positions they held, or the roles they performed. According to Webb (1940, p. 84), "Every cadet who enters the service does so in the knowledge that there are no barriers to his advancement to the highest positions, that his capacities will be impartially assessed, that his right of appeal against decisions affecting his status and salary is carefully safeguarded, and that he will be adequately pensioned on his retirement." Fairness was again a key value. Similarly, as Lipson (1948, p. 479) argued in his seminal commentary on New Zealand's egalitarianism, "there is a commendable absence of graft and a strict code of honesty," attributable in his view to job security, strict accounting, and audit requirements, and also to an "'inner check' reflecting public servants' professional commitment to the ideal of the public interest."

This "normative model" was in turn strongly reinforced by rigorous controls exercised over government officials, controls which allowed zero tolerance of any form of behavior that could be defined as corrupt or even unethical. As a leading New Zealand public service practitioner-scholar wrote in the late-1950s:

> There seems to be common in New Zealand a notion that the responsibilities and moral obligations of public servants are somehow substantially greater than those of other citizens ... . If his standard of conduct is more scrupulous – and, in some respects it is – the reason is to be found largely in the self-interest of the public servant. He is subject to more extensive controls than most private citizens: he is more likely to be caught if he commits an indiscretion: his career may suffer even if there is only suspicion of unsatisfactory conduct. (Polaschek, 1958, p. 283)

New Zealand was the first country to introduce the Danish institution of the Ombudsman, in 1962, as a further means of control over executive authority (Gilling, 1998; Hill, 1976). It also opened up official information to the public in the early 1980s, well before the abolition of the Official Secrets Act in Britain (Gregory, 1984). Interestingly, in 2012 the Office of the Ombudsman noted a "worrying trend in agencies seeking to exclude the application of the OIA [Official Information Act] to certain types of information, ostensibly because the OIA does not provide sufficient protection" (Office of the Ombudsman, 2012, p. 44).

Albeit heavily controlled, a career in the service of government gave employees secure and generously paid employment as long as they remained totally non-corrupt, and even if they were only adequately competent. Nor was the financial grass necessarily greener in the private sector. Security of tenure was not really bought at the cost of substantially lower wages than those available in the private sector. The "public service

discount" was not only generally minimal, but under the "mildly corporate" system of wage-fixing that characterized New Zealand's industrial
relations for several decades, state sector pay rates were often seen to be
ahead of those available in private employment (Roberts, 1978).[4]

New Zealand's first Labor Government, elected by a landslide in 1935 at
the tail-end of the Great Depression, and on the back of emergent growth
in the international economy, greatly expanded New Zealand's incipient
welfare state, largely through the Social Security Act 1938. This government not only developed a system of universal free education, but also
institutionalized a regime of generally fair and progressive taxation. It may
be significant that these two factors, along with a merit-based civil service
and high levels of gender equality (New Zealand was the first country to
give women the vote, in 1893), have been identified as key factors in
explaining low levels of corruption in some European countries (Charron,
Lapuente, & Rothstein, 2013).

As Lipson (1948, pp. 481—482) later argued, the state in New Zealand
was not some external force in the continental European tradition. It
was rather the people themselves in action, nation-building in pragmatic
rather than ideological ways, and only too ready and willing to develop
national infrastructure in the absence of commercial competition. In
this, public employment was not seen as having one's "snout in the public
trough," and although New Zealand never developed an institutionalized
administrative elite like that in Britain, its public service ethos similarly
embodied values like honor, duty, decency, and a strong sense of the public
interest. There was little if any scope or even temptation for corruption
in procurement, of the kinds that are commonplace elsewhere. The
Department of Public Works, established in 1876, later the Ministry of
Works, monopolized such development, and was itself firmly imbued with
the high standards of ethical probity that characterized the wider state
sector.

This strong normative ethos was greatly reinforced during the years of
World War II by the serendipitous convergence into top leadership positions in the New Zealand public service of a group of several highly capable
men, all able practitioners of "the profession of statecraft" (Martin, 1988).
One leading public administration scholar has suggested that the period
1940—1951 was "the age of mandarins" in New Zealand government
(Martin, 2010). If Ralph Waldo Emerson (1841) believed that "an institution is the lengthened shadow of one man," then as an institutional whole
the New Zealand public service could be seen to embody key values shared
by this group of men. They were fully committed to the tacit "Schafferian

Bargain" which shaped the relationship between the political executive and the top levels of the public service (Hood & Lodge, 2006), though the idea of "serial loyalty" (to successive governments of a different political stripe) on the part of the mandarins was not really tested, as the first Labor Government held office for 14 years, from 1935 to 1949.[5] Characterizing one of these men, as if describing them all, Duff (1941, p. 95) observed that, "He is a public servant. With his energy, ability and bold imagination, he could have had a half a dozen careers and made half a dozen reputations. But he entered the public service. He remained in the public service. He is the public service … ." The commitment to impartiality and the rule of law in the administration of public policy was very powerful in New Zealand (and remains so). This cohort of outstanding top officials clearly understood that the *opposite* of impartiality in public office was the use of that office for illegitimate private gain, and through their own behavior they set standards that became deeply embedded in the culture of New Zealand public service (Gregory, 1999).

Nor was it irrelevant that these public service "mandarins" lived and worked in the capital city of Wellington, located in the center of the country, at the foot of the North Island. They would, of course, have made their collective impression in the center of government, wherever it had been located, but the fact that Wellington had been chosen as the capital city in 1865 by New Zealand's then Governor, Sir George Grey, was a significant factor in the emergence of a largely non-corrupt governmental system. Prior to that choice, from 1841 to 1865, the capital city had been Auckland, in the north of the North Island. Auckland had always been, as it is today, by far New Zealand's largest city, but it was in those days not only the center of government, but also a city imbued with the spirit of commercial entrepreneurship and associated "wheeling and dealing," with money the predominant standard by which success was measured. (This remains largely the case today.) By choosing Wellington as the new capital city, albeit largely for logistical reasons, Governor Grey was also laying the foundation for a capital city whose culture would be shaped by governmental rather than commercial values and institutions, and thus would be less likely – especially in these earlier decades of cultural emergence – to become tainted with corruption.

The year 1865 was squarely in the middle of the New Zealand Wars, previously known as the "Land Wars," or the "Maori Wars," which were fought from 1845 to 1872 between the forces of the colonial government (the Crown) and many Maori *iwi* (tribes) (Belich, 1998; King, 2003). They involved the punitive confiscation of large areas of Maori land by the government, in apparent contravention of the country's founding constitutional charter, the Treaty of Waitangi, signed in 1840 between the Crown and many Maori *iwi*. More than 130 years later, about the mid-1970s, at the beginning of what many have seen as a Maori cultural and political renaissance, the New Zealand government began a process of Treaty Settlements, to provide redress for historical grievances, a process which continues to this day.

This whole issue is raised here because it shows how any consideration of corruption in the history of New Zealand government needs also to be viewed from the perspectives of Maori, who were victims of unjust practices perpetrated by the Crown and its agents mainly in the 19th century, notwithstanding the fact that the early colonial administration in New Zealand had been at pains to deal fairly and honestly with land acquisition and settlement issues. Indeed, it would not be drawing too long a bow to see much of this behavior by the Crown's agents as a form of "greed," corruption, even though public officials themselves may not have been the prime beneficiaries (Bauhr & Nasiritousi, 2011).[6] If corruption as a governmental phenomenon has to be gauged largely by perceptions of its incidence, then it clearly matters as to who is doing the perceiving. Just as "seeing is believing," so too is the converse the case: "believing is [not] seeing."

In this connection, it is worth quoting from two of the most acute historical observers of New Zealand society, to help understand why perhaps New Zealanders' national self-image, born of cultural insecurity, has tended to be self-congratulatory rather than self-critical. The French political commentator, André Siegfried, in 1914 published his observations of New Zealand society, wryly noting that, "Many New Zealanders are honestly convinced that the attention of the whole world is concentrated on them, waiting with curiosity and even with anxiety to see what they will say and do next ... they have become so accustomed to being taken seriously that they have become conscious of a mission to humanity" (Siegfried, 1914, pp. 58–59). Writing nearly half a century later, Lipson (1948, pp. 459–60), noted that this attitude was still prevalent. "The publicity of the government, the press, and a host of private organizations constantly assures the public that New Zealand leads the world in this, that, and the other," he noted. "So often is the point repeated and asserted about so many features of the Dominion's life that it is now earnestly believed by the majority. It is held as a faith which few call in question ... . Under its worst forms it can degenerate into smugness and complacency, the national delusion of the self-satisfied."

A CHANGING PICTURE OF CORRUPTION IN NEW ZEALAND

Several influences may have increasingly rendered such "smugness and complacency" more problematic than it has been in past times, when it comes to the question of corruption. There is no space here to discuss these influences in full, against the background provided by the preceding section of this chapter. Suffice it to say that prominent among them are the decline in New Zealand's egalitarian ethos, as indicated by a marked rise in income inequality since the early 1990s,[7] an associated weakening of New Zealand's welfare state, an open market economy more subject to negative international influences, and the possible attenuation of the normative model of public service compliance, largely as a result of the radical state sector reforms of the late 1980s and early 1990s, which − among other things − abolished the unified public service career structure and enabled the contracting-out of a great deal of public service provision (Boston, Martin, Pallot, & Walsh, 1996; Gregory, 1999).

In New Zealand, legal definitions of what constitutes corruption are narrow and orthodox. "Bribery and Corruption" as such is covered by two statutes − the Crimes Act 1961, and the Secret Commissions Act 1910. The Crimes Act (Part VI − "Crimes Affecting the Administration of Law and Justice − Bribery and Corruption") provides for prison sentences of up to 14 years for judicial officers and ministers of the Crown, who seek or accept bribes, and of up to seven years for anyone who offers a bribe to them; and sentences of up to seven years for any Member of Parliament (MP), law enforcement officer, or bureaucrat who accepts or seeks a bribe, and up to seven years for anyone offering bribes to them or to foreign officials (unless the bribe, offered outside of New Zealand, is not illegal in that other country). An official can receive a sentence of up to seven years in prison for using official information for personal advantage; and anyone who uses or discloses for his or her own advantage personal information illegally supplied by an official is liable for up to seven years in prison.

The Secret Commissions Act, which is perhaps mistakenly seen to cover "private sector" corruption, deals with the secret acceptance of "valuable considerations" (commissions) by agents unknown to their principals, including such commissions received in the procuring of contracts. The conduct of New Zealanders transacting business overseas is now subject to the provisions of Britain's forceful Bribery Act, which became operational in 2011, and which reflects the international anti-corruption strategies being pursued by organizations such as the World Bank, the International Monetary Fund (IMF), the Asia Development Bank (ADB), the Organisation for Economic Cooperation and Development (OECD), and so on. New Zealand businesses that have close dealings with enterprises in countries where corruption is endemic may be more at risk of falling foul of the provisions of this particular piece of legislation.

The penalties under the Secret Commissions Act are currently light, and are now under legislative reconsideration. Also, the government is considering extending the corruption provisions in the Crimes Act to cover "trading in influence" — whereby a public official, in exchange for advantages, undertakes to use his influence to benefit the person who provides the advantages. These initiatives follow governmental consideration of law changes that would be required in New Zealand were Parliament to ratify the UNCAC.

Following a series of highly publicized prosecutions for financial fraud, largely related to the share market crash of October 1987, the New Zealand government established the Serious Fraud Office (SFO) in 1990. The SFO is an independent agency dedicated to investigating major fraud cases, typically in excess of NZ$2 million, and instances of bribery and corruption. It is imbued with strong powers, including the ability to seize from anyone information and documents relating to an investigation, and to compel anyone to be interviewed and to respond to questions relating to a case, regardless of any self-incrimination in doing so. Decisions to initiate an investigation are the responsibility of the SFO's director, and are not open to review. Since its inception, the SFO has maintained a high success rate in prosecuting cases.[8]

Supplementing the SFO, is the Office of the Controller and Auditor-General (C & AG), which was first established in the middle of the 19th century and is answerable to Parliament but independent of the executive. The C & AG is the main agency responsible for ensuring the overall ethical probity of public sector administration in New Zealand.[9]

Even before the world financial crisis of 2008, financial fraud had become glaringly apparent in New Zealand. A former head of New Zealand's SFO publicly admonished corporate directors for doing too little about "financial crime and corruption" in their organizations, in the light of a series of high profile convictions of finance company executives following a spate of institutional collapses linked to the international financial crisis of the late 2000s, and involving the loss to investors of hundreds of millions of dollars. He argued that New Zealand is today socially, ethnically, and financially — "in terms of rich and poor in our society" — a "very different country than we were a few years ago and, particularly since the global financial crisis" (Birchfield, 2012). The former director dismissed the value of the CPI's rating of New Zealand: in his view, "company directors and legislators were sweeping the country's growing crime and corruption problem under the board table." In support of his arguments, he cited the results of an SFO survey, which indicated that a majority of New Zealanders did not share the CPI's view of corruption in their country: only 37 percent of respondents believed that the country was "largely free" of serious fraud and corruption. At the height of the share market boom before the October 1987 crash, illegal and dodgy commercial practices were rife. According to Bruce Jesson (1999, p. 126), "Not only did the ethical standards of business collapse during the share market boom, but so also did the notion that there should even be ethical standards ...."

A PricewaterhouseCoopers/Office of the Auditor-General New Zealand (2011) survey of fraud and corruption in New Zealand organizations of various sizes found that such events in the previous two years, with a cost of more than NZ$100,000, were reported by up to 8 percent of respondents. Fraud and/or corruption events in the previous two years, with a cost of between NZ$10,000 and 100,000, were reported by up to 9.5 percent of those surveyed. A KPMG survey in 2012 of fraud, bribery, and corruption in Australia and New Zealand, while not providing separate data on each country, found that "almost three-quarters of respondents reported that their organization has experienced behaviors that are defined as bribery or corruption" (KPMG, 2013, p. 34). Moreover, while perpetrators of fraud were more likely to be nonmanagement employees, a "real concern" was that fraud committed by senior executives and company directors had doubled since 2006 (KPMG, 2013, p. 9). The study also found that more than half of the respondents indicated that their organizations did not perform active monitoring of bribery and corruption payments. There is no central clearing house for information about the prosecution and conviction of New Zealand public officials on corruption or fraud charges, but some casual research only between 2001 and 2005 uncovered a not insubstantial list (Gregory, Zirker, & Scrimgeour, 2012, pp. 14—15; Gregory, 2002, 2006; and the appendix). It can also be noted in this connection that New Zealand has no common law offense of "Misconduct in Public Office," such as that which exists in Hong Kong.

More needs to be known about how New Zealanders perceive activities that could be called corrupt. Taito Philip Field, a Samoan New Zealander who became the first New Zealand MP to be convicted and imprisoned for corruption, claimed at his trial in 2009 that New Zealanders did not understand the time-honored Pacific tradition of gift-giving. The Supreme Court, which unanimously rejected his appeal, said that any gift-giving to officials with the power to influence a relevant case represented corruption.[10] The then head of New Zealand's immigration service, Mary Anne Thompson, was seen to have practiced nepotism in 2008, in attempting to gain residency to New Zealand for some of her Pacific Island extended family members. She also pleaded guilty to having falsely claimed to have received a doctorate from the London School of Economics and Political Science (Gregory, 2009). Donna Awatere Huata, an MP at the time of committing her offenses, was sentenced in 2005 to 33 months in jail for stealing from a Maori trust set up to help underprivileged children, and for perverting the course of justice. In 2011, a former Accident Compensation Corporation (ACC) National Property Manager was convicted on charges of corruption while in office and sentenced to 11 months of home detention. In recent years, there have been several cases of MPs "double-dipping" on accommodation allowances, and exorbitant uses of travel allowances. After public scrutiny the Deputy Prime Minister, Bill English, repaid NZ$12,000 worth of housing allowances. These public controversies are New Zealand's milder version of the much larger frauds perpetrated on British taxpayers in recent years by several Westminster MPs. While not comparable in scope or size to the most egregious cases that were uncovered in Britain, they do not help to sustain public trust in New Zealand's politicians. Commenting on practices that were commonplace in the late 1990s, criminologist Greg Newbold (2000, p. 42) observed that "The squandering of millions of dollars by politicians and public servants through expensive trips abroad, golden handshakes and opulent conferences is now well known."

In 2000, the then State Services Commissioner argued that there were two countervailing pressures against New Zealand's record of honesty in the public sector. The first related to documents of national identity and residents' permits, and their importance to an increasing level of Asian-based international organized crime activity in the Pacific region. In his words:

> ... since the end of the Cold War there has been an increase in both political instability and international criminal activity in our region. International organized crime based in Asia is having an impact in the Pacific, including in New Zealand. Documents of national identity and residents' permits have a particular value in this milieu. The criminals have large sums at their disposal. The sums of money that can be offered to officials are very large compared with officials' annual salaries. (State Services Commission, 2000, pp. 3–4)

The second risk factor, according to the Commissioner, was the fact that personal information had become "a marketable and valuable commodity."

CORRUPTION ISSUES AND REPUTATIONAL RISKS IN NEW ZEALAND

The relationship between corruption and national reputation in countries with a free press is typically mediated by the national news media. New Zealand's impressive successes in combating corruption, retaining its CPI status as the perceived least corrupt country in the world, and as the best place to do business (Smith & Fletcher, 2012), as well as a veritable parade of other impressive rankings and awards, are ceremonially and repeatedly recorded in the country's news media. Nevertheless, dire warnings of the "slippery slope" of corruption, and the need for "more transparency," also figure prominently, occasionally in the same reports (New Zealand Herald, 2012a). It is clear that New Zealanders have a lot to lose, although repeated sterling non-corruption rankings lead to complacency, and represent a potential disincentive to anti-corruption policy-making, and vigilance in defense against corruption. Even as national corruption scandals, "loopholes" in New Zealand's legislation, the apparent growth of organized crime, and, perhaps – most threatening of all – the rapid growth of income inequality in New Zealand, make their way into headlines, New Zealand's international reputation seems to prosper. How long will this last?

Corruption scandals have increased exponentially in the last five years, at least in their coverage in New Zealand's media. The most prominent recent example of these followed the New Zealand Police arrest (in concert with the United States Federal Bureau of Investigation) of Kim Dotcom, a multimillionaire German internet site operator with a shady past, residing in New Zealand and accused of massive copyright violations through his "Mega Upload" site, which at one point accounted for nearly 5 percent of the world's internet traffic. Dotcom (his name changed legally to reflect his occupation) seems to have had special support in his successful bid for New Zealand residency.[11] Soon after his arrest he announced that a member of the ruling National Party coalition, John Banks – the only Association of Consumers and Taxpayers (ACT) MP in the House of Representatives, had accepted an "illegally anonymous" NZ$50,000 campaign donation from him during Banks' unsuccessful 2010 Auckland mayoral campaign.[12] The rules are clear on this: if a candidate knows the source of a major campaign donation, it must be listed by source, not as "anonymous," as Dotcom's donation had been. A number of candidates, including Bank's former rival in the 2011 Parliamentary election (as head of the new Conservative Party), Colin Craig, have expressed outrage at this "corrupt behavior," and are moving to replace Banks at the first opportunity (Fairfax NZ News, 2012a). In any event, both Banks' and New Zealand's reputations were threatened by this, with the New Zealand Police investigating alleged campaign violations (Hartevelt, 2012a) before deciding, on apparently shaky grounds, not to press charges.[13]

It is beyond the scope of this chapter to list all of the recent corruption scandals that pose reputational risks to New Zealand. Suffice it to say that there has been a series of scandals of various kinds involving prison guards, police officers, and former and current officials (including a former Minister of Justice) involved with allegedly fraudulent investment schemes, and so on, some of which are listed in the appendix. While it can be argued that the public prosecution of such cases is in keeping with New Zealand's corruption-free reputation, the recently reported growth of organized crime in New Zealand, sometimes linked to the Chinese Triads and other groups involved in illegal drug manufacturing and distribution, has the potential to sully this reputation. In this context, the apparent reluctance of New Zealand to ratify (after signing in December 2003) the UNCAC, which would compel major public officials and their families to maintain full financial transparency, and the *belated* passage of the Anti-Money Laundering and Countering Financing of Terrorism Act (Public Act 2009 No. 35, which only went fully into effect in 2013), suggest a degree of inertia in New Zealand's defense of its clean, green image.[14] Regarding the latter, anti-money laundering legislation has been at the forefront of worldwide anti-corruption efforts over the past several decades, but New Zealand's belated adoption of this legislation required extraordinary training of local firms,[15] most of which have been engaged in high levels of foreign trade, apparently without formal/legal observation of international legal norms in combating corruption.[16] There is little doubt that the Anti-Money Laundering Act, as it is gradually implemented, will have a major remediating impact in this previously gray area of New Zealand's global financial linkages.

Revelations in 2012 that a loophole in New Zealand's trust laws allows off-shore parties with no legal connection to New Zealand to establish tax-free trust havens suggest a further challenge to the country's non-corrupt reputation.[17] As an intermediary for Cayman Islands-style banking secrecy, it is increasingly presumed that New Zealand is indirectly benefitting through its trust system from global financial malfeasance, at least some of which is very likely to be corruption.[18]

A recent Bill before the House to control the worst excesses of Parliamentary "lobbying" underscores yet another risk to New Zealand's non-corrupt reputation (Dudding, 2011). Largely uncontrolled lobbying in Parliament has increasingly been reported in the news media as a growing problem that is often linked to corruption. Efforts to regulate lobbying have encountered significant resistance (Hartevelt, 2012b),[19] raising further doubts about the authenticity of New Zealand's reputation.[20] Open access to the nation's MPs has long been seen as a hallmark of New Zealand's vibrant democracy. Lobbyists have quickly come to represent a direct threat to the country's non-corrupt reputation, and thus to its democratic tradition.

Arguably, the most corrosive change in New Zealand society is the marked growth in income inequality that has beset the country since the neo-liberalization of the state, beginning in 1988, and its impact upon a putative growth in corrupt tendencies. As news reports noted in 2011 and 2012, the gap between the rich and the poor has increased more than in any other OECD country over the past two decades, on top of a widening gap in all other OECD countries (Campbell, 2011; Cooke, 2012; Johnston, 2011).[21] A recent Salvation Army report stresses this, arguing that increasing numbers of New Zealanders had been marginalized in the last two years (Chapman, 2013). This manifests itself immediately in the well-being (or lack thereof) of children (Duff & Board, 2010),[22] and in deteriorating race relations (Dominion Post, 2012). With the wealthiest 1 percent of the population now owning three times more than "the combined cash and assets of the poorest 50 percent" (Nichols, 2011), the presumption is that increasing crime, including corruption, and even a surge in some diseases, might result (Francis, 2012).

Probably the most aggressive current assault on New Zealand's non-corrupt reputation is materializing in the city of Christchurch's rebuilding project, following the destructive earthquakes of September 4, 2010, and February 22, 2011. Despite explicit warnings in the national media of the potential for fraud and corruption in the multibillion dollar rebuilding project (Meadows, 2012; Slade, 2012; The Press, 2012), contractors using public funds have made significant use of illegal migrants, paying miniscule wages, and in violation of visa restrictions (Carville, 2013). Yet another alleged financial fraud, worth "tens of millions of dollars," was reported in the national media to be under investigation by the SFO in late 2012 (Wood, 2012).

CONCLUSION

In sum, several main factors largely explain New Zealand's long-standing reputation for low levels of official and business corruption. These factors are New Zealand's size and geographical location; its egalitarian and welfare state traditions; the strong bureaucratic and normative constraints exercised over official behavior; and its professional, merit-based, and impartial system of Westminster-style public administration.

In providing a set of largely narrative reasons as to why New Zealand has for a very long time been a country without significant levels of governmental and other corruption, and while suggesting that the country's top ranking on the CPI does not tell the full, or even the most interesting story, we do not mean to imply that all of a sudden corruption is becoming a major problem in New Zealand. Rather, we argue that there are significant recent signs that it is becoming an issue of increasing, if still little recognized, public importance, and that the country's strong international reputation may warrant closer scrutiny. While recent evidence may go nowhere near indicating that corruption in New Zealand may grow to a scale comparable to that in many other countries, nevertheless, if New Zealanders are genuinely concerned to maintain the standards they have been accustomed to in the past, then more public policy attention may soon need to be given to this complex and difficult issue.

NOTES

1. According to the 2006 official census, European New Zealanders comprised 68 percent of the population; Maori, 15 percent; Asian, 9 percent; Pacific Islands, 7 percent; and others, 1 percent.

2. The Australian and New Zealand Army Corps (ANZAC) was an expeditionary force that fought in the First World War's Battle of Gallipoli in 1915.

3. New Zealand's welfare state developed more along the lines of the British "model" rather than the more strongly social-democratic Scandinavian one. See Esping-Andersen (1990).

4. In this system, which endured until the radical reforms of the 1980s and 1990s, the government held the ring in negotiations among the three dominant

pressure groups — the Federation of Labor, the Employers' Federation, and Federated Farmers.

5. Essentially, the terms of this tacit bargain are that the political executive will forego involvement in the recruitment and promotion of public servants, who in turn will forego some political rights in return for security of employment and dutiful loyalty to the government of the day.

6. "Greed" corruption refers to actions of political and bureaucratic grandees who greedily capture state assets by virtue of their high positions in government. "Need" corruption occurs when people pay, to mainly lower level officials, bribes for governmental services that these citizens are legally entitled to.

7. In 1982 New Zealand's Gini coefficient (after housing costs) was around 27; in 2001, 38; and in 2011, 39. See Perry (2012). Figures derived from Statistics New Zealand's Household Economic Surveys.

8. For more details of the SFO's functions, operations, and performance, see SFO (2013).

9. For more information on the C & AG's role, see http://www.oag.govt.nz/about-us/cag-role.

10. An MP for 15 years, Field was sentenced to six years in jail.

11. The Dotcom scandal is sometimes portrayed in the media as representing a major threat to New Zealand's non-corrupt reputation (e.g., New Zealand Herald, 2012b).

12. It was listed as anonymous, and Banks has said that he was unaware of its source despite Dotcom's frequent testimony to the contrary.

13. Police found that Banks did solicit the donations but didn't have enough evidence under current legislation to charge him, specifically, that "they could not establish Banks had the necessary knowledge that a $15,000 donation from SkyCity was recorded as anonymous before he signed and submitted his return. They made the same finding about anonymous radio advertisements worth $15,690 and two $25,000 donations from internet millionaire Kim Dotcom" (Fairfax News NZ, 2012b).

14. See http://www.legislation.govt.nz/act/public/2009/latest/DLM2140720.html. Retrieved on February 8, 2013.

15. For example, barristers Wilson and Harle in Auckland launched a website in 2010 to begin training corporate executives in the nuances of the new bill. As the website notes, "A long-awaited upgrade of New Zealand's Anti-Money Laundering (AML) law was finally passed by Parliament late last year. But although this is one of the most far-reaching pieces of law reform to hit the financial sector in recent years, it remains an over-arching framework only — it is not yet properly in force, and a lot of specific detail is still to be developed for particular sectors via subsidiary regulations and guidelines. Now the 'rubber' is starting to hit the road, with the Ministry of Justice starting to develop those details in a consultation paper covering the specific AML regime likely to apply to regulated 'reporting entities.' The Ministry and the other supervising agencies are keen 'to test some initial thinking with industry' on the matters that will find their way into the detailed aspects of the regime: the regulations, codes of practice, and guidelines that will flesh out the bare bones of the Anti-Money Laundering and Countering Financing of Terrorism Act 2009 (AML/CFT Act)." This article recaps the essentials of New Zealand's

new AML framework, and then examines some key aspects of the Ministry's detailed proposals, which are available at www.justice.govt.nz. See http://www.wilsonharle.com/new-zealand-s-anti-money-laundering-law-now-the-rubber-hits-the-road/. Retrieved on February 10, 2013.

16. It is difficult to avoid the central importance of this fight against the most extreme forms of corruption. The British Bank, the Hongkong and Shanghai Banking Corporation (HSBC), for example, agreed in December 2012 to pay nearly US$2 billion to US authorities after admitting to laundering at least US$881 million in drug trafficking money in a case that received close attention in the New Zealand media. The *New Zealand Herald* described it as "the latest scandal to hit banks since the financial crisis started in 2008. Standard Chartered PLC, another British bank, signed an agreement with New York regulators on Monday to settle a money-laundering investigation involving Iran with a $340 million payment" (New Zealand Herald, 2012c).

17. A recent New Zealand TV-3 exposé underscored the use of New Zealand trust laws to establish anonymous tax-free trusts for off-shore interests. See http://www.tv3.co.nz/October-7th—Treasure-Islands/tabid/2059/articleID/79738/Default.aspx. Retrieved on February 8, 2013.

18. For an informed commentary on these trusts, see http://www.stuff.co.nz/business/opinion-analysis/7521775/NZ-foreign-trusts-among-global-tax-havens. Retrieved on May 9, 2013.

19. In an editorial in the *Dominion Post*, a constitutional lawyer stridently criticized the bill, arguing that the bill is badly drafted and would distance MPs from "the people" (Williams, 2012).

20. Dudding (2011) quotes the late Jeremy Pope in his article. Pope, a New Zealander and one of the founders of Transparency International, argued that the lack of transparency in New Zealand, and particularly in such activities as lobbying, was "an accident waiting to happen. No one knows how many there are and who they're lobbying for and who they're lobbying to."

21. Campbell observes that the 10 wealthiest New Zealanders own approximately 11 percent of the country's GDP, while the 10 wealthiest Australians own just over 4 percent of the Australian GDP; Cooke notes that New Zealand household incomes declined by 3 percent between July 2010 and June 2011, that the incomes of the lowest decile declined markedly, while the incomes of the top deciles increased, and that 21 percent of New Zealand children now live in poverty, again a marked change over the past decade.

22. Duff and Board (2010) note, for example, that New Zealand has had the second worst record for child safety among 30 developed countries, and that child abuse and gang violence are natural extensions of this development.

ACKNOWLEDGMENT

The authors would like to thank their New Zealand colleagues, Peter Jones and John Martin, for their valuable contributions to our discussion in the historical section. The usual disclaimer applies.

REFERENCES

Bassett, M., & King, M. (2000). *Tomorrow comes the song: A life of Peter Fraser*. Auckland: Penguin.

Bauhr, M., & Nasiritousi, N. (2011). *Why pay bribes? Collective action and anti-corruption efforts*. Working Paper Series 2011: 18. Quality of Government Institute, University of Gothenburg, Gothenburg.

Belich, J. (1998). *The New Zealand wars and the Victorian interpretation of racial conflict*. Auckland: Penguin.

Birchfield, R. (2012). Cover story: Boards blasé about management. *New Zealand Management*, September. Retrieved from http://www.management.co.nz/Editorial.asp?eID = 61744& Wcat = 7. Accessed on February 8, 2013.

Boston, J., Martin, J., Pallot, J., & Walsh, P. (1996). *Public management: The New Zealand model*. Auckland: Oxford University Press.

Campbell, G. (2011). Putting the focus on income inequality. *The Wellingtonian*, August 11. Retrieved from http://www.stuff.co.nz/dominion-post/news/local-papers/the-wellingtonian/opinion/5423125/Putting-the-focus-on-income-inequality. Accessed on February 8, 2013.

Cardona, F. (2013). Spain: Corruption, weak institutionalization, unfinished democratization. *Public Administration Review*, *73*(1), 95–96.

Carville, O. (2013). Quake rebuild sparks job scam, *Fairfax NZ News*, January 13. Retrieved from http://www.stuff.co.nz/national/christchurch-earthquake/8171833/Quake-rebuild-sparks-job-scam. Accessed on February 8, 2013.

Chapman, K. (2013). Poor Kiwis left behind, says Salvation Army. *Fairfax NZ News*, February 13. Retrieved from http://www.stuff.co.nz/national/8295161/Poor-Kiwis-left-behind-says-Salvation-Army. Accessed on February 8, 2013.

Charron, N., Lapuente, V., & Rothstein, B. (2013). *Quality of government and corruption from a European perspective: A comparative study of good government in EU regions*. Cheltenham: Edward Elgar.

Cooke, M. (2012). Poor get poorer, inequality reigns – Survey. *Fairfax NZ News*, August 23. Retrieved from http://www.stuff.co.nz/national/politics/7536914/Poor-get-poorer-inequality-reigns-survey. Accessed on February 8, 2013.

Dominion Post. (2012). Racial prejudice, inequality still entrenched in NZ. *Dominion Post*, March 8. Retrieved from http://www.stuff.co.nz/dominion-post/news/6541003/Racial-prejudice-inequality-still-entrenched-in-NZ. Accessed on February 8, 2013.

Dudding, A. (2011). Inside political lobbying. *Fairfax NZ News*, July 17. Retrieved from http://www.stuff.co.nz/national/politics/5297632/Inside-political-lobbying. Accessed on February 8, 2013.

Duff, O. (1941). *New Zealand now*. Wellington: Department of Internal Affairs.

Duff, M., & Board, A. (2010). "Shameful record" as Kiwi kids suffer. *Fairfax NZ News*, December 6. Retrieved from http://www.stuff.co.nz/national/4425416/Shameful-record-as-Kiwi-kids-suffer. Accessed on February 8, 2013.

Economist. (2012). *Pocket world in figure 2013 edition*. London: Profile Books.

Emerson, R. W. (1841). *Self-reliance*. Hoboken, NJ: BiblioBytes.

Esping-Andersen, G. (1990). *The three worlds of welfare capitalism*. Princeton, NJ: Princeton University Press.

Fairfax NZ News. (2012a). Colin Craig and John Banks compared. *Fairfax NZ News*, May 8. Retrieved from http://www.stuff.co.nz/national/politics/6877074/Colin-Craig-And-John-Banks-Compared. Accessed on February 8, 2013.

Fairfax NZ News. (2012b). Banks won't be charged, police say. *Fairfax NZ News*, July 26. Retrieved from http://www.stuff.co.nz/national/politics/7353754/Banks-won-t-be-charged-police-say. Accessed on February 8, 2013.

Fischer, D.H. (2012). *Fairness and freedom: A history of two open societies: New Zealand and the United States*. New York, NY: Oxford University Press.

Francis, C. (2012). Surge in disease blamed on social inequality. *Dominion Post*, February 20. Retrieved from http://www.stuff.co.nz/dominion-post/news/6448733/Surge-in-disease-blamed-on-social-inequality. Accessed on February 8, 2013.

Galtung, F. (2006). Measuring the immeasurable: Boundaries and functions of (macro) corruption indices. In C. Sampford, A. Shacklock, C. Connors, & F. Galtung (Eds.), *Measuring corruption* (pp. 101–130). Aldershot: Ashgate. Chap. 6.

Gilling, B. (1998). *The Ombudsman in New Zealand*. Auckland: Dunmore Publishing.

Gregory, R. (Ed.) (1984). *The official information act: A beginning*. Wellington: New Zealand Institute of Public Administration.

Gregory, R. (1999). Social capital theory and administrative reform: Maintaining ethical probity in public service. *Public Administration Review*, 59(1), 63–75.

Gregory, R. (2002). Governmental corruption in New Zealand: A view through Nelson's telescope?. *Asian Journal of Political Science*, 10(1), 17–36.

Gregory, R. (2003). New Zealand – The end of egalitarianism?. In C. Hood, B.G. Peters, & G. Lee (Eds.), *Reward for high public office: Asian and Pacific rim states* (pp. 88–104). London: Routledge. Chap. 5.

Gregory, R. (2006). Governmental corruption and social change in New Zealand: Using scenarios, 1950–2020. *Asian Journal of Political Science*, 14(2), 117–139.

Gregory, R. (2009). No suspicious circumstances? Contractualism and reputation-protection in political-bureaucratic relations – The case of New Zealand immigration. In P. Roness & H. Sætren (Eds.), *Change and continuity in public sector organizations: Essays in honor of Per Laegreid* (pp. 279–297). Bergen: Fagbokforlaget. Chap. 14.

Gregory, R., Zirker, D., & Scrimgeour, F. (2012). A Kiwi halo? Defining and assessing corruption in a 'non-corrupt' system. *Asia Pacific Journal of Public Administration*, 34(1), 1–29.

Griffin, J. (1990). Wren, John (1871–1953). *Australian Dictionary of Biography* (Vol. 12). Melbourne: Melbourne University Press. Retrieved from http://adb.anu.edu.au/biography/wren-john-9198. Accessed on February 8, 2013.

Griffin, J. (2004). *John Wren: A life reconsidered*. Melbourne: Scribe.

Hartevelt, J. (2012a). Widening banks campaign donations probe. *Fairfax NZ News*, April 30. Retrieved from http://www.stuff.co.nz/national/politics/6826949/Widening-Banks-campaign-donations-probe. Accessed on February 8, 2013.

Hartevelt, J. (2012b). Lobbyists push back against bill. *Fairfax NZ News*, October 25. Retrieved from http://www.stuff.co.nz/national/politics/7859944/Lobbyists-push-back-against-bill. Accessed on February 8, 2013.

Hill, L.B. (1976). *The model Ombudsman: Institutionalizing New Zealand's democratic experiment*. Princeton, NJ: Princeton University Press.

Holmes, L. (2010). Australian police corruption in comparative perspective. Paper presented at the 58th annual conference of the Australian Political Studies Association, University of Melbourne, in Melbourne, September 26–29.

Hood, C., & Lodge, M. (2006). *The politics of public service bargains: Reward, competency, loyalty – and blame*. New York, NY: Oxford University Press.

Jesson, B. (1999). *Only their purpose is mad.* Palmerston North: Dunmore Press.

Johnston, K. (2011). New Zealand's wealth gap widens. *Dominion Post*, December 6. Retrieved from http://www.stuff.co.nz/dominion-post/news/6092339/New-Zealands-wealth-gap-widens. Accessed on February 8, 2013.

King, M. (2003). *New Zealanders at war.* Auckland: Penguin.

KPMG. (2013). *A survey of fraud, bribery and corruption in Australia and New Zealand 2012.* Retrieved from http://www.kpmg.com/au/en/issuesandinsights/articlespublications/fraud-survey/pages/fraud-bribery-corruption-survey-2012.aspx?chan=story1. Accessed on February 8, 2013.

Larmour, P. (2006). *Culture and corruption in the Pacific Islands: Some conceptual issues and findings from studies of national integrity systems.* Discussion Papers, Policy and Governance, Asia Pacific School of Economics and Government, Australian National University, Canberra.

Lipson, L. (1948). *The politics of equality: New Zealand's adventures in democracy.* Chicago, IL: University of Chicago Press.

Martin, J. (1988). *A profession of statecraft? Three essays on some current issues in the New Zealand public service.* Wellington: Victoria University Institute of Policy Studies.

Martin, J. (2010). The age of the mandarins? Government in New Zealand 1940–1951. Paper presented at the conference on the seven dwarfs and the age of the mandarins: Australian government administration 1940s to 60s at the Australian National University in Canberra, November 3.

Meadows, R. (2012). Huge fraud potential in Chch rebuild. *Fairfax NZ News*, September 18. Retrieved from http://www.stuff.co.nz/business/rebuilding-christchurch/7696127/Huge-fraud-potential-in-Chch-rebuild. Accessed on February 8, 2013.

Newbold, G. (2000). *Crime in New Zealand.* Palmerston North: Dunmore Press.

New Zealand Herald. (2012a). Editorial: The time has come for more transparency. *New Zealand Herald*, April 11.

New Zealand Herald. (2012b). Editorial: Kim Dotcom sets off year of fireworks for politicians. *New Zealand Herald*, December 27.

New Zealand Herald. (2012c). HSBC to pay $1.9b to settle money-laundering case. *New Zealand Herald*, December 12.

Nichols, L. (2011). Revealing the gap between NZ's rich and poor. *Fairfax NZ News*, November 18. Retrieved from http://www.stuff.co.nz/national/politics/5989843/Revealing-the-gap-between-NZs-rich-and-poor. Accessed on February 8, 2013.

Office of the Ombudsman. (2012). *Annual report to Parliament for the year ending 30 June 2012.* Wellington: Office of the Ombudsman.

Perry, B. (2012). *Household incomes in New Zealand: Trends in indicators of inequality and hardship 1982 to 2011.* Wellington: Ministry of Social Development.

Polaschek, R. (1958). *Government administration in New Zealand.* London: Oxford University Press.

PricewaterhouseCoopers/Office of the Auditor-General New Zealand (2011). *Global economic crime survey: New Zealand results.* Wellington: Office of the Auditor-General.

Quah, J. S. T. (2003). *Curbing corruption in Asia: A comparative study of six countries.* Singapore: Eastern Universities Press.

Quah, J. S. T. (2010). Curbing corruption in Asian countries: The difference between success and failure. Paper presented at the Fourth International Conference on Public management in the 21st century: Opportunities and challenges in Macau, SAR, October 22–23.

Quah, J. S. T. (2011). *Curbing corruption in Asian countries: An impossible dream?* Bingley: Emerald Group Publishing.

Roberts, J. (1978). Society and its politics. In I. Wards (Ed.), *Thirteen facets: The silver jubilee essays surveying the new Elizabethan age, a period of unprecedented change.* Wellington: Government Printer.

Schwab, K. (Ed.) (2012). *The global competitiveness report 2012–2013.* Geneva: World Economic Forum.

SFO (Serious Fraud Office). (2013). *Annual report 2012.* Auckland. Retrieved from http://www.sfo.govt.nz/f55,18661/SFO_Annual_Report_2012.pdf. Accessed on July 27, 2013.

Siegfried, A. (1914). *Democracy in New Zealand* (E. V. Burns, Trans.). London: Bell.

Slade, M. (2012). Lax Kiwi systems "open to bribery." *Fairfax NZ News,* September 13. Retrieved from http://www.stuff.co.nz/business/rebuilding-christchurch/7664577/Lax-Kiwi-systems-open-to-bribery. Accessed on February 8, 2013.

Smith, B. C. & Fletcher, H. (2012). NZ ranked best in world to do business. *New Zealand Herald,* November 16. Retrieved from http://www.nzherald.co.nz/business/news/article.cfm?c_id = 3&objectid = 10847700. Accessed on February 8, 2013.

State Services Commission. (2000). *Annual report of the State Services Commission for the year ended 30 June 2000.* Wellington.

Sutch, W. (1969). *Poverty and progress in New Zealand: A reassessment.* Wellington: Reed.

Temple, P. (2002). *A sort of conscience: The Wakefields.* Auckland: Auckland University Press.

The Press. (2012). Editorial: Vigilance needed during rebuild. *The Press,* October 24. Retrieved from http://www.stuff.co.nz/the-press/opinion/editorials/7854624/Editorial-Vigilance-needed-during-rebuild. Accessed on February 8, 2013.

Webb, L. (1940). *Government in New Zealand.* Wellington: Department of Internal Affairs.

Weller, P., Wanna, J. & Patapan, H. (Eds.) (2005). *Westminster legacies: Democracy and responsible government in Asia and the Pacific.* Sydney: University of New South Wales Press.

Williams, J. (2012). Lobbying bill will distance people from MPs. *Dominion Post,* September 21. Retrieved from http://www.stuff.co.nz/dominion-post/7708988/Lobbying-bill-will-distance-people-from-MPs. Accessed on February 8, 2013.

Wood, A. (2012). Monster Christchurch rebuild fraud feared. *Fairfax NZ News,* September 28. Retrieved from http://www.stuff.co.nz/business/rebuilding-christchurch/7740372/Monster-Christchurch-rebuild-fraud-feared. Accessed on February 8, 2013.

Zirker, D., Gregory, R., & Scrimgeour, F. (2012). Iceland Agonistes and a Kiwi halo: Comparative perceptions of corruption and the rapid descent of a leading "non-corrupt" country, 2005–2012. Paper presented at the annual New Zealand Political Studies Association conference in Wellington, November 28–30.

APPENDIX: CORRUPTION AND FRAUD CASES INVOLVING NEW ZEALAND GOVERNMENT OFFICIALS (REPORTED IN NEWS MEDIA, 2001–2005)

1. An Immigration Department officer pleaded guilty to accepting NZ $100,000 in bribes to secure permanent residency for Korean immigrants and was jailed for two-and-a-half years.
2. A Housing New Zealand employee was jailed for accepting bribes amounting to NZ$60,000.
3. A Department of Conservation senior manager was jailed for defrauding his department of NZ$180,000.
4. A case manager with the former Department of Work and Income (DWI) was imprisoned for selling confidential beneficiary information to a repossession agent and for stealing more than NZ$30,000 from the department.
5. A senior property manager for the same department was jailed for three years after receiving nearly NZ$640,000 in bribes.
6. Another official of this department pleaded guilty to 32 charges of misappropriation totaling more than NZ$30,000.
7. In March 2002 yet another employee of DWI, who had worked for the department for 16 years, was jailed for defrauding the agency of more than NZ$81,000.
8. A Customs Service official was jailed after pleading guilty to bribery and fraud charges involving the importation of luxury stolen cars.
9. An official with the Ministry of Economic Development was jailed for 18 months for using official information to set up his own business.
10. A clerk in the same ministry was convicted of stealing more than NZ $25,000 from her employer.
11. A Fire Service national commander resigned after an internal investigation found he had spent "a significant amount" of public money on family travel and private international phone calls.
12. A Customs Service officer sentenced to nine years in jail for his involvement in drug smuggling by organized crime.
13. An Inland Revenue Department (IRD) officer pleaded guilty to six charges of failing to maintain the secrecy of taxpayers' and the department's information.
14. Another IRD officer was jailed for selling taxpayers' details to debt collectors.
15. A ministerial secretary was convicted for her part in passing on confidential IRD information to a family member chasing a debt.

16. Forty-three staff members of the Ministry of Social Development were caught committing fraud totaling NZ$729,442 during 2000–2003.
17. An Immigration Service official was sacked after requesting sexual favors from a female applicant.
18. An Immigration Service worker charged with stealing from foreigners in the course of his work faces seven years' jail if found guilty (case pending).
19. In a very high profile case, a manager in the Ministry of Social Development was jailed for five-and-a-half-years for defrauding the agency of NZ$1.9 million over a period of 28 months, and for receiving a benefit while working full-time in the organization.

Earlier in the 1990s, the Executive Director of New Zealand's Sports Foundation was imprisoned for stealing over NZ$1 million from the organization; a former railways consultant was sent to jail for defrauding New Zealand Railways of NZ$46,000; a commercial manager of the Electricity Corporation of New Zealand, was jailed for defrauding the organization of NZ$1.1 million; and a former Controller and Auditor-General himself was jailed for defrauding the public purse of about NZ$56,000 while in office.

CHAPTER 6

CURBING CORRUPTION IN SINGAPORE: THE IMPORTANCE OF POLITICAL WILL, EXPERTISE, ENFORCEMENT, AND CONTEXT

Jon S. T. Quah

ABSTRACT

Corruption was a serious problem in Singapore during the British colonial period and especially after the Japanese Occupation (February 1942–August 1945) mainly because of the lack of political will to curb it by the incumbent governments. In contrast, the People's Action Party (PAP) government, which assumed office in June 1959 after winning the May 1959 general election, demonstrated its political will with the enactment of the Prevention of Corruption Act (POCA) in June 1960, which strengthened the capacity of the Corrupt Practices Investigation Bureau (CPIB) to combat corruption effectively. Indeed, Singapore's success in curbing corruption is reflected in its consistently high scores on Transparency International's Corruption Perceptions Index (CPI) from 1995 to 2012 as the least corrupt country in Asia. Singapore was ranked first with Denmark and New Zealand in the 2010 CPI with a score of 9.30. Similarly, Singapore has been ranked first in the Political and

Different Paths to Curbing Corruption: Lessons from Denmark, Finland, Hong Kong, New Zealand and Singapore

Research in Public Policy Analysis and Management, Volume 23, 137–166
ISSN: 0732-1317/doi:10.1108/S0732-1317(2013)0000023006

Economic Risk Consultancy (PERC) annual surveys on corruption from 1995 to 2013. Why has Singapore succeeded in minimizing the problem of corruption when many other Asian countries have failed to do so? What lessons can these countries learn from Singapore's experience in combating corruption? This chapter addresses these two questions by first describing Singapore's favorable policy context, followed by an identification of the major causes of corruption during the British colonial period and Japanese Occupation, and an evaluation of the PAP government's anti-corruption strategy.

INTRODUCTION: SINGAPORE'S FAVORABLE POLICY CONTEXT

The policy context refers to the geographical, historical, economic, demographic, and political factors which influence the formulation and implementation of public policies in a country (Quah, 2011, p. 30). These contextual factors hinder the implementation of the incumbent governments' anti-corruption strategies in those large countries or archipelagoes, which lack a tradition of meritocracy, or the economic affluence to provide the anti-corruption agencies (ACAs) with the necessary legal powers, adequate budgets, and personnel to enforce the anti-corruption laws impartially. On the other hand, Singapore's policy context promotes the impartial implementation of the anti-corruption laws because of its small land area, the introduction of meritocracy in January 1951 with the establishment of the Public Service Commission (PSC), its economic affluence which enables the PAP government to provide the Corrupt Practices Investigation Bureau (CPIB) with adequate budget and personnel, its small population, and the political stability and continuity arising during the PAP government's more than 54 years in power.

Singapore's policy context is advantageous for the effective implementation of its anti-corruption strategy for five reasons, which are summarized in Table 1. First, as a city-state with a land area of 715.8 sq km, which is equivalent to the size of Lake Taupo in North Island, New Zealand, Singapore's smallness enables the CPIB to enforce the anti-corruption laws impartially and effectively because of the effective political control, communication, administrative coordination, and absence of a large hinterland or rural sector (Quah, 2011, p. 202).

Table 1. Singapore's Favorable Policy Context for Combating
Corruption.

Factor	Contribution
Small land area of 715.8 sq km.	Enhances communication and control and the impartial enforcement of the anti-corruption laws.
Introduction of meritocracy with the creation of the Public Service Commission in January 1951.	Civil servants are recruited and promoted on the basis of merit and relevant qualifications and not patronage; those found guilty of misconduct are punished and dismissed for serious offenses.
Substantial increase in GDP per capita from S$1,200 (US$400) in June 1959 to S$65,048 (US$52,051) in June 2012.	Singapore's economic affluence enables the PAP government to provide the CPIB with the required budget and personnel to perform its functions effectively.
Small population of 5,312,400 persons in June 2012.	Singapore's high literacy rate of 96.4 percent and population density of 7,422 persons per sq km enables the CPIB to enforce the POCA impartially and effectively.
The PAP government has been in power for more than 54 years after assuming power in June 1959.	Singapore's political continuity and stability and policy of zero tolerance for corruption have attracted substantial foreign investment from other countries.

Source: The latest data are taken from Department of Statistics, Singapore (2013).

Second, the introduction of meritocracy by the British colonial government in January 1951 with the establishment of the PSC has strengthened
considerably the CPIB's effectiveness. The PSC was created to ensure that
the recruitment and promotion of civil servants was based on merit and
not patronage, and to accelerate the pace of localization in the Singapore
Civil Service (SCS). When the PAP government assumed power in June
1959, it decided to continue the tradition of meritocracy by retaining
the PSC to attract the "best and brightest" citizens to join the SCS by
awarding scholarships to the best students in each cohort (Quah, 2010,
pp. 74, 91).

Third, Singapore's dramatic transformation from a poor country with a
per capita GDP of US$400 and an unemployment rate of 14 percent in
June 1959 to an economically affluent country with a per capita GDP of
US$52,051 and a low unemployment rate of 1.9 percent in June 2012 is an
important factor contributing to the CPIB's success in curbing corruption.
Indeed, as will be shown later, Singapore's economic affluence means that

the PAP government can demonstrate its political will in combating corruption by providing the CPIB with sufficient personnel and budget to enable it to implement the anti-corruption laws effectively (Quah, 2011, pp. 203–204).

Fourth, as Singapore's population of 5,312,400 persons is multiracial, multilingual, and multireligious, the PAP government has promoted racial harmony and minimized discrimination against the minority groups by ensuring that both public and private organizations are fair and impartial in their treatment of all citizens, regardless of their ethnic origin, language, or religion. This means that anyone found guilty of corruption in multiracial Singapore is punished according to the law, regardless of his or her ethnic group, language, or religion (Quah, 2011, p. 204).

Fifth, the PAP government has been in power in Singapore for more than 54 years as it was reelected for 12 times after winning the May 1959 general election. Singapore's political stability and continuity is an important asset for the PAP government because it is highly conducive for attracting foreign investment and for improving the effective implementation of public policies as the political leaders can focus on meeting the long-term goals instead of being constrained by short-term considerations. More importantly, in terms of fighting corruption, the continuity of the PAP government and its commitment to curbing corruption for more than 54 years has certainly enhanced the effectiveness of its anti-corruption strategy (Quah, 2011, p. 205).

CORRUPTION DURING THE BRITISH COLONIAL PERIOD

Corruption was a serious problem in Singapore during the British colonial period for two reasons: the British colonial government lacked the political will to curb corruption and this weakness was reflected in the adoption of ineffective anti-corruption measures.

Weak Political Will

Singapore initiated its battle against corruption in 1871, when corruption was made illegal with the enactment of the Penal Code of the Straits

Settlements of Malacca, Penang, and Singapore. To deal with the increase in the number of criminal cases and complaints against the Singapore Police Force (SPF), the British colonial government appointed a Commission of Inquiry in 1879 to investigate the causes of the SPF's inefficiency. The Commission found that corruption was rampant among the European inspectors and the Malay and Indian junior officers (Quah, 1979, pp. 24—25).

In April 1886, another Commission was appointed to investigate public gambling in the Straits Settlements. A total of 44 witnesses gave evidence before the Commission in Singapore and of these, 10 witnesses testified to the prevalence of police corruption on the basis of their observations and own experiences (Quah, 1979, pp. 25—26). The testimonies of these witnesses provided convincing proof of the SPF's involvement with the illegal gambling houses because of their different background. Consequently, the Commission concluded that there was "a systematic arrangement, both in Singapore and Penang, for corrupting the Police Force" and such corruption had "reached the Inspector class" (Straits Settlements, 1887, pp. i—ii).

The British colonial government's lack of political will in combating corruption was reflected in the 66-year delay in enacting the first anti-corruption law — the Prevention of Corruption Ordinance (POCO) — in December 1937 after corruption was made an offense with the enactment of the Penal Code in 1871. Indeed, nothing was done by the British colonial government to curb police corruption in the Straits Settlements even though the 1879 and 1886 Commissions had provided convincing proof of the prevalence of police corruption.

The reliance on appointing commissions to delay the implementation of political reforms was an important feature of British imperialism. K. B. Krishna (1939, p. 306) has observed that "whenever British imperialism is faced with a major or minor crisis in the colonies" it responded by appointing Royal Commissions and Conferences. However, the purpose of appointing these Commissions was political and "not to find facts." More specifically, there were three reasons for the establishment of Commissions of Inquiry by the British colonial government. First, these Commissions served to register "the benevolent intentions" of British imperialism. Second, the Commissions were used to discredit the demands of political parties opposed to British imperialism. Third, and most important, the Commissions were employed "to gain and bide time, to carry on the same exploitation with a promise of thorough investigation" (Krishna, 1939, pp. 307—309).

Ineffective Anti-Corruption Measures

Apart from the delay in enacting legislation to combat police corruption, the British colonial government also made a serious error in passing the POCO in December 1937, which made the SPF's Anti-Corruption Branch (ACB) responsible for corruption control even though police corruption was rampant in Singapore.

The POCO's aim was to prevent "bribery and secret commissions in public and private business." However, it was ineffective for two reasons. First, the POCO's offenses were not seizable and limited the powers of arrest, search, and investigation of police officers as warrants were required before arrests could be made. The second reason for the POCO's ineffectiveness was that the penalty of imprisonment for two years and/or a S$10,000 fine for those found guilty of corruption did not deter corrupt behavior. This defect of the POCO was only rectified nine years later when it was amended in 1946 to increase the penalty to a prison term of three years, thus making corrupt offenses seizable and automatically giving police officers more powers of arrest, search, and investigation (Quah, 2007, pp. 12–13).

According to the POCO, the ACB within the SPF's Criminal Investigation Department (CID) was responsible for curbing corruption in Singapore. However, the ACB was ineffective for three reasons. First, the ACB was a small unit of 17 personnel and was clearly inadequate in performing the difficult task of eradicating corruption in the SCS and SPF. As the CID was mainly concerned with the detection and solving such serious crimes like murder and kidnapping, the task of corruption control was accordingly given much lower priority. This meant that the ACB had to compete with other branches of the CID for limited personnel and other resources (Quah, 2007, p. 14).

The second reason for the ACB's ineffectiveness was that it was not a specialized ACA because the CID was saddled with many priorities, and the function of corruption control was only one of the 16 duties of the Assistant Commissioner of the CID in May 1952. Apart from curbing corruption, he was also responsible for these duties: secret societies; gambling promoters; fraud (commercial crime); anti-vice (traffickers); pawnshops; second-hand dealers; narcotics (traffickers); criminal records; banishment; naturalization; missing persons; fingerprints; photography; Police Gazette; and house-to-house and street collections (Colony of Singapore, 1952, p. 31). Hence, it was not surprising that combating corruption was not the CID's top priority, especially when the police were corrupt themselves.

The final and most important reason for the ACB's ineffectiveness was the prevalence of police corruption. In 1950, the Commissioner of Police, J. P. Pennefather-Evans, confirmed the existence of widespread police corruption documented by the 1879 and 1886 Commissions of Inquiry, and reported that corruption was rife in government departments in Singapore. A few days later, the ACB Chief admitted that the problem of corruption was "getting worse." Mrs. Elizabeth Choy, a member of the Second Legislative Council, criticized the British colonial government for its "weak and feeble attempt" to fight corruption in Singapore. Accordingly, she urged the government to implement without delay the ACB's proposals for amending the POCO and to increase the personnel of the ACB and separate it from the SPF (Quah, 2007, p. 15).

Police corruption was rampant in Singapore during the British colonial period mainly because of the low salaries of the local junior policemen, whose monthly salaries ranged from S$4 for a second-class peon to S$15 for a sergeant. Second, the poor working conditions of the local policemen also contributed to police corruption because they were not provided with free uniforms, rations, or accommodation, which made life more difficult for them to cope with the rising cost of living. Third, being poorly paid, the local policemen took advantage of the ample opportunities for corruption by accepting bribes from the gambling house owners, or to take on second jobs to supplement their meager salaries even though they were not legally permitted to do so. In other words, police corruption was widespread because of the low salaries of junior policemen, their unfavorable working conditions, and the lack of control over them in corruption-prone areas (Quah, 1979, pp. 28–31).

However, corruption in colonial Singapore was not confined to the SPF, but was widespread throughout the entire public bureaucracy. Indeed, apart from the SPF, other government agencies like the customs, immigration, and internal revenue departments also provided more opportunities for corruption than those public agencies that had limited contact with members of the public, did not issue licenses or permits, or collected fees or taxes. An important reason for the Singapore Improvement Trust's failure to provide low-cost public housing was the corruption of its senior expatriate officers and local junior officers in contracts procedure, planning and development control, and the allocation of housing units (Quah, 1975, pp. 281–290). In short, corruption was prevalent in those government departments concerned with granting licenses, "food and price control action, protection rackets connected with the smuggling of gold bars and opium, and gambling" (Yoong, 1972, p. 56).

CORRUPTION DURING THE JAPANESE OCCUPATION AND POSTWAR PERIOD

The problem of corruption worsened during the Japanese Occupation from February 1942 to August 1945 because the rampant inflation made it difficult for civil servants to live on their low salaries. The low value of the Japanese military currency compelled many civil servants to supplement their incomes by accepting bribes or doing business on the side line to prevent their families from starving (Yoong, 1972, p. 55). Mothers were forced to sell their jewelry in the black market to feed their children (Pitt & Leong, 2009, p. 193). Trading in the black market became a way of life because "shortages created the black market and a culture of thievery to fuel the market" (Lee, 2005, p. 205). The black market was important for many people as it "allowed them to act as brokers between a buyer and seller and earn a commission from each transaction to supplement their wages" (Pitt & Leong, 2009, p. 194).

In December 1942, the Japanese military administration introduced the *kumiai* system of grouping suppliers of commodities into distribution monopolies to prevent profiteering and inflation by keeping all stocks and controlling their distribution. However, in practice, the *kumiai* exacerbated the situation because the "monopolistic situation encouraged unscrupulous businessmen to turn to bribery and other methods to get supplies" (Lee, 2005, pp. 158–159). The *kumiai* system was "greatly abused" because "its members engaged in black-market activities under the cloak of government authority and fleeced the public" (Lee, 1956, p. 29). The food shortages also resulted in widespread pilfering and theft as "many workers seized opportunities to steal something from their workplaces to make ends meet" (Lee, 2005, p. 159).

The Japanese Occupation bred corruption into Singaporean society because practices of "bribery, blackmail, and extortion grew out of the violence and fear" that the Japanese used to rule their occupied territories (Lee, 2005, p. 205). Lee Geok Boi contended that "bribery worked wonders" during the Japanese Occupation because:

> From generals to the ordinary soldier, gifts and money smoothed the way. Nothing was transparent and everything was about connections and payoffs. Nothing was impossible with the right connections. ... Everyone – the Japanese included – did black marketing. The Japanese Occupation culture brought out the basic survival instincts in people and produced a society where all manner of evils could be justified because it was all about survival. ... It would take years to undo the corruption and address the social evils that Japanese military occupation bred in Singapore. (Lee, 2005, p. 205)

Similarly, Turnbull (1977, p. 225) contended that the Japanese Occupation's worst legacy was "the corruption of public and private integrity" because of the "flourishing gambling dens and brothels, both legalized by the Japanese, the resurgence of opium smoking, universal profiteering, and bribery."

Conditions in Singapore deteriorated during the postwar period, and corruption spread among civil servants as a result of their low wages, inflation, and inadequate supervision by their superior officers, thus providing them with ample opportunities for corruption with a low probability of being caught (Quah, 1982, pp. 161–162). Corruption was a way of life for many people and the British Military Administration (BMA), which had taken over after the Japanese surrender in August 1945, was described pejoratively as the "Black Market Administration" because of its arbitrary requisition of private property, gross mismanagement of the distribution of rice, financial inefficiency, and "scandalous corruption" (Turnbull, 1977, p. 225).

In the 1950s, "bribes and kickbacks were part of the way of life" in Singapore because "people had to grease palms to obtain licenses, permits, immigration papers, public housing, and coveted places in schools." Lee Kip Lin, a retired architect, described the Lim Yew Hock administration as "being corrupt from head to toe." Singapore was described as "a journalist's paradise" and "a Marxist recipe for revolution" because it was afflicted by "riots, strikes, pickets, protests, demonstrations, squalor, poverty, joblessness, corruption, vice, crime, fires, floods, diseases" (Yap, Lim, & Leong, 2009, pp. 555–556).

In October 1951, 1,800 pounds of opium worth S$400,000 (US$133,333) were stolen at Ponggol by a gang of robbers, which included three police detectives. The British colonial government appointed a special team led by a senior ACB officer to investigate the robbery. Investigations revealed that some senior police officers were involved in the racket with both the hijackers and the importers of the opium. In April 1952, the British colonial authorities formed another special investigation team to find out what went wrong with the previous investigation conducted by the ACB. When the special team completed its investigation in September 1952, the British colonial government decided to replace the ACB with the special team, which became the CPIB.

Thus, the Opium Hijacking scandal of October 1951 was the triggering mechanism that catalyzed the CPIB's birth. Furthermore, it should be noted that the scandal also made the British colonial government realize that it had made a serious policy mistake in December 1937, when the

ACB was entrusted with the task of curbing corruption even though police corruption was rampant in Singapore.

CORRUPT PRACTICES INVESTIGATION BUREAU

The CPIB began its operations with a small staff of 13 seconded police officers in October 1952. However, the CPIB's reliance on these officers on short secondment undermined its effectiveness during its formative years because they had "limited time and capacity to conduct thorough investigations" and "were not fully committed in investigating their fellow police officers" (CPIB, 2012b, p. 18; Ali, 2000, pp. 3−4).

Learning from the British colonial government's lack of political will in combating corruption as reflected in the CPIB's lack of legal powers, manpower, and budget during its first eight years, the PAP government realized from the outset the critical importance of enhancing the CPIB's powers and providing it with the required personnel and budget for performing its functions effectively. Lee Kuan Yew, Singapore's first prime minister, explained in his memoirs why his government was committed from the outset to keep Singapore free from corruption:

> When the PAP government took office in 1959, we set out to have a clean administration. We were sickened by the greed, corruption, and decadence of many Asian leaders. … We had a deep sense of mission to establish a clean and effective government. When we took the oath of office … in June 1959, we all wore white shirts and white slacks to symbolize purity and honesty in our personal behavior and our public life. … We made sure from the day we took office in June 1959 that every dollar in revenue would be properly accounted for and would reach the beneficiaries at the grassroots as one dollar, without being siphoned off along the way. So from the very beginning we gave special attention to the areas where discretionary powers had been exploited for personal gain and sharpened the instruments that could prevent, detect or deter such practices. (Lee, 2000, pp. 182−184)

Accordingly, the PAP government initiated a comprehensive anti-corruption strategy by enacting the POCA in June 1960 to strengthen the CPIB. In moving for the second reading of the Prevention of Corruption Bill in the Legislative Assembly on February 13, 1960, Ong Pang Boon, the Minister for Home Affairs, elaborated on its rationale thus:

> The Prevention of Corruption Bill is in keeping with the new Government's determination to stamp out bribery and corruption in the country, especially in the public services. … Therefore, this government is determined to take all possible steps to see that all necessary legislative and administrative measures are taken to reduce the

opportunities of corruption, to make its detection easier and to deter and punish severely those who are susceptible to it and who engage in it shamelessly. Therefore, in this Bill, the Government is asking for new and wider powers to fight bribery and corruption. (State of Singapore, 1960, cols. 376–377)

As Singapore's sole ACA, the CPIB enforces the POCA by performing these three functions: (1) receiving and investigating complaints alleging corrupt practices; (2) investigating corrupt malpractices and misconduct by public officers; and (3) preventing corruption in the SCS by minimizing opportunities for corrupt practices by examining their practices and procedures (CPIB, 2004, p. 3). The Budget has described the Corrupt Practices Investigation Program as the administration of the CPIB, the investigation of corruption and malpractices, and the review of administrative weaknesses in the public sector that "provides avenues for corruption and the screening of officers for appointment in the public service" (Republic of Singapore, 1994, p. 638). In other words, in relation to its preventive function, the CPIB is also responsible for screening candidates selected for positions in the SCS and statutory boards to ensure that only those candidates without any taint of corruption or misconduct are actually appointed.

The POCA has five important features which remove the POCO's weaknesses, enhance the CPIB's legal powers, and increase its personnel. First, in contrast with the POCO's 12 sections, the POCA has a broader scope with 32 sections.[1] Second, corruption is defined explicitly in terms of five forms of "gratification" in section 2. Third, section 5 increases the penalty for corruption to five years imprisonment and/or a fine of S$10,000 to enhance the POCA's deterrent effect.[2] Fourth, according to section 13, a person found guilty of accepting an illegal gratification had to pay the amount that he or she had taken as a bribe in addition to any other punishment imposed by a court. Finally, the POCA's most important feature is that it has given the CPIB more powers and a new lease of life. Section 15 gives CPIB officers powers of arrest and search of arrested persons. Section 18 empowers the public prosecutor to authorize the CPIB's Director and his senior officers to investigate "any bank account, share account, or purchase account" of anyone suspected of having committed an offense against the POCA. Section 20 enables the CPIB officers to inspect a civil servant's banker's books and those of his wife, child, or agent, if necessary. Section 21 empowers the public prosecutor to obtain information on an individual's property, income tax, and bank accounts from the relevant government departments and banks. Section 22 enables police officers and CPIB officers to enter any suspected place and search, seize, and detain incriminating documents under a warrant issued by a magistrate or the CPIB's Director. Section 24 is perhaps the CPIB's most important asset in its investigation of corruption offenses because "the fact that an accused person is in possession, for which he cannot satisfactorily account, of pecuniary resources or property dispro- portionate to his known sources of income" is evidence that he or she had obtained these pecuniary resources or property "corruptly as an inducement or reward" (Quah, 2011, pp. 219−220).

Table 2 shows that the CPIB has grown by nearly 11 times from its initial staff of 13 officers in 1952 to its current strength of 138 officers in 2011. Even though the CPIB has grown during its first six decades, it is still a relatively small agency on two counts. First, the CPIB's staff of 138 mem- bers constitutes only 0.10 percent of the 77,540 civil servants and the 53,688 members of the statutory boards in Singapore in 2011 (Department of Statistics, Singapore, 2012, p. 52). Second, Hong Kong's Independent Commission Against Corruption (ICAC) is more than nine times larger than the CPIB as it has 1,298 personnel in 2011 (ICAC, 2012, p. 22).

Table 2.   Increase in CPIB's Personnel, 1952−2011.

Year	No. of Personnel
1952	13
1959	8
1961	9
1963	33
1965	36
1968	40
1969	41
1970	50
1971	51
1972	52
1973	53
1974	54
1975	55
1976	61
1980	69
1998	79
2000	84
2005	82
2007	89
2009	93
2010	138
2011	138

Sources: Quah (1978, p. 17; 2011, p. 222); Republic of Singapore (2011, p. 378).

Table 3. CPIB's Budget, 1978–2011.

Year	Budget	Percentage Increase
1978	S$1,024,370	100
1987	S$4,147,230	405
1997	S$10,225,463	998
2007	S$14,619,718	1,427
2008	S$15,790,811	1,542
2009	S$16,386,900	1,600
2010	S$21,087,600	2,059
2011	S$34,073,400	3,326

Sources: Quah (2011, p. 223); Republic of Singapore (2011, p. 378).

Unlike the ICAC, the CPIB does not require as much manpower as its location within the Prime Minister's Office and its legal powers have enabled the CPIB to obtain the necessary cooperation from both the public and private organizations (Quah, 1995, p. 397).

The CPIB is divided into the Operations Division and the Administration and Specialist Support Division. The Operations Division is subdivided into the Operations Branch and the Operations Support Branch, which includes the Intelligence Unit and Field Research and Technical Support Unit. The Operations Branch consists of the Special Investigation Team, which handles major and complex cases, and Units I, II, and III. The Administration and Specialist Support Division comprises of the Administration Unit, Prevention and Review Unit, and the Plans and Projects Unit. The Administration Unit is subdivided into these units: Finance, Records and Screening, Personnel, and Computer Information System Unit (CPIB, 2004, p. 11).

Table 3 provides details of the substantial growth in the CPIB's budget from S$1,024,370 in 1978 to S$34,073,400 in 2011, reflecting an increase of more than 33 times during this period. In other words, the PAP government has demonstrated its political will in combating corruption in Singapore by providing the CPIB with the required budget to perform its functions.

EVALUATING THE CPIB'S EFFECTIVENESS IN CURBING CORRUPTION

The CPIB's effectiveness in curbing corruption in Singapore is ascertained by examining Singapore's performance on these five indicators:

(1) Transparency International's CPI from 1995 to 2012; (2) PERC's annual surveys on corruption from 1995 to 2013; (3) World Bank's Control of Corruption governance indicator from 1996 to 2011; (4) World Bank's Ease of Doing Business rank from 2007 to 2013; and (5) the *Global Competitiveness Report's* Public Trust of Politicians indicator from 1999 to 2012.

Table 4 shows first that Singapore has been consistently ranked as the least corrupt country in Asia from 1995 to 2013. In 2010, Singapore was jointly ranked first with Denmark and New Zealand with a score of 9.3 among the 178 countries included in the CPI for that year. Singapore retained its ranking as the fifth least corrupt country in the CPI for 2011 and 2012. Second, PERC's annual surveys of corruption from 1995 to 2013

Table 4. Singapore's Performance on the CPI, PERC, and Control of Corruption, 1995–2013.

Year	CPI Rank and Score[a]	PERC Rank and Score[b]	Control of Corruption Percentile Rank
1995	3rd (9.26)	1st (1.20)	NA
1996	7th (8.80)	1st (1.09)	96.6
1997	9th (8.66)	1st (1.05)	NA
1998	7th (9.1)	1st (1.43)	96.1
1999	7th (9.1)	1st (1.55)	NA
2000	6th (9.1)	1st (0.71)	96.6
2001	4th (9.2)	1st (0.83)	NA
2002	5th (9.3)	1st (0.90)	98.5
2003	5th (9.4)	1st (0.38)	98.0
2004	5th (9.3)	1st (0.50)	98.5
2005	5th (9.4)	1st (0.65)	98.0
2006	5th (9.3)	1st (1.30)	97.6
2007	4th (9.3)	1st (1.20)	97.6
2008	4th (9.2)	1st (1.13)	98.1
2009	3rd (9.2)	1st (0.92)	98.1
2010	1st (9.3)	1st (0.99)	98.6
2011	5th (9.2)	1st (0.37)	96.2
2012	5th (87)	1st (0.67)	NA
2013	NA	1st (0.74)	NA

Sources: http://www.transparency.org; PERC (2001, 2008, p. 7; 2012, p. 4; 2013, p. 6); http://info. worldbank.org/governance/wgi/sc_chart.asp.
[a]The CPI score from 1995 to 2011 ranges from 0 (highly corrupt) to 10 (very clean). The CPI 2012 score ranges from 0 (highly corrupt) to 100 (very clean).
[b]The PERC score ranges from 0 (least corrupt) to 10 (most corrupt).

also confirm Singapore's status as the least corrupt Asian country. Third, the World Bank's Control of Corruption indicator from 1996 to 2011 shows that Singapore has the highest percentile rank among all the Asian countries included in the surveys.

Fourth, Table 5 confirms that red tape is not a problem at all in Singapore, which has consistently been ranked first in terms of the ease of doing business among the 175–185 economies included in the World Bank's *Doing Business Surveys* from 2007 to 2013. The relative absence of red tape in Singapore is also an indicator that corruption is not a serious problem, as reflected in Singapore's consistently high ranking and scores on the CPI from 2007 to 2012.

Fifth, Table 6 shows the high level of public trust of politicians in Singapore from 1999 to 2012. More specifically, Singapore has been ranked first with a score between 6.30 and 6.50 among the 59–144 countries surveyed during 1999 to 2012. This finding is not surprising because it is another indication of the high level of public trust of politicians and the low level of corruption in Singapore.

Singapore's consistently good performance on the above five indicators is also reflected in the small number of corruption cases investigated by the

Table 5. Ease of Doing Business in Singapore, 2007–2013.

Indicator	2007	2008	2009	2010	2011	2012	2013
Ease of doing business (rank)	1st	1st	1st	1st	1st	1st	1st
Starting a business (rank)	11th	9th	10th	4th	4th	4th	4th
Number of procedures	6	5	4	3	3	3	3
Time (days)	6	5	4	3	3	3	3
Cost (% of income per capita)	0.8	0.8	0.7	0.7	0.7	0.7	0.6
Dealing with construction permits (rank)	8th	5th	2nd	2nd	2nd	3rd	2nd
Number of procedures	11	11	11	11	11	11	11
Time (days)	129	102	38	25	25	26	26
Cost (% of income per capita)	22.0	22.9	21.2	19.9	19.7	18.1	16.7
Registering property (rank)	12th	13th	16th	16th	15th	14th	36th
Number of procedures	3	3	3	3	3	3	5
Time (days)	9	9	9	5	5	5	21
Cost (% of income per capita)	2.8	2.8	2.8	2.8	2.8	2.8	2.9
CPI rank and score	4th	4th	3rd	1st	5th	5th	NA
	(9.3)	(9.2)	(9.2)	(9.3)	(9.2)	(87)	

Sources: World Bank (2006, p. 140; 2007, p. 149; 2008, p. 133; 2009, p. 150; 2010, p. 192; 2012, p. 125; 2013, p. 193).

Table 6. Public Trust of Politicians in Singapore, 1999−2012.

Year	Rank	Score[a]	No. of Countries
1999	1st	6.36	59
2000	1st	6.50	59
2001	1st	6.40	75
2002	1st	6.40	80
2003	1st	6.50	102
2007	1st	6.40	131
2008	1st	6.50	134
2009	1st	6.40	133
2010	1st	6.40	139
2011	1st	6.40	142
2012	1st	6.30	144
Average	1st	6.41	-

Sources: Quah (2011, p. 227); Schwab (2011, p. 393; 2012, p. 391).
[a]The score ranges from 1 (very low) to 7 (very high) for the respondents' answers to this question: "How would you rate the level of public trust in the ethical standards of politicians in your country?"

Table 7. Corruption Cases Investigated by the CPIB by Sector, 2008−2012.

Sector	2008	2009	2010	2011	2012	Average
Public sector cases	45 (18.8%)	49 (20.9%)	37 (18.0%)	31 (22.5%)	35 (19.6%)	39 (20%)
Private sector cases	194 (81.2%)	185 (79.1%)	169 (82.0%)	107 (77.5%)	144 (80.4%)	160 (80%)
Total	239 (100%)	234 (100%)	206 (100%)	138 (100%)	179 (100%)	199 (100%)

Source: Singh (2013b, p. A8).

CPIB from 2008 to 2012, according to the findings of a recent study commissioned by the Prime Minister's Office. Table 7 shows that an average of 80 percent of the cases investigated by the CPIB came from the private sector, with the remaining 20 percent originating from the public sector. Indeed, the number of public sector corruption cases investigated by the CPIB ranges from 31 in 2011 to 49 in 2009, with an average of 39 cases during 2008−2012. However, the number of private sector corruption cases has decreased from 194 in 2008 to 144 in 2012.

LESSONS FROM SINGAPORE'S EXPERIENCE IN CURBING CORRUPTION

Why has Singapore succeeded in curbing corruption and what lessons can other Asian countries learn from its experience in combating corruption? The factors responsible for Singapore's success in curbing corruption can also serve as lessons for those Asian countries interested in improving their anti-corruption strategies.

Lesson 1: Political Will Is Needed to Curb Corruption Effectively in a Country

Political will or the commitment of the political leaders is the critical factor responsible for the effectiveness of a country's anti-corruption measures because the lack of political will is the most important reason for the failure of anti-corruption efforts in many Asian countries (Quah, 2011, pp. 22, 453–456). Ian Senior (2006, pp. 184, 187) has explained why political will is needed to ensure success in a country's anti-corruption strategy:

> The principal people who can change a culture of corruption if they wish to do so are politicians. This is because they make the laws and allocate the funds that enable the laws to be enforced. If, however, politicians at the top of the hierarchy have routinely worked their way up by accepting bribes to fund their parties and themselves, there is little prospect that they will wish to cleanse their colleagues or their nation of corruption. ... The very people who are the greatest beneficiaries of corruption have the greatest power and use the corrupt nature of government to maintain that power.

If political will is the most important factor for ensuring the effective implementation of a comprehensive anti-corruption strategy in a country, how can it be ascertained? Political will exists when these three conditions are met: comprehensive anti-corruption laws exist; the independent ACA is provided with sufficient personnel and resources; and the anti-corruption laws are impartially enforced by an independent ACA (Quah, 2007, pp. 37–38). To assess whether the CPIB has been provided with adequate personnel and budget by the PAP government to perform its functions, these two indicators are used:

1. Per capita expenditure – that is, the CPIB's budget for a selected year in US\$ (to ensure comparability), divided by the total population in Singapore for the same year.

2. Staff—population ratio — that is, the ratio of Singapore's population in a selected year to the number of CPIB personnel in the same year (Quah, 2009, p. 182).

Table 8 shows that the CPIB's per capita expenditure has increased from US$1.80 in 2005 to US$2.31 in 2008, and to US$5.11 in 2011. On the other hand, according to Table 9, the CPIB's staff—population ratio has increased from 1:52,022 in 2005 to 1:56,272 in 2008. However, with the increase of 52 personnel in 2011, the CPIB's staff—population ratio has decreased to 1:38,406.

Lesson 2: CPIB's Reliance on Expertise and Total Enforcement

An ACA is a specialized agency established by a government to minimize corruption in a country. Nicholls, Daniel, Polaine, and Hatchard (2006, p. 476) have identified these four advantages of an ACA: reduced administrative costs; enhanced public profile; concentration of expertise; and reduced uncertainty over the jurisdiction by avoiding duplication of powers and work. Perhaps, the most important advantage of creating an ACA is that it sends a powerful signal to the citizens in the country that the government is committed to fighting corruption (United Nations Office on Drugs and

Table 8.   Increase in Per Capita Expenditure of CPIB from 2005 to 2011.

Year	CPIB's Budget	Population of Singapore	Per Capita Expenditure
2005	US$7.7 million	4,265,800	US$1.80
2008	US$11.2 million	4,839,400	US$2.31
2011	US$27.08 million	5,300,000	US$5.11

Sources: Department of Statistics, Singapore (2012, p. 23); Republic of Singapore (2007, 2008, 2011); Schwab (2012, p. 383).

Table 9.   Staff—Population Ratio of CPIB from 2005 to 2011.

Year	CPIB's Personnel	Population of Singapore	Staff—Population Ratio
2005	82	4,265,800	1:52,022
2008	86	4,839,400	1:56,272
2011	138	5,300,000	1:38,406

Sources: As in Table 8.

Crime, 2004, p. 90). However, this initial advantage is eroded if the government does not demonstrate its commitment by providing the ACA with sufficient legal powers and adequate human and financial resources. Also, the government should provide the ACA with operational autonomy so that it can investigate anyone, regardless of status or position. All the above operational advantages will count for naught if the government does not support the ACA by allowing it to operate independently and by providing it with adequate resources for performing its functions effectively (Quah, 2009, p. 174).

The CPIB adopts a "total approach to enforcement" by dealing with both "big and small cases" of public and private sector corruption, "both giver and receiver of bribes" and "other crimes uncovered in the course of [the] corruption investigation" (Soh, 2008, pp. 1–2). According to Soh Kee Hean (2008, pp. 2–3), a former CPIB Director, the CPIB has succeeded in its enforcement efforts because of its reliance on skilful interview techniques, careful planning and execution of field operations, and computer forensics. Indeed, the CPIB's effective enforcement capacity can be attributed to its threefold emphasis on the capability building of its enforcement officers, building networks and partnerships with other public agencies in Singapore, and organizational excellence.

To improve the capabilities of its enforcement officers, the CPIB has exposed them to both in-house and external training programs in Singapore and abroad on relevant management and professional topics. The CPIB has also organized three Anti-Corruption Expertise (ACE) regional training workshops on the "bread-and-butter issues" for ACAs in Singapore from 2006 to 2008 for anti-corruption practitioners. The August 2006 ACE workshop focused on "Excellence in Investigation," a very important topic for ACAs. The second ACE workshop held in Singapore on September 10, 2007, dealt with "Excellence in Computer Forensics" and was attended by 50 participants from the ACAs in Brunei Darussalam, Cambodia, Indonesia, Lao PDR, Malaysia, Philippines, Singapore, Thailand, and Vietnam. The third ACE workshop in Singapore held on October 14–16, 2008 focused on "Excellence in Management of ACAs" and was well attended by many officers from the ACAs in Australia, Bhutan, Brunei Darussalam, China, Hong Kong SAR, Indonesia, Macao SAR, Malaysia, Mongolia, New Zealand, Pakistan, Philippines, Singapore, South Korea, and Thailand. To build networks and partnerships with other public agencies in Singapore, the CPIB has conducted joint operations with the Commercial Affairs Department and the Immigration and Checkpoints Authority (Soh, 2008, pp. 3–4).

The CPIB's focus on organizational excellence is important and perhaps unique among the ACAs in Asia. Its commitment to organizational excellence is reflected in the many awards it has won, beginning with its certification as an ISO 9000: 2001, since 1997. The significance of this award is that the key processes of the CPIB are documented and followed by its officers, and there is also a "regular surveillance audit by the ISO inspectors and regular reviews" of these processes "to keep them up-to-date" (Soh, 2008, p. 4). In 1998, the CPIB was awarded the Singapore Quality Class, which certifies the excellence of both public and private organizations in Singapore. In 2003, the CPIB became the first government agency in Singapore to receive the People Excellence Award. Finally, the CPIB was given the Distinguished Public Service Award for Organizational Excellence in 2005 (CPIB, 2008).

To further enhance its expertise, the CPIB formed a Computer Forensic Unit in July 2004 to improve its investigative and evidence-gathering capabilities. It has also developed a Technology Masterplan to provide support for its operations and management systems. In 2006, the CPIB improved its system of recruiting investigation officers by introducing a three-stage process involving the use of psychometric tests to evaluate the candidates' aptitudes and competence, case analysis exercises to assess their thinking and people skills, and a structured interview (CPIB, 2008).

To supplement its emphasis on investigation and enforcement, the CPIB adopts a proactive approach to its activities on corruption prevention and education. To prevent corruption, the CPIB reviews the procedures and practices in those government agencies where corruption has occurred and makes recommendations to remove the "loopholes and vulnerabilities." The CPIB relies on this review process "to identify potential problem areas and loopholes" in order to reduce the opportunities for corruption (Soh, 2008, p. 8). The CPIB has an extensive outreach program for Singaporeans and visitors from other countries. It has a Public Education Group which conducts prevention and education talks for pre-university students, principals and teachers, newly appointed civil servants, law-enforcement agencies like the police and immigration, and the management and staff of major organizations in key industries. The CPIB's effectiveness has attracted worldwide attention and it has received 13,031 visitors from other countries from 2005 to 2011, including the staff of ACAs and those foreign officials visiting Singapore under the auspices of the Singapore Cooperation Program. Table 10 shows that the number of persons visiting the CPIB and attending its prevention and education talks has increased by more than three times from 3,670 in 2005 to 12,320 in 2010. However, the number of

Table 10. Attendance at CPIB's Corruption Prevention and Education Activities, 2005–2011.

Activity	2005	2006	2007	2008	2009	2010	2011
Prevention and education talks	2,500	4,500	7,073	5,823	7,441	9,193	5,928
Visits by foreign delegates	1,000	1,500	2,142	2,520	2,358	2,538	973
Visitors from local organizations	20	200	357	424	403	56	NA[a]
Student visitors	150	200	432	433	791	533	971
Total	3,670	6,400	10,004	9,200	10,993	12,320	7,872

Sources: CPIB (2008; 2011, p. 9; 2012a, p. 11).

[a]The figures for visitors from local organizations in 2011 were included in the number of persons attending the prevention and education talks.

visitors to the CPIB in 2011 dropped to 7,872 because of the decline in the number of participants attending the prevention and education talks and the number of foreign delegates.

Lesson 3: Punish Corrupt Offenders by Enforcing the Law Impartially

As corruption is a crime, the most effective way to curb it is to punish those found guilty of corrupt offenses. Indeed, Singapore's experience demonstrates the importance of punishing corrupt offenders, regardless of their status or position, in order to deter others from being involved in corruption. During the British colonial period, corruption was perceived by the population as a "low-risk, high-reward" activity as the probability of being detected and punished for corrupt offenses was low because of the ineffectiveness of the ACB. However, the empowerment of the CPIB by the enactment of the POCA in June 1960 by the PAP government, which was committed to eradicating corruption, led to the transformation of the public perception of corruption in Singapore to a "high-risk, low-reward" activity.

As mentioned above, the POCA's deterrent effect was enhanced by increasing the penalty for corruption to imprisonment for five years and/or a fine of S$10,000. In 1981, the POCA was amended to increase its deterrent effect by requiring those convicted of corruption to repay all the money received in addition to facing the usual court sentence (Section 13). Offenders who could not make full restitution were given heavier court sentences. Eight years later, the fine for corrupt offenses was further increased by 10 times, from S$10,000 to S$100,000, to enhance the POCA's deterrent effect. Sections 11 and 12 stipulate that Members of Parliament (MPs) and members of public bodies found guilty of corrupt offenses would be fined S$100,000 and imprisoned for a term of seven years (Quah, 2011, p. 221).

Apart from enhancing the penalty for corruption offenses, the CPIB has enforced the POCA impartially by not hesitating to investigate allegations of corruption against political leaders and senior civil servants in Singapore. It has investigated these four PAP leaders for corruption: (1) Tan Kia Gan, the Minister for National Development, in 1966 for assisting his friend in the sale of Boeing aircraft to Malaysian Airways; (2) Wee Toon Boon, Minister of State, in 1975 for accepting bribes from a property developer; (3) Phey Yew Kok, an MP and trade union leader, in 1979 for criminal breach of trust; and (4) Teh Cheang Wan, Minister for National Development, in 1986 for accepting bribes of S$1 million from two property developers. Tan was stripped of all his public appointments as the witnesses did not give evidence against him. Wee was found guilty and sentenced to four and a half years of imprisonment. Phey jumped bail and fled abroad and remains a fugitive. Teh committed suicide before he could be charged in court (CPIB, 2003, pp. 6.45–6.47).

Corrupt senior civil servants have also not been spared by the CPIB. In March 1991, the Director of the Commercial Affairs Department, Glenn Knight, was investigated and sentenced to three months' jail in October 1991 for attempted cheating and giving false information to obtain a government car loan. In 1993, Yeo Seng Teck, the Chief Executive Officer of the Trade Development Board, was investigated for cheating offenses and charged for 22 counts of forgery, cheating, and using forged invoices involving the purchases of Chinese antiques worth S$2 million. Yeo was found guilty and sentenced to four years' imprisonment. In 1995, Choy Hon Tim, the Deputy Chief Executive (Operations) of the Public Utilities Board, was investigated for receiving kickbacks from some contractors. He was convicted for receiving bribes amounting to S$13.85 million and sentenced to 14 years' imprisonment (CPIB, 2003, pp. 6.48–6.49).

More recently, two senior civil servants were arrested by the CPIB for "serious personal conduct": Ng Boon Gay, the Director of the Central Narcotics Bureau (CNB), was arrested on December 19, 2011; followed 16 days later, with the arrest of Peter Lim, Director of the Singapore Civil Defense Force (SCDF), on January 4, 2012. Lim was charged on June 6 with 10 counts of corruption involving sex with three female information technology (IT) executives, who were seeking government contracts for their companies (Lim & Tham, 2012a, p. A1). Ng was charged on June 12 with four counts of corruptly obtaining sexual favors from a former IT sales manager, Cecilia Sue, between July and December 2011 (Lim & Tham, 2012b, p. A1). Ng's trial began on September 25 and was adjourned on November 22 after 14 days of testimony from 10 witnesses, which included Ng himself. When the trial resumed on January 28, 2013, the prosecution contended that, according to the POCA, the onus was on Ng to prove that he was not corrupt. However, the defense countered that the prosecution had not provided evidence that Ng was corrupt and had favored Cecilia Sue or the two companies (Tham, 2013, p. A6; Lim, 2013, p. A6). Ng was acquitted on February 14, 2013 by District Judge Siva Shanmugam because there was no evidence to show that Ng was aware that Cecilia Sue's employer, Hitachi Data Systems, was involved in a contract that he had approved as the CNB's Director. Furthermore, the trysts between Ng and Cecilia Sue occurred because of their intimate relationship and were not bribes (Tham & Lim, 2013, p. A1).

Peter Lim's trial began on February 18, 2013 and he was found guilty of corruptly obtaining sexual gratification from the former General Manager of Nimrod Engineering in exchange for business favors with the SCDF on May 31, after a 12-day trial that spanned over two months (Spykerman, 2013). He was sentenced to six months' imprisonment on June 13 and began serving his sentence on June 26 (Today online, 2013). The most recent corruption case involves Edwin Yeo, the CPIB's Assistant Director responsible for field research and technical support, who was accused on July 24, 2013 for misappropriating more than S$1.7 million from the CPIB. Yeo was charged on 21 counts: 12 for using the proceeds of his crimes for gambling, eight for criminal breach of trust, and one for forgery (Singh, 2013a, p. A1).

In his opening speech at the 60th-anniversary celebrations of the CPIB on September 18, 2012, Prime Minister Lee Hsien Loong reiterated his government's commitment to its policy of zero tolerance toward corruption and stressed that the CPIB's investigation and arrest of Ng and Lim reflects "our determination to clamp down on corruption and wrongdoing even when it's awkward or embarrassing for the Government" (Lee, 2012, p. A23). Lee elaborated on his government's unequivocal stand against corruption thus:

> Let me be quite clear: We will never tolerate corruption and we will not accept any slackening. Anyone who breaks the rules will be caught and punished − no cover ups, no matter how senior the officer or how embarrassing it may be. It is far better to suffer the embarrassment and keep the system clean, than to pretend that nothing went wrong and let the rot spread. (Lee, 2012, p. A23)

On the other hand, another important reason why some Asian countries have not succeeded in curbing corruption is the low risk of detection and punishment for corrupt offenses. For example, in South Korea, those persons found guilty of corruption offenses are not punished severely as they can be pardoned by the President. The most recent example of this phenomenon was the special pardons granted by President Lee Myung-bak on January 29, 2013 to 55 persons who were imprisoned for bribery. Among those pardoned were Lee's confidant and former minister, Choi See-joong; his friend and businessman, Chun Shin-il; former parliamentary speaker, Park Hee-tae; and Lee's former senior political affairs aide. This latest round was the seventh time that President Lee had exercised his right to pardon those found guilty of offenses during his term of office (Straits Times, 2013, p. A12). Yoon Gwan-seok, spokesperson for the Democratic United Party, criticized President Lee's action because "using pardons to let off friends and family at the end of one's presidency is more than shameless − it is a deliberate insult to the Korean people" (Ahn, 2013).

Thus, to minimize corruption and deter those who are not involved in corrupt practices from doing so, honesty and incorruptibility among civil servants and political leaders must be recognized and rewarded instead of being punished. The lack of punishment of corrupt civil servants and political leaders in a country sends the wrong signal to their honest counterparts and the population at large as it makes a mockery of the anti-corruption laws and encourage others to become corrupt as the probability of being caught and punished is low. In short, the political system in a country plagued with corruption rewards those who are corrupt and punishes those who are honest. Hence, this system of reward and punishment must be reversed by punishing the corrupt offenders and rewarding those who have abstained from being corrupt.

Lesson 4: Singapore's Favorable Policy Context Has Enhanced Its Anti-Corruption Efforts

As mentioned in the introductory section, Singapore's policy context has enhanced its anti-corruption efforts because of its small size, its retention of the tradition of meritocracy it inherited from British colonial rule, its economic affluence, the impartial enforcement of the anti-corruption laws regardless of a person's race, language or religion, and the durability of the PAP government, which has been in power in Singapore for more than 54 years.

Table 11 provides data on the land area, population, and GDP per capita for 2011, and the CPI 2012 Rank and Score for 26 Asian countries. First, in terms of size, Singapore has the smallest land area of 715.8 sq km, in contrast to such larger countries like China (9,560,900 sq km), India (3,287,263 sq km), Indonesia (1,904,443 sq km), and Mongolia (1,565,000 sq km). Second, the populations of the 26 countries range from 400,000 for Brunei to 1,367 million for China. Singapore's population of 5.3 million is ranked 22nd among the 26 Asian countries, with only Mongolia, Timor-Leste, Bhutan, and Brunei having smaller populations. Third, Singapore is also the richest country with its GDP per capita of US$49,271 in 2011, which is higher than those of Japan (US$45,920), Brunei (US$36,584), and Hong Kong

Table 11. Policy Contexts of 26 Asian Countries.

Country	Land area (sq km)	Population (2011)	GDP per capita (2011)	CPI 2012 Rank and Score
Singapore	715.8	5,300,000	US$49,271	5th (87)
Hong Kong	1,075	7,400,000	US$34,049	14th (77)
Japan	377,727	134,900,000	US$45,920	17th (74)
Bhutan	47,000	700,000	US$1,920	33rd (63)
Taiwan	36,179	23,200,000	US$20,101	37th (61)
South Korea	99,274	49,400,000	US$22,778	45th (56)
Brunei	6,000	400,000	US$36,584	46th (55)
Malaysia	332,665	29,000,000	US$9,700	54th (49)
Sri Lanka	66,000	21,400,000	US$2,877	79th (40)
China	9,560,900	1,367,000,000	US$5,414	80th (39)
Thailand	513,115	70,700,000	US$5,394	88th (37)
India	3,287,263	1,250,200,000	US$1,389	94th (36)
Mongolia	1,565,000	2,800,000	US$3,042	94th (36)
Philippines	300,000	95,300,000	US$2,223	105th (34)
Timor-Leste	15,000	1,200,000	US$3,949	113th (33)
Indonesia	1,904,443	244,200,000	US$3,509	118th (32)
Vietnam	331,114	90,000,000	US$1,374	123rd (31)
Nepal	147,000	30,600,000	US$653	139th (27)
Pakistan	803,940	177,800,000	US$1,201	139th (27)
Bangladesh	143,998	151,600,000	US$678	144th (26)
Papua New G.	463,000	6,900,000	US$1,300	150th (25)
Cambodia	181,000	14,400,000	US$852	157th (22)
Laos	237,000	6,400,000	US$1,010	160th (21)
Myanmar	677,000	50,500,000	US$1,300	172nd (15)
Afghanistan	652,000	30,600,000	US$517	174th (8)
North Korea	121,000	24,000,000	US$1,800	174th (8)

Sources: CIA (2013); Economist (2012); Schwab (2012, pp. 383–384).

Table 12. World Bank's Governance Indicators for Singapore, 1996–2011.

Year	Political Stability	Government Effectiveness	Rule of Law	Regulatory Quality	Control of Corruption
1996	85.1	100.0	89.5	100.0	96.6
1998	75.0	100.0	90.0	100.0	96.1
2000	81.3	100.0	87.6	100.0	96.6
2002	88.5	93.7	90.9	100.0	98.5
2003	77.9	96.6	93.3	99.0	98.0
2004	87.0	96.1	94.7	99.0	98.5
2005	87.0	99.0	95.7	99.5	98.0
2006	93.3	99.5	92.3	98.0	97.6
2007	91.8	100.0	92.3	98.1	97.6
2008	96.2	100.0	92.3	99.0	98.1
2009	90.0	99.5	92.4	98.6	98.1
2010	89.6	100.0	92.9	98.6	98.6
2011	90.1	99.1	93.4	97.2	96.2
Average	87.1	98.7	92.1	99.0	97.6

Source: http://info.worldbank.org/governance/wgi/sc_chart.asp.

SAR (US$34,049). In other words, Singapore has the most favorable policy context among the 26 Asian countries listed in Table 11 because it is the smallest country in terms of land area but also the most affluent with the highest GDP per capita, with a small population of 5.3 million persons.

The other important advantage which Singapore has, which is not shared by the other Asian countries, is its political stability as the PAP government has been in power for more than 54 years, after its assumption of office in June 1959. Furthermore, Singapore has also performed well on the World Bank's governance indicators for government effectiveness, rule of law, regulatory quality, and control of corruption from 1996 to 2011. Table 12 confirms that Singapore has performed well on these five indicators with its average percentile ranks of 87.1 for political stability, 98.7 for government effectiveness, 92.1 for rule of law, 99.0 for regulatory quality, and 97.6 for control of corruption.

CONCLUSION

In sum, unlike many Asian countries, Singapore has succeeded in minimizing corruption as reflected in its consistently good performance on these five indicators: Transparency International's CPI from 1995 to 2012; PERC's annual surveys on corruption from 1995 to 2013; World Bank's control of corruption indicator from 1996 to 2011; World Bank's ease of doing business rank from 2007 to 2013; and the *Global Competitiveness Report's* public trust of politicians from 1999 to 2012. Singapore's success in curbing corruption can be attributed to the PAP government's political will, which is reflected in the enactment of the POCA in June 1960, and its provision of the necessary legal powers, personnel, and budget to the CPIB to enable it to enforce the POCA impartially. The CPIB has been effective because of its reliance on expertise and a total enforcement approach and its ability to enforce the POCA impartially, without any interference from the PAP government. Finally, Singapore's efforts in combating corruption have also been aided considerably by its favorable policy context namely, its small size and population, its economic affluence, and its political stability.

Singapore's success in minimizing corruption is an important factor contributing to its development during the more than 54 years under the PAP government. When Lee Kuan Yew, who was Singapore's Prime Minister from June 1959 to November 1990, was asked this question: "What do you think were the critical success factors for Singapore?" on August 31, 2012, his answer was:

> First, you must have an efficient administration. … It cannot be one-off. It has to be regularly done and there must be an organization or several organizations that see to this. …
>
> Second, it must be a level playing field for all. … You must have a society that people believe is fair. We have a heterogeneous population − Chinese, Indians, Malays and others − so policy is color-blind. …
>
> Third, it must be corruption-free. … The basis for that was a non-corrupt bureaucracy, especially the police, heavy penalties for corruption, rigorous enforcement of the law. Today, people accept it as a fact − you've just got to obey the law. (Lee, 2013, p. D7)

In short, according to former Prime Minister Lee Kuan Yew, Singapore's success can be attributed to its efficient civil service, which implements public policies impartially regardless of a person's race, gender, language or religion, and the effective implementation of its policy of zero tolerance for corruption.

NOTES

1. As result of several amendments, the POCA now has 37 sections.
2. The fine was increased to S$100,000 in 1989.

REFERENCES

Ahn, C. H. (2013). President Lee's corrupt relatives and associates could be pardoned. *Hankyoreh*, January 10.

Ali, M. (2000). Eradicating corruption – The Singapore experience. Paper presented at the Seminar on International Experiences on Good Governance and Fighting Corruption at the Grand Hotel in Bangkok, Thailand, February 17.

CIA (Central Intelligence Agency). (2013). *The world factbook*. Retrieved from https://www.cia.gov/library/publications/the-world-factbook/. Accessed on June 21, 2013.

Colony of Singapore (1952). *Distribution of work 1st May, 1952*. Singapore: Government Printing Office.

CPIB (Corrupt Practices Investigation Bureau). (2003). *Swift and sure action: Four decades of anti-corruption work*. Singapore.

CPIB. (2004). *Corrupt Practices Investigation Bureau*. Singapore.

CPIB. (2008). Interview with Soh Kee Hean, CPIB Director, and two senior officers on June 27 and subsequent information provided in e-mail correspondence on July 3 and 11.

CPIB. (2011). *CPIB report 2010*. Singapore.

CPIB. (2012a). *CPIB report 2011*. Singapore.

CPIB. (2012b). *The journey: 60 years of fighting corruption in Singapore*. Singapore.

Department of Statistics, Singapore. (2012). *Yearbook of statistics Singapore*, 2012. Singapore.

Department of Statistics, Singapore. (2013). *"Latest data." Singapore*. Retrieved from http://www.singstat.gov.sg/statistics/latest_data.html. Accessed on July 15, 2013.

Economist (2012). *Pocket world in figures 2013 edition*. London: Profile Books.

ICAC (Independent Commission Against Corruption). (2012). *2011 annual report*. Hong Kong.

Krishna, K. B. (1939). *The problem of minorities or communal representation in India*. London: George Allen & Unwin.

Lee, A. C. (1956). *Singapore under the Japanese 1942–1945*. B.A. academic exercise, Department of History, University of Malaya, Singapore.

Lee, G. B. (2005). *The Synonan years: Singapore under Japanese rule 1942–1945*. Singapore: National Archives of Singapore and Epigram.

Lee, H. L. (2012). Incorruptibility ingrained in S'porean psyche. *Straits Times*, September 19, p. A23.

Lee, K. Y. (2000). *From third world to first, The Singapore story (1965–2000)*. Singapore: Times Media Private.

Lee, K. Y. (2013). Lee Kuan Yew's chance of a lifetime. *Straits Times*, February 16, p. D7.

Lim, J. (2013). DPP: Onus of proof is on Ng. *Straits Times*, January 29, p. A6.

Lim, L. & Tham, Y.-C. (2012a). Former SCDF chief faces 10 charges. *Straits Times*, June 7, p. A1.

Lim, L. & Tham,Y.-C. (2012b). Former CNB chief faces graft charges. *Straits Times*, June 13, p. A1.

Nicholls, C., Daniel, T., Polaine, M., & Hatchard, J. (2006). *Corruption and misuse of public office*. Oxford: Oxford University Press.

PERC (Political and Economic Risk Consultancy). (2001). Corruption in Asia in 2001. *Asian Intelligence*, No. 579, March 7. Hong Kong.

PERC. (2008). Corruption as a force destabilizing the business environment. *Asian Intelligence*, No. 750, March 12. Hong Kong.

PERC. (2012). The web of corruption in Asia. *Asian Intelligence*, No. 847, March 21. Hong Kong.

PERC. (2013). Corruption's impact on the business environment. *Asian Intelligence*, No. 871, March 13. Hong Kong.

Pitt, K. W. & Leong, W. K. (Eds.) (2009). *Syonan years 1942–1945: Living beneath the rising sun.* Singapore: National Archives of Singapore.

Quah, J. S. T. (1975). *Administrative reform and development administration in Singapore: A comparative study of the Singapore Improvement Trust and the Housing and Development Board.* Ph.D. dissertation, Department of Government, Florida State University, Tallahassee, FL, USA.

Quah, J. S. T. (1978). *Administrative and legal measures for combating bureaucratic corruption in Singapore.* Occasional Paper No. 34. Department of Political Science, University of Singapore, Singapore.

Quah, J. S. T. (1979). Police corruption in Singapore: An analysis of its forms, extent and causes. *Singapore Police Journal, 10*(1), 7–43.

Quah, J. S. T. (1982). Bureaucratic corruption in the ASEAN Countries: A comparative analysis of their anti-corruption strategies. *Journal of Southeast Asian Studies, 13*(1), 153–177.

Quah, J. S. T. (1995). Controlling corruption in city-states: A comparative study of Hong Kong and Singapore. *Crime, Law and Social Change, 22*, 391–414.

Quah, J. S. T. (2007). *Combating corruption Singapore-style: Lessons for other Asian countries.* Baltimore, MD: School of Law, University of Maryland.

Quah, J. S. T. (2009). Benchmarking for excellence: A comparative analysis of seven Asian anti-corruption agencies. *Asia Pacific Journal of Public Administration, 31*(2), 171–195.

Quah, J. S. T. (2010). *Public administration Singapore-style.* Bingley: Emerald Group Publishing.

Quah, J. S. T. (2011). *Curbing corruption in Asian countries: An impossible dream?* Bingley: Emerald Group Publishing.

Republic of Singapore (1994). *The Budget for the Financial Year 1994/95.* Singapore: Budget Division, Ministry of Finance.

Republic of Singapore (2007). *The Budget for the Financial Year 2007/2008.* Singapore: Budget Division, Ministry of Finance.

Republic of Singapore (2008). *The Budget for the Financial Year 2008/2009.* Singapore: Budget Division, Ministry of Finance.

Republic of Singapore (2011). *The Budget for the Financial Year 2011: Annex to the Expenditure Estimates.* Singapore: Budget Division, Ministry of Finance.

Schwab, K. (Ed.) (2011). *The global competitiveness report 2011–2012.* Geneva: World Economic Forum.

Schwab, K. (Ed.) (2012). *The global competitiveness report 2012–2013.* Geneva: World Economic Forum.

Senior, I. (2006). *Corruption – the World's big C: Cases, causes, consequences, cures.* London: Institute of Economic Affairs.

Singh, B. (2013a). CPIB officer accused of embezzling over $1.7 m. *Straits Times*, July 25, p. A1.

Singh, B. (2013b). Public service graft cases: Half were in enforcement. *Straits Times*, July 27, p. A8.

Soh, K. H. (2008). Corruption enforcement. Paper presented at the Second Seminar of the International Association of Anti-Corruption Associations in Chongqing, China, May 17–18.

Spykerman, K. (2013). Ex-SCDF chief Peter Lim found guilty of corruption. *Channel News Asia*, May 31. Retrieved from http://channelnewsasia.com/news/singapore/ex-scdf-chief-peter-lim-found-guilty-of-/693694.html. Accessed on June 21, 2013.

State of Singapore (1960). *Legislative Assembly debates, First Session of the First Legislative Assembly (Vol. 12)*. Singapore: Government Printing Office.

Straits Settlements (1887). *Report of Commission appointed to enquire into the question of public gambling in the Straits Settlements*. Singapore: Colonial Secretary's Office.

Straits Times. (2013). South Korean leader pardons ex-aides. *Straits Times*, January 30.

Tham, Y.-C. (2013). Defense: No evidence to show accused was corrupt. *Straits Times*, January 29, p. A6.

Tham, Y.-C. & Lim, J. (2013). Court finds Ng Boon Gay not guilty of corruption. *Straits Times*, February 15, p. A1.

Today Online. (2013). Ex-SCDF chief Peter Lim to start prison sentence today. *Today Online*, June 26. Retrieved from http://www.todayonline.com/singapore/ex-scdf-chief-peter-lim-start-prison-sentence-today. Accessed on June 21, 2013.

Turnbull, C. M. (1977). *A history of Singapore: 1819–1975*. Kuala Lumpur: Oxford University Press.

UNODC (United Nations Office on Drugs and Crime) (2004). *The global program against corruption: United Nations anti-corruption toolkit*. 3rd ed. Vienna.

World Bank. (2006). *Doing business 2007*. Washington, DC.

World Bank. (2007). *Doing business 2008*. Washington, DC.

World Bank. (2008). *Doing business 2009*. Washington, DC.

World Bank. (2009). *Doing business 2010*. Washington, DC.

World Bank. (2010). *Doing business 2011*. Washington, DC.

World Bank. (2012). *Doing business 2012*. Washington, DC.

World Bank. (2013). *Doing business 2013*. Washington, DC.

Yap, S., Lim, R., & Leong, W. K. (2009). *Men in white: The untold story of Singapore's ruling political party*. Singapore: Singapore Press Holdings.

Yoong, S. W. (1972). Some aspects of corruption. *National youth leadership training institute Journal* (January), 54–59.

CHAPTER 7

CAN INDIA COMBAT CORRUPTION?

Krishna K. Tummala

ABSTRACT

Corruption in India reached a crescendo between 2011 and 2013, with the exposure of the 2G Spectrum scandal and the "Coalgate" report fiasco at the top of all recent events. The largest working democracy is under the scanner. As the third largest economy in Asia, a nuclear power, and an information technology powerhouse, India has a lot to clean up. Current experience shows the failure of the top investigative agencies and the lack of political will to tackle corruption. The spate of high-level corruption scandals has also led to a popular movement in 2011, which also fizzled out, including the newly introduced "Anti-Corruption, Grievance Redressal and Whistleblower Protection Act, 2011." This chapter examines the several issues involved.

INTRODUCTION

India did not invent but excels in corruption. Much has been written and will continue to be written on corruption in India. India's preoccupation with corruption can be traced to Kautilya's work written during 321−296

Different Paths to Curbing Corruption: Lessons from Denmark, Finland, Hong Kong, New Zealand and Singapore
Research in Public Policy Analysis and Management, Volume 23, 167−187
ISSN: 0732-1317/doi:10.1108/S0732-1317(2013)0000023007

BCE, which identified at least 40 ways of "embezzlement" alone (Shama Sastry, 1967, pp. 67–71). In modern India, Section 161 of the 1860 Indian Penal Code dealt with combating corruption, which is still the basis for much legal action. The 1964 *Report of the Committee on Prevention of Corruption* (popularly known as the *Santhanam Committee*, after its Chairman) identified 33 different forms of corruption under two headings (involving the public and internal to administration) and made far reaching recommendations, all for nothing.

Despite many laws and several institutions to fight corruption in India, not much has been accomplished in controlling or eradicating it. The latest movement against corruption was the agitation started by Anna Hazare, which in itself had fizzled out after a very promising start. Corruption continues and is ubiquitous in India, involving both petty and grand corruption. While in the past the bureaucracy was pilloried for corruption, it is the mix of political and business class who are at the forefront today. This chapter analyzes the phenomenon of corruption in India, and identifies lessons that India can learn from the effective anti-corruption strategies of Denmark, Finland, Hong Kong, New Zealand, and Singapore, which are perceived to be among the least corrupt countries on Transparency International's 2012 Corruption Perceptions Index (CPI). In contrast, India is ranked 94th among the 176 countries included in the 2012 CPI with a score of 36 (out of a possible 100).

This chapter is divided into eight sections. The first section sets the stage by describing the context in India. The second section provides several vignettes of some recent major corruption scandals. The third section focuses on the anti-corruption measures in India, followed by an evaluation of their performance in the fourth section. The fifth section discusses the Hazare movement and provides an explanation for its failure in the sixth section. The seventh section draws some lessons from the experiences of the least corrupt nations. The concluding section provides some reasons for optimism. As a *caveat*, the subject is so vast and complex that it cannot be studied exhaustively in this chapter, which only attempts to highlight the major issues involved.

CONTEXT

To begin, it is important to show the relevance and context of India's experience. With 1.25 billion people (Schwab, 2012, p. 198), India has the second largest population in the world. It is also the largest working democracy with well-established and reasonably well functioning parliamentary institutions. It conducts relatively peaceful and corruption-free elections on schedule, and on a massive scale. Its economy was growing at a fast rate of 8–9 percent, albeit its 2011–2012 growth rate was 5 percent. It is a nuclear power, though not a signatory to the nonproliferation treaty, and a powerhouse in information technology (IT). More importantly, India is held up as an example for the rest of the less developed world. Thus, what happens in India is a matter of interest and concern.

To understand the behavior of people, it is important to dwell upon the predominant Hindu tradition that includes over 82 percent of the Indian population. Under the Hindu system, four human pursuits (*purushaartha*) are identified. They are *dharma* (that which upholds and maintains society); *artha* (material wealth); *kaama* (all physical, emotional, and intellectual desires, not only sex, as is commonly misunderstood); and *moksha* (liberation/salvation). The four different stages of life, which are not coterminous, are *brahmacharya* (student life while a bachelor); *grihastha* (married, householder); *vaanaprastha* (hermit); and *sanyaasa* (wandering ascetic around the end of life). Given that, it is easy to postulate that while in the *grihastha* stage one's duty is to indulge in the pursuit of *artha*. In fact, it so happens that this stage becomes a lifetime pursuit for many.

The worship of the Goddess of wealth, *Lakshmi*, is important in the Hindu culture, which led Lloyd and Susanne Rudolph (1987) to name their book accordingly! There does not seem to be any guilt attached to the acquisition of wealth (although nowhere does it appear how it ought to be acquired). Not many questions are raised, but in fact such munificence is praised so long as a part of the wealth is offered in the name of god, charity, and the current fleet of "Godmen" and "Godwomen."

Great tolerance is also attributed to Hinduism. However, this does not mean that Hindus do not commit acts of intolerance as can be seen in the case of the Gujarat riots as an example of Hindu atrocity against the Muslims. Other writers dispute the tolerance that is attributed to Hinduism as a virtue. For example, Ambedkar (1995, p. 54) argued that this was because the Hindu was either too weak or indifferent to oppose intolerance.

Hinduism is also known for its infinite capacity for forgiveness. As the great critic, Nirad Chowdhury (1987, p. 787) observed: "The unlimited capacity to be a villain of the worst kind with an unlimited capacity for self-abasement before virtue and nobility is one of the most disarming traits of the Indian character ...." More importantly, the Hindu lives in a state of dissonance, in that life is seen at two levels of existence. The present is *maya* or *midhya* − an illusion; it is the later higher abstraction, after death, which is more desirable, and sought after. This phenomenon accords an opportunity for escaping political and personal responsibility, while seeking religious vindication (Tummala, 2009a, p. 39).

There is also the great tradition of gift giving. While visiting an elder, or someone of substance, one is expected to carry a gift, however inconsequential it is. This is also true when seeking the blessing of gods and goddesses.

EXAMPLES OF HIGH-PROFILE CORRUPTION

Corruption is so ubiquitous that it has been acknowledged by a background paper prepared by the Ministry of Personnel, Public Grievances, and Pensions in April 2012, which stated that: "At senior levels it [corruption] is usually a result of [the] strong nexus between politicians and civil servants and, at lower levels, it is a result of poor systems and ill-defined public service levels" (India Today, 2012).

There have been many major corruption scandals in India in the past. The 1987 Bofors gun purchases, where bribes of about US$11.5 million (US$1 = Rs. 50) allegedly involved even the then Prime Minister Rajiv Gandhi (who was later exonerated). However, the Bofors scandal pales in comparison with the recent corruption scandals between 2010 and 2013. First, among the 543 Indian Members of Parliament (MPs) in 2012, 158 have pending criminal charges. Seventy-four of them have "serious" charges such as murder and abduction. As no party is above reproach, the net result is the general criminalization of politics and politicization of criminals. Ironically, two State Home Ministers (who are in charge of law and order), Amit Shah in Gujarat and Gulabchand Kataria in Rajasthan, are booked for murder by the Central Bureau of Investigation (CBI)!

A second example is provided by the Commonwealth Games, which cost nearly US$2.1 billion in 2010, when it was originally estimated by the Indian Olympic Association in 2003 to cost about US$300 million. With all other sundry expenses, the total expenditure was estimated to be around US$11 billion, the costliest event ever. In the process, as much as US$1 billion to US$1.7 billion were lost because of alleged malfeasance by the chief of the games, Suresh Kalmadi, who is also a Congress Party *Rajya Sabha* (Upper House of Parliament) member, and one time General Secretary of the Congress Party. He was jailed, but is out on bail.

Third, the Adarsh Housing Scheme in Bombay where apartments built for heroes of the Kargil war (with Pakistan), and army widows, were allotted at cut-rate prices to several politicians including the then Chief Minister of Maharashtra, Ashok Chavan (who was forced to resign). The then Chief of Army Staff, General Deepak Kapoor, in order to be eligible for a flat, had underdeclared his income at about US$4,900 when in fact it was over US$13,000. A fourth scandal involved Ketan Desai, President of the Medical Council of India, who collected large bribes for according recognition to private medical schools. He was arrested while taking a bribe of about US$364,000 in one of those deals (and was dismissed from his job).

Fifth, black money, or the underground economy, is estimated to be nearly US$640 billion or about half of India's annual Gross Domestic Product of US$1.3 trillion. In a study conducted by the US Global Financial Integrity, between 1948 and 2008, at least US$500 billion were stashed away in foreign banks (Nayyar & Unnithan, 2011, p. 13). Consequent to a Public Interest Litigation (PIL) petition, the Supreme Court of India expressed its disgust, and appointed on July 4, 2011, a Special Investigative Tribunal to monitor the government investigation in this regard. The final outcome is yet to be seen.

Sixth, land scams involving the forceful eviction of poor farmers by paying a pittance of compensation, in the name of "development" and the creation of Special Economic Zones, by governments such as West Bengal and Uttar Pradesh (UP), have led to alleged personal fortunes made by influential political personalities such as B. S. Yeddyurappa (the Bharatiya Janata Party [BJP], Chief Minister of Karnataka, who was forced to resign in 2011). In this regard, the then President Nitin Gadkari of BJP (which always claimed a moral high ground) advanced a novel argument that what Yeddyurappa did may have been "immoral," but not "illegal"!

The Communist government of West Bengal (which always claimed to be standing for the downtrodden) forced out several poor farmers by buying out nearly 400 acres of land to facilitate the building of the cheap car, Nano, by the renowned industrial giant, Tata. Under pressure from several sources, Tata moved the factory to Gujarat, anyway. Later, Chief Minister Mamata Banarjee restored that land to the farmers. On July 5, 2011, the Supreme Court ordered the government of UP to return the land to 185 similarly dispossessed farmers in the Greater Noida Extension. The Court expressed its anger at the government's argument that the land was obtained for "development," when in fact it was being used to build apartment complexes and multiplexes by private builders. It called the effort "anti-people," "sinister," and "an engine of oppression" (All India Radio, 2011).

Two major corruption scandals are the 2G Spectrum case in 2010, which became a catalyst in the rise of a civil society movement led by Anna Hazare, and the "Coalgate" scandal, which occurred in 2012 when it was revealed that coal blocks were allotted to companies arbitrarily and without verifying their credentials during 2004–2011 at a loss of nearly US$210 billion. (More details of these two scandals are provided below.)

Finally, there are three recent corruption scandals. First, a US$64 million bribe was allegedly paid by Anglo-Italian firms, Augusta Westland and Finmeccanica, to swing a 12 helicopter contract worth about US$655 billion in their favor; and the then Chief of Airforce, S. P. Tyagi, along with other high-ranking air force officers, are being investigated for allegedly taking the bribe. The second scandal involves a nephew of the Railway Minister Pawan Bansal, who was arrested for allegedly taking hefty bribes to arrange a plum job for a railway employee. The third scandal refers to the case where the CBI report was shown to the Minister for Law, Ashwani Kumar, the Attorney General, and two other officials of the Prime Minister's Office (PMO) who edited the report before it was submitted to the Supreme Court (see below). While both Ministers were compelled to resign, Ashwani Kumar did not admit to any wrongdoing, but boldly stated that he was resigning to end an "unnecessary controversy"!

All the above corruption scandals lead to these questions: Why is corruption so rampant in India and why is it so difficult to curb it?

ANTI-CORRUPTION MEASURES

Stripped off of all the analytical niceties, there are two major reasons for corruption: need and greed. Need could be addressed by generous pay and benefit packages, which of course is a function of the economy, available human resource skills, and competition for the same between the public and private sectors. But even in the presence of generous emoluments, there is neither a guarantee nor evidence that corruption could be eradicated.

Certainly, the temptation to take a bribe is far greater for a person whose pay may not allow existence at subsistence level. However, better pay would not preclude corruption as such as may be seen from several high-profile cases from the so-called "developed" countries. Rich nations are not bereft of corruption. The difference is a matter of scale and frequency, and whether the client is taken hostage. That leaves us with greed, which is a matter of character that in itself is a product of tradition and societal norms. Laws and institutions are needed to fight greed.

The fight against corruption again has two aspects: investigation and punishment. Investigation is the responsibility of the several institutions designed to fight corruption whereas according punishment is the domain of the courts. There are five institutions created to fight corruption. The first agency is the Central Intelligence Bureau (CIB), which was created by the Ministry of Home Affairs in 1947 to gather intelligence within India and execute counter intelligence and counterterrorism measures. Second, the Research and Analysis Wing (RAW) is responsible for obtaining external intelligence. The National Technical Research Organization, which comes under RAW's jurisdiction, is the third agency. However, these agencies have no statutory backing as they are created by executive fiat, and are not known to the public at large. As they do not have a direct bearing on fighting corruption, this chapter focuses instead on the other two major institutions: the Central Vigilance Commission (CVC) and the CBI.

The CVC was created under an Office Memorandum of the Home Ministry in February 1964 on the recommendation of the Santhanam Committee. The Supreme Court of India in the *Vineet Narain* decision, was highly critical of the working of the CVC and asked the Government of India to come up with legislation to strengthen it (Tummala, 2002, pp. 43–69). Consequently, an Ordinance was issued, and the CVC obtained its statutory basis further to an Act of Parliament in 2003. Under this Act, the CVC has the responsibility to supervise the functioning of the Delhi Special Police Establishment (DSPE), and inquire into cases allegedly committed under the Prevention of Corruption Act, 1988.

The CVC is headed by a Central Vigilance Commissioner, who works with two other Commissioners. They are drawn from higher civil service, or from those who hold office in a corporation or company created by the government. They are selected by a Committee consisting of the Prime Minister, Minister for Home Affairs, and the leader of the Opposition in *Lok Sabha* (Lower House of Parliament), and appointed by the President of India for a four-year term of office, or till the attainment of 65 years of age (whichever comes first). While the Commissioner is not entitled for reappointment, the other two members are eligible for appointment as Commissioner. After retirement, they are ineligible for any other office of profit under the government. They may be removed from office by the President on grounds of misbehavior or incapacity.

The CVC is deemed to be a civil court, and all matters before it are considered to be judicial proceedings. It is noteworthy that the CVC's ambit, however, is limited in various ways. First, it pertains only to the Center and excludes the States. Second, its jurisdiction was confined to

Group A public servants (the top of civil service) and other public sector undertakings. (Other civil servants remain under the control of the individual Ministries and Departments where they are employed.) Third, the CVC's jurisdiction does not cover politicians, contractors, and others. Finally, the CVC has only advisory powers, without any enforcement authority. However, Clause (v) of the Act empowered the CVC to "exercise superintendence over the vigilance administration," which was interpreted by the then newly appointed Commissioner, N. Vittal, to give directions as well (Vittal, 2012, p. 3).

The CBI is a police agency investigating both serious crimes and corruption. Its progenitor, the DSPE, created in 1941 within the War Department was the first agency to investigate corruption in India during World War II. After independence, the DSPE became the CBI within the Home Ministry (whose responsibility is maintenance of law and order), with expanded powers in April 1963. Currently, it has three separate Investigative Divisions: Anti-Corruption, Economic Crimes, and Special Crimes. It has a total of 166 zones and 60 branches, spread all over the nation. Other than cases falling under the jurisdiction of the Center, it cannot pursue any case out of a State unless it is requested, or permitted by the concerned State.

Consequent to the *Vineet Narain* decision (mentioned above), where the Supreme Court expressed its disappointment at the working of the CBI, a new Act was passed in 2003. Under this Act, the Director of CBI (who must be an Indian Police Service officer of the rank of Director General) is appointed from a panel recommended by a selection committee headed by the Commissioner and two other members of CVC, and Secretaries of the Home Ministry and the Department of Public Grievances (in the Ministry of Personnel). Once an appointment is made, the Director cannot be transferred for two years without the CVC's permission. Within the CBI, there is also the Enforcement Directorate (ED), which deals with financial crimes.

As an organization, the CBI is a nightmare as it serves multiple masters. The Ministry of Home Affairs has to clear the cadre of the Commissioners. For funds, it depends on the Ministry of Personnel, Training and Public Grievances, and reports to it for its daily operations. For hiring all officers above the rank of Superintendent of Police, the Union Public Service Commission's approval is needed. For all corruption cases, it faces the supervision of the CVC. The Ministry of Law and Justice pays the salaries of prosecutors arguing cases of corruption for the CBI. The CBI's annual report for 2012 shows that it had an authorized strength of 6,586, with 831 vacancies, and a budget of about US$720 million (Rs.3,958 crores) (CBI, 2013, pp. 82, 108).

Punishment following a trial is accorded by the courts. The Indian court system operates at a notoriously slow pace — what with the cumbersome jurisprudence and case overload. It is estimated that there are about 30 million pending cases, and at the present rate of disposal it would take about 300 years to clear such a backlog (i.e., without taking any new cases). On an average, a court case takes about 15 years to be cleared (Vittal, 2012, p. 154). The already clogged and slow judicial process is made worse since the inauguration of PIL using which a person could drag another to the court on the flimsiest cause or no cause at all — just being vindictive, or be a nuisance, or to settle past scores. PIL, which does not seem to have any statutory basis, began when Justice Krishna Iyer allowed in 1976 a few outsiders to file a petition on behalf of others in the Supreme Court. Without going through the cumbersome legal procedures, any simple petition, even simple letters or telegrams, could start this process. T. S. Tulsi, a Supreme Court lawyer indicated that hardly 6 percent of cases led to conviction in the Indian courts (Vittal, 2012, p. 53). The BBC reported on May 27, 2013, that there were as many as 300,000 inmates in various jails, 70 percent of whom are yet to face trial. It also reported the strange case of one young son bailing out his mother who was rotting in a jail for 19 years for having not paid a bond of a paltry sum of less than US\$200 (Rs. 10,000), and was forgotten by the authorities.

The judiciary is generally considered beyond reproach with some exceptions. For example, there is an affidavit filed with the Supreme Court alleging that 8 of the last 16 Chief Justices were corrupt (Vittal, 2011, p. 36). In particular, three names may be mentioned: Justices V. Ramaswamy, Soumitra Sen, and J. D. Dinakaran. Justice Ramaswamy of the Supreme Court was charged for his ostentatious lifestyle while he was Chief Justice of Punjab/Haryana. The charges were drafted by the Supreme Court Bar Association, but his impeachment fell through because of lack of sufficient votes in the *Lok Sabha* (when Congress members voted against his impeachment en bloc). Justice Soumitra Sen of the Calcutta High Court was impeached for misappropriation of funds. Chief Justice J. D. Dinakaran of the Sikkim High Court resigned before corruption charges came before a judicial panel prior to impeachment.

The judiciary has also been criticized for being very active, which is to an extent correct in that some of the judicial pronouncements actually tended to be matters pertaining to policymaking by the government. Surely, the disgruntled politicians object to such "judicial activism." Perhaps this activism is necessary where no other alternative seems to be available.

EVALUATION OF ANTI-CORRUPTION MEASURES

The CVC and CBI do not engender much trust or respect among the general public. Their own statements are revealing. For example, regarding the advice they rendered, the CVC in its 2011 annual report noted "with concern that in some of the cases, either the due consultation process with the Commission have not been followed ... or the advices have been partly acted upon or badly delayed. There have also been instances where the advice of the Commission has been diluted considerably without approaching the Commission. ... The Commission takes a serious view of such cases of non-compliance and non-consultation with it" (CVC, 2012, pp. 33, 39). The CVC cannot compel compliance as its opinions are only advisory. It also claimed that of the total 7,037 cases, it disposed of 75.9 percent of the cases, and 1,696 cases were still pending. Among the individual entities of the government, each of which has its own vigilance office headed by a Chief Vigilance Officer, a total of 16,987 complaints were pending, of which 6,910 complaints were pending for over six months.

In its annual report for the year 2012, the CBI reported that it dealt with a total of 1,048 cases, 52 of which were at the request of States, and at the end of the year a total of 861 cases were pending investigation with as many as 194 cases for more than a year. It was also reported that 9,734 corruption cases were pending in various courts. But, it claimed a conviction rate of 67 percent (CBI, 2013, p. 8). Despite such a high conviction rate, it must be noted, as the saying goes, only the flies are caught, not the elephants, as is evident from several Chief Ministers of States and Cabinet Ministers at the Center, continuing in their positions. Some former Chief Ministers ended in the Central Cabinet, just as a few Central Ministers tended to serve as Chief Ministers. And every Minister who was caught and charged with corruption ended up on bail. The few who are in jail get special consideration as they are allowed perks. As far back as in 1997, in its *Vineet Narain* decision (cited above), the Supreme Court, inter alia, observed thus:

> The Constitution and the working of the investigating agencies revealed the lacuna of its [sic] inability to perform whenever powerful persons were involved. For this reason, a close examination of the constitution of these agencies and their control assumes significance. No doubt, the overall control of the agencies and responsibility for their functioning has to be in the executive, but then a scheme giving the needed insulation from extraneous influences even of the controlling executive is imperative.

The Supreme Court further observed that "inertia was the common rule whenever the alleged offender was a powerful person." It found out that the CBI and other police investigators had not performed their primary duties, and directed them to do just that by saying that "none stands above the law so that an alleged offense by him is not required to be investigated."

The CBI in particular came under severe criticism not only for its inactivity when high dignitaries were concerned but also for the fact that it became a political pawn. Given the latter, a former Director General of Police of Haryana, who served with the CBI, raised the not so rhetorical question: "Who Owns the CBI?" (Lall, 2007, 2011). The CBI's operating strength of personnel has dwindled in recent years. Furthermore, of those CBI officers in service, as many as 55 were facing departmental inquiries, four were being investigated and 35 others are on trial (India Today, 2011a, p. 10).

There is the striking case of the Superintendent of Police heading the team investigating the Coalgate case, who was caught taking a bribe from a businessman for settling an unrelated land dispute, and was suspended, pending investigation (India Today, 2013). Furthermore, the lure of further employment on retirement makes the CBI Director tow the line of the government. For example, the 2013 appointment of former CBI Director (2008–2010), Ashwani Kumar, as Governor of Nagaland raised not only several eyebrows but also an uproar from the Opposition parties. The government took shelter behind the argument that there are no rules against any such further appointment, and moreover his appointment as Governor came two years after his retirement.

The prosecution of the "Coalgate" case also showed how defunct the CBI is. At the behest of the Supreme Court, a report of its investigation was prepared by the CBI. But, before it was submitted to the Supreme Court, the Law Minister, Ashwani Kumar, asked the Attorney General (AG) to inquire into the status of the report. The AG convened a secret meeting where the newly appointed CBI Director Ranjit Sinha was present. The Additional Solicitor General deposed before the Supreme Court that there was no political interference, and the AG insisted that he did not see the report. But neither was telling the truth as it turned out (Nayyar & Vij-Arora 2013, pp. 10–15). As the Supreme Court eventually demanded an affidavit, not a status report, Director Sinha had no alternative (as he would not have liked to be held in contempt by the Supreme Court, or worse taken to task for lying) but said on May 6, 2013, that the report indeed was vetted by the Law Minister, among others. Initially, Ranjit Sinha did not see anything wrong in sending the report to the Law Minister and other officials in the PMO, as he claimed that after all the CBI is a government agency. Though he is technically correct, he seems to have been insensitive to the CBI's bad reputation, and the underlying moral imperatives. (He did in fact later show some contrition.) The

Supreme Court was not amused, and gave him a literal thrashing on the subject, calling the CBI a "caged parrot" serving many masters, and concluded that the "heart of the report" was in fact changed by those who had no business to look into the report. It also demanded that the Government of India should come up with legislation insulating the CBI from political pressures by July 10, 2013 (Nayyar & Sriram, 2013, pp. 32–34). Consequently, the Prime Minister appointed a five-member Group of Ministers, heading the Ministries of Telecom, Finance, External Affairs, Personnel, and Information and Broadcasting, to look into the matter.

THE 2G SPECTRUM SCANDAL AND
ANNA HAZARE'S PROTEST

Into this bleak picture a little bit of sunshine appeared under the leadership of Anna Hazare and his team consequent to the 2G Spectrum case, touching the conscience of the nation and raising its ire. But his movement also fizzled out.

The 2G Spectrum case is rather complex. But briefly, a "spectrum" is an electromagnetic frequency used by cell phones. It is a scarce resource. However, the then Telecom Minister, A. Raja, ignoring advice from several officials to open it for competitive bidding, followed the existing policy of "first come first served" among the applications received by September 25, 2007, on his own. Moreover, arbitrarily, he advanced the deadline for submission of applications, and issued licenses to 122 applicants out of turn, several of whom had nothing to do with the telecom business. The Comptroller and Auditor-General (C & A-G) in his report made no bones: "The Honorable Minister of Communications and IT (Raja) for no apparent logical or valid reasons ignored the advice of Ministry of Law, Ministry of Finance, avoided the deliberations of the Telecom Commission to allocate 2G spectrum, a scarce finite national asset, at less than its true value on flexible criteria and procedures adopted to benefit a few operators." (Nayyar & Vij-Arora, 2013, p. 10). The consequent loss to the exchequer was estimated to be about US$39 billion (about 3 percent of India's GDP).

The Opposition parties raised a storm in Parliament, calling it "crony capitalism." But the government disregarded all pressures to investigate. In response to a PIL, the Supreme Court was puzzled as to what was preventing the Prime Minister from acting, and felt it was "troubling." It is not difficult to find the reasons. Prime Minister Manmohan Singh was leading a coalition government, and for its survival, he needed every partner's support. The Dravida Munnetra Kazhgam (DMK) party of Tamil Nadu, headed by M. Karunanidhi, with 18 MPs and six Minister in the Singh government provided crucial support. Initially, Karunanidhi was not willing to support any action taken against Minister Raja, but he later relented under severe pressure and did not oppose Raja's resignation in November 2010. Raja thus survived as a Cabinet Minister for 400 days after the scandal broke, and was sent to jail (but is now on bail).

The initial inaction of the government prompted Anna Hazare to step into the fray. Kisan Bapat Baburao Hazare was a former army driver. He is recognized, and respected, as a simple person committed to social service, in the Gandhian style. He picked up the cause, and went on a fast in April 2011 to pressure the government to act swiftly and firmly, demanding the creation of the office of *Lok Pal* (Ombudsman in vernacular) – a subject that has been discussed since 1968. After endless debates, the government introduced a Bill: "Anti-Corruption, Grievance Redressal and Whistleblower Protection Act, 2010." There were several disagreements between Hazare and the government such as the very appointment of the *Lok Pal,* whether the Prime Minister, judges, and all the civil servants should be subjected to its control, what to do with the CVC, and how to protect the independence of CBI, and so on. Despite Hazare's protestations, the *Lok Sabha* passed the Bill in December 2011 with some modifications. But as the Bill moved to the *Rajya Sabha* (the Upper House), as many as 200 amendments were proposed. One of the most contested provisions of the Bill was the appointment of all State level *Lokayukta*s by the Center, which was considered to be an assault on the federal form of government. Even as the government suggested dropping that provision, the Bill did not clear the *Rajya Sabha* when the session ended on March 30, 2012. Neither was it taken up during the following winter session that ended in June 2013. Thus, the Bill is left in a limbo with Hazare threatening yet another fast. The Hazare team, no doubt, succeeded in bringing corruption to the front page leading to a national movement. Yet, they seem to have lost the momentum (see below). And the government showed neither urgency nor good faith in this venture. So the 45-year saga continues.

WHY ALL THESE FAILURES?

There are several reasons for India's inability to deal effectively with corruption, which Vittal (2012, p. 5) has described as a "multiple organ failure." First, time and again, leaders argue that corruption is a British legacy. But the British left India over 66 years ago! Since independence in

1947, under the Nehruvian era of Democratic Socialism, the state made every effort to capture the "commanding heights of the economy." This facilitated further corruption as the citizens were taken hostage and forced to seek permission and licenses from the government for all sorts of activity, private and public. "Permit Raj" was the slogan of the day! The New Economic Policy inaugurated in 1990 by the then Finance Minister, and current Prime Minister Manmohan Singh, led to economic liberalization by easing, if not abolishing, state control of the economy. Private entrepreneurship that was stifled previously was unshackled and looked toward globalization and international capital. More importantly, the common Indian became a voracious consumer, contrary to the age old hoarder of what little he or she had. The widening economic opportunity in itself unleashed a new wave of greed in the name of enterprise. Greater emphasis on economic success has seen a new consumer/citizen in India who appears to be amoral in pursuit of wealth. Cultural traits mentioned in the beginning of the chapter helped. The globalization process itself is also theorized to have contributed to burgeoning corruption (Rotberg, 2009).

The second reason is that the criminalization of politics and the politicization of criminals in India have resulted in turning the "lawmakers" into "lawbreakers," as the Election Commission has observed. There have also been one coalition government after another. After the 1996 elections, the BJP's coalition lasted for 13 days, and the following United Front government survived for 7 months. The 1998 National Democratic Alliance led by Atal Bihari Vajpayee completed its five-year term. The 2004 elections resulted in the first United Progressive Alliance (UPA I) government of Manmohan Singh. In the 2009 elections, 37 different parties returned 543 MPs, leading to the UPA II coalition led by Prime Minister Manmohan Singh of the Congress Party (Tummala, 2009b, pp. 323−348; 2010, pp. 78−94). Coalition governments, which are often dubbed as "unholy alliances," turned out to be less effective due to all sorts of pressures and accommodations among the several partners. Coalition partners pursuing separate agendas, and the government depending on their support for its very survival, have precluded any concerted action.

Third, both the CVC and the CBI failed in pursuing corrupt individuals under the pressure of incumbent governments, which have been under their own stress, as the coalition government phenomenon, which has become the norm, did not do much good. Independent investigative arms were also politicized.

Fourth, the very insistence on the rule of law itself seems to have become an impediment. Article 311 of the Constitution of India protects civil servants from mala fide actions of government, and provides security in the job by stating that no civil servant can be "dismissed or disciplined by an authority subordinate to that which he was appointed." Section 197 of the Criminal Procedure Code also stipulates that no civil servant can be prosecuted without the permission of the appropriate authority. The appointing authority in principle is the President of India, but in practice it is the Minister heading the Ministry or Department who exercises this power. It is no secret that a Minister would not let his/her employee be indicted easily, which also meant the politicization of cases. Yet, higher civil servants are always in the thick of policymaking in that they are the advisors to the Minister concerned, and thus their activity and testimony tend to be crucial. And the refusal of the parent department to question them, much less prosecute them, is detrimental to the prosecution of a high-level case. For example, in trying to investigate the "Coalgate" scam, the CBI's plea to question H. C. Gupta, who was Secretary, Ministry of Coal, during 2006–2009, was denied in June 2013 (relented later) by the Ministry of Corporate Affairs (where he currently is). Suggestions to repeal, at least ease, Clause 6 (A) of the Prevention of Corruption Act, which prevents the CBI from investigating an officer of the level of Joint Secretary or higher without the permission of the Minister concerned have fallen on deaf years with the government arguing strangely that the threat of a CBI inquiry would impede decision making as high officials would be afraid of coming under scrutiny later. In fact, the government wants to extend the ban for even retired officials!

Fifth, the last appointment of the head of CVC did not inspire much confidence in the bona fides of the government. P. J. Thomas was appointed to that post in 2010 despite pending charges against him on a Pamolein import scandal while he was the Secretary in Kerala. The Department of Personnel and Training (DOPT) had noted during 2000 to 2004 on at least six occasions recommending proceedings against Thomas. However, neither the CVC's briefing in 2008, nor the DOPT's own briefing in 2010, had mentioned the DOPT's previous recommendations when Thomas' appointment as the head of CVC was being considered (India Today, 2011b, p. 32). The Prime Minister claimed that he was not aware of the charges, and the Home Minister kept quiet. The other member of the Committee that selected him, Sushma Swaraj, the Opposition party leader, was the only one to claim later that she had objected to the appointment. Thomas himself boldly claimed that he was eminently qualified for the appointment! The Supreme Court, however, invalidated that appointment. On July 2, 2011, Pradeep Kumar, Defense Secretary, was unanimously approved for the job by the same Committee. Just as Kumar was to take office, Thomas asked the Delhi High Court on July 13 to stop the finalization of that appointment, but the Court did not oblige.

In the 2G Spectrum case, the C & A-G, Arun Rai, came under severe attack by the government, to which he responded that he was not there to be a cheerleader for the government. As he retired, Shashi Kant Sharma, who served as Secretary of Defense, was appointed in his place in 2013. Considering there are a slew of defense-related corruption cases pending, that appointment was considered insensitive on the part of the government. Not without surprise, Prashant Bhushan (a Supreme Court lawyer), who led the fight in the 2G Spectrum case, joined by eight other prominent personalities, had gone on a PIL challenging his appointment. (The case is yet to come up for hearing at the time of this writing.)

Sixth, Anna Hazare's movement failed because his team had shown chinks in their armor and suffered many setbacks, some of which were self-inflicted. The "Team Hazare" consisted of several individuals with their own personal agendas to push using this movement, thus resulting in the hazards of "cooptation" (Selznick, 1949). Some of these persons, in fact, found themselves under a cloud. For example, Kiran Bedi, who was the first female Indian Police Service officer (since retired) was shown to have charged first or business class fares when she went on lecture tours, but traveled on economy class. When challenged, she explained that her intention was to save money for her own nongovernmental organization (NGO). Another team member, Arvind Kejriwal, a former tax official himself, was charged for tax evasion. He distanced himself from Hazare eventually, and started a political party, *Aam Aadmi*, wanting to fight corruption on his own. Hazare himself proved that he was not above politics as he went on canvassing against the Congress Party and Prime Minister Singh in State elections (where the Congress Party lost eventually). He was charged as supporting the BJP/RSS opposition.

Even though Hazare's group was effective in exposing the latest corruption scandals, the role of civil societies and their activism themselves need to be examined more closely. Active civil societies could indeed serve as the peoples' representatives as participation is a bedrock principle of democracy. However, whose interests do the civil society organizations serve, and to whom are they responsible? More importantly, what shall be the relationship between them and the duly elected governments? Should they be subjected to the control of government, or should they be allowed to operate independently, even contentiously? The Hazare movement does not provide clear answers to these questions.

Finally, the current *Lokpal* Bill is but the latest in the contemplated control measures; neither would it be the last. It would be foolish to believe that a simple creation of a *Lokpal* in itself would be a panacea. It might in fact add yet another layer of bureaucracy if it were not to function properly. What has been lacking in India is a determined political will to enable the existing institutions to fight corruption effectively. For that matter, it might be noted that there are the *Lok Ayuktas* at several States' level with rather spotty records, which inspire not much confidence. Could the working of *Lokpal* be any different?

LESSONS FROM THE LEAST CORRUPT COUNTRIES

The experiences of Denmark, Finland, Hong Kong, New Zealand, and Singapore, which are analyzed in the previous five chapters, and are perceived to be among the least corrupt countries on Transparency International's 2012 CPI, yield some interesting lessons, though not all are relevant to a country like India because of the contextual differences. First, unlike India, these five countries are smaller in terms of land area and population. Indeed, there are many individual States in India, which are much larger than the five countries combined together, either in land size or population (about 28.7 million people compared with India's 1.25 billion). Second, India's diversity is mind boggling when compared with these five countries. While New Zealand, Hong Kong, and Singapore have relatively heterogeneous populations, Denmark and Finland have more homogeneous populations.

Third, despite their diversity, there is some homogeneity in Denmark and New Zealand in terms of their striking work ethic and simplicity of lifestyle. Most politicians in Denmark adopt a modest lifestyle as they still ride their bicycles to work. Furthermore, social norms in New Zealand in terms of seeking social respectability are striking as it is a country of innocence, populated by the straightlaced and endowed with the Calvinist work ethic. However, in India, tolerance and forgiveness abet corrupt practices. Moreover, unlike the modest lifestyle of Danish politicians, in India status is very important as public officials try to outdo each other. Even the lowest legislator moves around with a security detail and retired Cabinet Ministers are demanding high security details, not because they are threatened somehow (although it should not matter once they are out of office) but as a matter of status.

Fourth, like Hong Kong, New Zealand, and Singapore, India is also a former British colony. However, unlike these three former British colonies, India has not succeeded in curbing corruption as reflected in its much lower ranking and score on Transparency International's 2012 CPI, even though it has been independent for 66 years.

Fifth, the issue of political stability is also an important variable. While India is politically stable, it suffers from coalition governments that tend to be powerless in trying to satisfy the individual demands of each of the coalition partners. One might argue that Denmark, despite being run by coalitions of eight parties due to proportional representation, is politically stable. But, there is a qualitative difference in that there is a firm understanding among the coalition parties in Denmark. Until 1969, the Congress Party had control of the government (albeit without ever being in a complete majority). Since then, coalition governments became the norm where small coalition partners take the leading party in government as a hostage, despite the fact that they all agree initially on a "common minimum program," which is largely honored in the breach. Furthermore, the four Communist parties in India support the current government without being in the government, but they push their own policy agendas, thus taking their pound of flesh without ever being accountable.

Yet, two lessons in comparison come out strongly. First, it is all a matter of ecology, and second, much depends on the prevailing social norms. The importance of the ecological approach was long advocated by writers such as Fred Riggs (1964) who popularized the concept introduced by John M. Gaus (1947). For that matter, this is not all that modern an idea in itself. After all, Plato made this argument around 386 BCE. In the *Republic*, Socrates said to Glaucon: "Do you know … that governments vary as the dispositions of men vary, and that there must be as many of the one as there are of the other? For we cannot suppose that the States are made of 'oak and stock,' and not out of human nature …. The States are as the men are; they grow out of human character" (Jowett, 1937, Book VIII, p. 544). Thus, each nation in its fight must find its own ways, while looking at those who have been successful in fighting corruption.

CONCLUSION

Some scholars have asked the not so rhetorical question, whether curbing corruption is an impossible dream in India (Quah, 2008)? While the outlook does not look bright, there are nevertheless six reasons for optimism.

First, economic liberalization, which undid past state control, also led to numerous media outlets sprout, followed by aggressive reportage by outfits such as *Aaj Tak* and *tehelka.com*. But this also saw several other private and partisan outlets, both in print and television, each grinding its own personal axe, exposing real or feigned corruption.

Second, the Right to Information Act (RTI), 2005, led to such to an active, even zealous, media that several journalists have been killed for relentlessly pursuing unsavory stories of the high and mighty. The nation itself is yet to come to grips with the fundamental issue of protecting the whistle-blower. However, it is now rather difficult for the government to hide behind the Official Secrets Act of 1923.

Third, several NGOs have emerged such as the *Forum for Democratic Reform* and the Hazare movement itself. These civil society organizations, while raising their own issues, have also exposed some of the rot.

Fourth, the judiciary, which has been held up as the only bulwark of integrity, has become more active of late in going so far as giving numerous directions to various governments, some of which in the normal process have a policymaking flavor. The Supreme Court, led by the previous Chief Justice S. H. Kapadia, demonstrated that it is ready to pounce on the various errant government agencies. The slow court system, however, needs to be expedited.

Fifth, the new instrument called PIL allows any person to approach a court on any issue, thus helping the courts to step in. Although these suits do serve (or meant to serve) the public interest, on occasion they tend to be not only frivolous but also vindictive (to settle old scores) while also clogging the already overburdened and slow court system. This delay needs to be checked because, by the time the cases come to a court to be judged, the lapse of time plays havoc as memories fade, evidence are lost or destroyed, and witnesses can be bought and sold.

Finally, perhaps, a more important phenomenon is the progressive disappearance of the mystique and awe of government. The common citizen who was in the past reluctant, or afraid, to approach a public servant with a complaint is, of late, ready to confront to the point of ignoring some important traditional taboos. Indians have always shown respect, almost to the point of deference or even subservience, to their elders and authority figures. However, now, it is not uncommon for citizens to throw *chappal* (common footwear) at them, which tradition considers as disgraceful and disgusting. Yet, the government is brought down to earth, in a way.

In short, perhaps there is some hope and a hint of optimism, that one day corruption in India might after all be brought under control, although the expectation that it would be eradicated is naive, impractical, and even foolhardy.

REFERENCES

All India Radio. (2011). July 5.

Ambedkar, B. R. (1995). *Annihilation of caste* (3rd ed.). Jalandhar: Bheem Publications.

Central Bureau of Investigation (CBI). (2013). *Annual report 2012.* New Delhi. Retrieved from http://cbi.nic.in/annualreport/cbi_annual_report_2012.pdf. Accessed on July 11, 2013.

Central Vigilance Commission (CVC). (2012). *Annual report 2011.* New Delhi. Retrieved from http://cvc.nic.in/ar2011.pdf. Accessed on July 11, 2013.

Chowdhury, N. C. (1987). *Thy hand! The great anarch! India: 1921–1952.* London: Chatto & Windus.

Gaus, J. M. (1947). *Reflections on public administration.* University, AL: University of Alabama Press.

India Today. (2011a). June 22.

India Today. (2011b). September 9.

India Today. (2012). Government paper admits corruption at all levels in civil service. *India Today,* March 14.

India Today. (2013). Bribery in CBI. *India Today,* June 17 & 22.

Jowett, B. (Trans.). (1937). *Plato's Republic.* New York, NY: Vintage Books.

Lall, B. R. (2007). *Who owns the CBI? The naked truth.* New Delhi: Manas.

Lall, B. R. (2011). *Free the CBI.* New Delhi: Manas.

Nayyar, D., & Sriram, J. (2013). Nowhere to hide. *India Today,* May 20.

Nayyar, D., & Unnithan, S. (2011). The great Indian robbery. *India Today,* March 31.

Nayyar, D., & Vij-Arora, B. (2013). From asset to liability. *India Today,* May 13.

Quah, J. S. T. (2008). Curbing corruption in India: An impossible dream? *Asian Journal of Political Science, 16*(3), 240–259.

Riggs, F. W. (1964). *The theory of prismatic society.* Boston, MA: Houghton, Mifflin.

Rotberg, R. (Ed.). (2009). *Corruption, global security, and world order.* Washington, D.C: Brookings Institution Press.

Rudolph, L. I., & Rudolph, S. H. (1987). *In pursuit of Lakshmi: The political economy of the Indian state.* Chicago, IL: University of Chicago Press.

Schwab, K. (Ed.). (2012). *The global competitiveness report 2012-2013.* Geneva: World Economic Forum.

Selznick, P. (1949). *The TVA and grassroots: A study in the sociology of formal organization.* Berkeley, CA: University of California Press.

Shama Sastry, R. (Trans.). (1967). *Kautilya's arthsastra* (8th ed). Mysore: Mysore Printing & Publishing House.

Tummala, K. K. (2002). Corruption in India: Control measures and consequences. *Asian Journal of Political Science, 10*(2), 43–69.

Tummala, K. K. (2009a). Combating corruption: Lessons out of India. *International Public Management Review, 10*(1), 34–57.

Tummala, K. K. (2009b). Coalition politics in India: 2004-2009. *Asian Journal of Political Science, 17*(3), 323–348.

Tummala, K. K. (2010). Political corruption in India: Coalition *Dharma? International Public Management Review, 11*(2), 78–94.

Vineet Narain et al. v. Union of India et al. (1998). AIR 1998 SC 889.

Vittal, N. (2011). The grand sham of things. *India Today*, January 10.

Vittal, N. (2012). *Ending corruption? How to clean up India.* New Delhi: Penguin Books India.

CHAPTER 8

ACCOUNTING FOR SUCCESS IN COMBATING CORRUPTION

Gerald E. Caiden

ABSTRACT

In nature, the adaptable survive best. In human affairs, elites do better than others, much better when they take advantage of both fair and foul means to exercise public authority and influence. Where absolutism prevails, the disadvantaged cannot make much headway unless their betters make concessions to share communal treasures, govern responsibly and accountably, and refrain from abusing social norms. The evolution of the welfare democracy has brought about the greatest success in making communal benefits more accessible and attainable to all, recognizing the universal dignity and rights of every individual, and, above all, curbing corrupt institutions and practices wherever revealed. Although the ideals of the welfare democracy have been confined to relatively few countries, they illustrate what is achievable. They also have been active in convincing the international community to recognize two landmark United Nations conventions concerning both private and public sectors to strive for greater global success in combating corruption, despite unpromising circumstances and the many obstacles that still favor the corrupt and corrupted at everyone's cost. Context is the most important variable.

Different Paths to Curbing Corruption: Lessons from Denmark, Finland, Hong Kong, New Zealand and Singapore
Research in Public Policy Analysis and Management, Volume 23, 189–217
Copyright © 2013 by Emerald Group Publishing Limited
All rights of reproduction in any form reserved
ISSN: 0732-1317/doi:10.1108/S0732-1317(2013)0000023008

Success in curbing corruption requires the adaptation of reforms to the specific context. It cannot be imposed without thorough knowledge of the circumstances and devoted agents on the ground.

INTRODUCTION

Accounting for success in combating corruption (defined here as unacceptable conduct even if committed in secret) is difficult to fathom out as the whole subject is ambiguous, the facts are difficult to substantiate, and the methodological puzzles belie easy solution. Presumably, success refers to preventing offensive wrongdoing committed by people entrusted with exercising public trust (hereafter called public authorities). This worthy aim is fraught with mixed and conflicting interpretations. It changes from era to era, ever moving on as culture, attitudes, values, circumstances, and technology transform, rejecting outmoded tradition and institutions, embracing new ideas, and dealing with new contexts. Every locality has to find its own answers to the following list of philosophical, ethical, cultural, political, economic, pragmatic, and technical questions:

1. What exactly constitutes success? How can the expected outcome be ascertained? Who judges the measure of success and by what criteria? Over what period of time?
2. Is prevention eliminating such wrongdoing altogether or reducing it to the rare isolated incident? How can the unexpected be prevented in advance?
3. Is keeping things under tolerable control enough? How much effort should be further invested in reducing wrongdoing?
4. What is understood by wrongdoing that constitutes corruption even when it is unintended or causes no intentional harm or actually turns out to be beneficial?
5. Which categories of public authority could be dealt with more leniently than others and on what grounds?
6. How clear are prevailing social norms in regard to rightdoing and acceptable conduct? What circumstances justify transgressions?
7. What locally is considered proper conduct expected of public authorities? How are offenders dealt with? Does punishment really deter wrongdoing?
8. Is investment in combating corruption worthwhile, given that the costs are so high and the results often disappointing?

Every generation since the dawn of civilization has struggled to find convincing arguments to these and other questions to justify its attempts to combat conduct unbecoming of public authorities. Every so often, the answers and methods used to apply them have had more than local significance and have been copied and adjusted elsewhere to changing times and circumstances. Over the years, much progress has been made as to identify what should work and be more likely to succeed than fail. After all, community sanctions against cannibalism, incest, murder, and theft are almost universal and offenders hunted down and relieved of their public authority until rehabilitated simply because they defy social norms and ideals, place narcissism over caring for others and self-gratification over virtuous intent, and fail to take responsibility for their actions (Levine, 2013).

HISTORY OF GOVERNMENT ACTION MAKES GLOOMY READING

Most history records the decline and fall of peoples, societies, and regimes attributed to treachery and horrid events blamed on corruption. This makes grim reading mostly of disasters, mistakes and missteps, offset occasionally by heroic deeds, noble self sacrifices, and exemplary conduct. The stress is largely placed on villainy or misplaced trust such that most everything that went and goes wrong can be traced to unscrupulous public authorities. History is past and cannot be undone. Can it teach anything? Is all irrelevant and can be ignored? A more careful study of surviving records reveals that in every age somewhere around the world, there has been timeless wisdom that went beyond local circumstances. Among the dross are portraits of ideal leaders, moral traits desired of public authorities, and what action should be taken to curb misgovernment, maladministration, and mismanagement, including all forms of corruption, however defined or interpreted. Almost all preaching about ethics stresses personal integrity and the need to hold leaders to much higher moral standards than their followers. Responsible practitioners emphasize the need for adequate and competent governance, effective execution, the rule of law, high quality public goods and services, strict financial supervision, and transparent accountability and discipline, especially within public organizations (Raadschelders, 1998) and socially responsible business (O'Sullivan, Smith, & Esposito, 2012). The assumption is made that private organizations hold or should hold themselves to the same standards of right conduct but as they are not using public property and resources, they are or should be free to use their private property as they like unless forbidden by law in which case they are subject to both civil and criminal charges. In reality, where absolutism rules, nothing prevents public authorities from doing anything they want to do but once it is upset, public authorities find that there are limitations on wrongdoing.

Significant to contemporary society, the Age of Enlightenment rationalists opposed all forms of absolutism, especially unaccountable and irresponsible government. Public officials, that is, career employees of public organizations, as masters of affairs of state were no longer to be considered just the servants of an imperial regime. Instead, the *philosophes* thought such public officials should be transformed into servants of the ruled as well as the rulers, offering wise advice to the people's representatives and administering public policies and laws ethically, economically, efficiently, and effectively. As public professionals devoted to public service, virtue, the public interest, they had to be properly qualified, motivated, loyal, honest, trustworthy, and responsible. They were to be technically competent and politically accountable, skilled in knowledge useful to improving public administration. They were to be meritorious, politically impartial, professionally objective, and bound to follow both the spirit and letter of the law. These ideas, when put into practice, have probably been the most successful in curbing official corruption, less so in private employment where employers continue to uphold their freedom of action, their responsibility only to themselves, and in business their obligation to make profits to their shareholders (Friedman, 1970), including unethical and illegal actions. So, almost all attempts to combat corruption rely on government/official/public support and enforcement.

Following the appealing cries of the French revolutionaries for liberty, equality, and fraternity, victorious Napoleon realized the potential of transforming aristocratic traditions into this new concept of professional public service. Building on previous reform efforts, he demonstrated what could be accomplished by reforming the machinery of state along more rational lines although he never overcame systemic corruption, financial mismanagement, and patronage (Kahan, 1998). Nevertheless, his example was soon followed throughout much of Europe through a combination of pressures for greater democratization and failures in the most rotten areas of public administration held responsible for military setbacks, local government inadequacies, and urban discontent. More and more progressive reform was being advocated throughout the 19th century as the modern administrative state took shape. To head off such increasing radicalism, the conservative Chancellor Otto Bismarck in the new Germany compromised by introducing guaranteed welfare measures and added the alleviation of social and individual ills to more traditional government activities. Thus, by the beginning of the 20th century, progressive reform was in full flood with its demands for increased state intervention, economic and social regulation and professional public service now politically respectable, promoted by its enthusiastic supporters and welcomed by an expanding electorate. This tide did not diminish in countries that within a few decades became welfare democracies in Australasia and Scandinavia staffed by career public professionals (Caiden, 2013b) that took some of the strictest measures yet against corruption.

After a century of gradually combating official corruption, disillusion dampened further progress. Well-meaning professionals were still no match for their ambitious political masters who could exploit their technical and managerial talents for partisan ends. Either one conformed or exited. Protest, never mind sabotage, was out of the question as retribution would be swift and merciless. During extreme emergencies between 1900 and 1945, such as the two world wars, revolution in Russia, the coming to power of Fascist regimes in Italy, Germany, and Spain, and during national labor strikes, governments now reassumed (where they had not retained) absolutist power to fight wars, restore law and order in insurrections, seize private property, conscript, prosecute alleged traitors, and disregard civil liberties. The machinery of government could be used for both good and bad. Just to avoid doing harm or suffering harm, both public bureaucrats and their clients found ways of getting around their formal administrative systems just as they had always done. Their informal channels opened up new avenues of corruption not just to avoid harm but for more devious motives to obtaining special privileges and dispensations for smart operators. In any event, the bureaupathologies inherent in large-scale organizations could always be exploited for personal gain (Caiden, 1991) despite the progress that was proceeding by governments resolute on stamping down on corrupt practices both within and without the public sector. When between the world wars, the international community split into different ideological camps, corrupt practices on a partisan basis spread globally if only as yet on a small scale.

During the Second World War, the United Nations (UN) formed by the victorious Allies resolved to establish an international network of public agencies to deal with issues that might foment another disastrous global war. These agencies were to be staffed by a new international professional civil service to avoid their being corrupted (Mazower, 2012), although international partisan politics again could not be thwarted and corrupted global undertakings. It was not until the early 1970s that international bribery between multinational corporations and developing countries was officially brought to the attention of the UN which merely called for further research. Pressures concerning the globalization of corruption could not be denied as poor countries protested that their development prospects were being thereby undermined and obstructed. Another twenty years passed before the international community took action against the global dysfunctions of international and national corruption that had become so serious that nothing short of a binding comprehensive treaty to combat it would satisfy.

The breakthrough came in the late 1990s when the UN Secretary General Kofi Annan at the 1999 World Economic Forum in Davos called upon the business community to initiate a global compact of shared principles and values to provide a human face to globalization that would cover human rights, labor rights, environmental quality, and anti-corruption. The UN Compact for Business (UNCB) was launched in 2000 to work against all forms of corruption including extortion and bribery (O'Sullivan et al., 2012). Behind the scenes, the UN had been putting together a comprehensive convention against official corruption that it had hoped would coincide with its fiftieth anniversary. Agreement was not reached until the landmark 2003 UN Convention Against Corruption (UNCAC) (Caiden, 2013b). To date, about 75 percent of the member countries have signed it. No longer can any country plead ignorance for there is now an International Anti-Corruption Day celebrated on December 9, jointly sponsored by the UN Development Programme (UNDP) and the UN Office on Drugs and Crime (UNODC). Does this mean success at last? The UN Compact and the UNCAC are formal statements of the international community that corruption, both public and private, is at last, after some two hundred years of agitation, within its firing range. Resources are now being spent to bring corruption under control and that those proven corrupt will no longer be so sheltered to enjoy their ill-gotten gains. Does this mean we can now afford to relax?

MASS MEDIA DEPRESSES

In the past when public education was sparse, few people were literate. Newspapers had small circulations and were expensive. Knowledge of corruption was largely confined to inner circles sworn to secrecy to limit knowledge of embarrassing scandals from spreading farther. Much was hushed up for self-protection. Even so, gossip was inevitable as to who might be suspect and unprotected from exposure. Spies and informants abounded to detect wrongdoing, real, or alleged. Disgrace could well spell ruination and might extend to expected suicide. Almost everywhere, public executions seem to have been well attended although poor rural folk would rarely hear of such events and were unlikely to be able to attend as they lived too far away and had limited means of transportation. Most people just would not know of any widespread corruption unless they were the local victims in which case it was safer for them to keep quiet so as not to offend public authorities and arouse undue attention to themselves. Talk about corruption was taboo.

This situation still exists in the contemporary world but is fast disappearing as mass media extend their reach and illiteracy shrinks. Most adults now possess transistor radios, have access to television sets, and are being linked by relatively cheap cell phones. They are no longer so isolated or unaware of what goes on elsewhere. Mass media consider corruption hot news everywhere. Every day, from just a few sources, information about official corruption can be gleaned from wherever there is a local reporter able to spread the word although there are places where nobody is allowed to pass on any information about wrongdoing (Spector, 2012). In contrast, some countries, currently in southern and Eastern Europe, central Asia, the Indian subcontinent, Africa, and Latin America, receive extraordinary coverage. During February 2013, from just the *New York Times*, *Wall Street Journal*, and the *Economist* alone and accessible from the Internet, one could read about alleged ongoing corruption scandals involving participants in Russia, China, South Korea, India, Bangladesh, Pakistan, Sri Lanka, Afghanistan, Greece, Cyprus, Italy, Spain, Portugal, Bulgaria, Brazil, Venezuela, Mexico, United States, United Kingdom, France, and many countries in Africa and the Middle East stretching from South Africa to Iran, involving public leaders, world figures, and organizations in almost every area of human activity. Every month, this pattern is repeated perhaps with a different cast and serious readers can extend their search to many different sources.

Frequent targets are corporate crime, insider trading, price fixing, nepotism and patronage, election fraud, unseemly conduct by religious figures, police misconduct, tax dodging, money laundering, illegal trafficking, underground economies, entertainers, researchers, and celebrities in sports. There is no avoiding the topic in dailies, weeklies, and monthlies, involving scandals, public demonstrations, and official inquiries. The airwaves are swamped with chit chat about official misconduct. All one needs to do is to get into the Internet and its overwhelming detail of facts and allegations, court trials and accusations, and the fast expanding corruption investigating industry comprised of investigators, researchers, consultants, analysts, tabulators, and publicists. Despite suppression and censorship, information leaks out. Public denials only make matters worse when it is suspected that something incriminating, unbecoming, and immoral is being secreted from general knowledge.

The impression conveyed is that corruption is everywhere. No place is immune. Misdeeds are ubiquitous. Nobody can be trusted. One should always be on one's guard. The corrupt are devious, innovative, sly, and deceiving actors. They look out for likely victims. They have institutional supports that protect them. They are clever at covering up their tracks. Corruption is so rewarding that there is no scarcity of willing participants who believe that the risks are worth taking. Who is not attracted and who does not have the opportunity? Indeed, the evidence is so slanted and selected that reality gets distorted. The other side of the picture is by comparison rarely stated, that the examples cited are taken out of context, exaggerated, and unrepresentative and the alleged offenders are assumed guilty and not given a fair hearing. The obvious message is that things are bad and getting worse. The fact is that the public are just getting much more information and more aware about the possibility and proof of corruption than ever before, and somewhat slanted to convey the message that nothing is sacred anymore, that most public authorities are contaminated, certainly more in the public than private sector (until the latter is exposed as being just if not more guilty only cleverer at secrecy), and that nobody should be taken at face value.

Unfortunately, there is no way of telling accurately the extent of corruption. There remains the lingering suspicion that irrespective of more scientific research, all that is coming to light is merely that part of the iceberg above water. Too much corruption still remains hidden. What is known is bad enough so that the unknown must be even worse and for peace of mind best left unexplored. Underplayed is the fact that, ever since the *philosophes*, there have been continuous successes in combating corruption through greater democratization, the criminalization of wrongdoing, the professionalization of public careers, and the multiplication of enforced curbs. Some of the reputed 10 least corrupt countries according to the 2012 Corruption Perceptions Index (Denmark, Finland, New Zealand, Sweden, Singapore, Switzerland, Australia, Norway, Canada, and the Netherlands), organizations, and societies have been that way for at least a century if not longer and anyone dealing with them has been aware of their reputation for honesty and trustworthiness is well deserved. They may have had their occasional setbacks and failings. After all, nothing is perfect. Year after year, the same countries top the evaluations as the least corrupt now being conducted by the World Bank, the UNDP, Transparency International, the Organisation for Economic Co-operation and Development, Amnesty International, the International Red Cross, the International Labour Organization, the International Criminal Police Organization, and other bodies that make it their business to keep tabs on corrupt activities. Pointers to success are contained in many of their publications besides those emanating out of the 2000 UNCB and the 2003 UNCAC. To keep harping on failure is depressing and breeds pessimism if not fatalism that failure rather than success is inevitable.

Is the situation as bad as it is made out to be? Nobody knows but it is not from want of trying. Now that corruption is in the open more than ever before, there is so much more new information that has to be properly digested, analyzed, and assessed. The original crude measures are becoming more sophisticated (Serra & Wantchekon, 2012). There is more empirical research carefully conducted in the laboratory and in the field. There is closer analysis of the causes of corruption (Graaf, Maravic, & Wagenaar, 2010; Treisman, 2000, 2006). And there are accounts of successful technical anti-corruption actions, such as that against bribery (Porta & Vannucci, 2012) and exposing corrupt networks (Jancsics & Javor, 2012). Unfortunately, just as one corrupt practice is closed down, so another seems to take its place. The corrupt become more inventive, experimental, and clever at avoiding detection, leaving behind few traces although clearly guilty of fraud and deceit. The computer has opened a whole new world to intervention, interference, and theft. All information within it can be manipulated, erased, and distorted, including state secrets, military intelligence, and financial systems. Everything is now so vulnerable that among the next international priorities is likely to be anti-corruption safeguards in information technology before a man-made disaster of global proportions occurs (Marichal, 2012; Redner, 2013).

SOME MAJOR CAUSES OF ACKNOWLEDGED CORRUPTION

Since corrupt practices are committed by individuals, much attention is given to why people go astray. In this, public authorities are not much different from anyone who does not stick to ideals, gets greedy, becomes arrogant, and sees norms as obstacles to overcome. There may be many residents of all ages and disposition who are less susceptible to misconduct because they are descended from long-respected families or readily conform to community expectations and norms or have the self-discipline to avoid being tempted into corruption by opportunity, connivance, and self-gratification. Guilt can only be ascertained when the alleged offender is caught red-handed. Otherwise, people have to be taken at face value and trusted to behave as expected unless there is good reason to suspect that all is not well. Corrupt individuals slip through any net set to trap criminals and the really smart ones escape detection altogether or it is too late to catch them. Some individual corruption is inevitable. Since both human nature and human arrangements are imperfect, elimination is unlikely. *Homo sapiens* is flawed.

What is more likely to be combated is institutional corruption when corrupt activities are shared by more than one person. Too many people know, participate, and are expected to keep silent. They may shelter pragmatically behind such adages as "one cannot make an omelet without breaking eggs" or "the ends justify the means." Should the misconduct be considered petty and insignificant (petty theft, ubiquitous sleaze, even "honest graft"), it may be dismissed as a common human failing better dealt with as a minor breach of discipline. However, when it occurs on a larger scale, becomes institutionalized (common practice), and is socially dysfunction, then it is too serious to ignore. Practice contradicts public profession. Offenders violate public expectations when absolved or treated lightly. Whistle blowers who expose such institutional hypocrisy are the ones more likely to suffer (Caiden & Caiden, 1977, pp. 306–307). Such organizational arrogance is resented for upsetting the community's sense of decency, fair play, equal consideration, and social justice. Its victims feel that they are being exploited and unfairly treated. Should their complaints and calls for change be ignored, their discontent mounts and eventually finds subversive ways to express their opposition to what is felt to be oppressive. Such alienation goes well beyond their annoyance at routine theft, cheating, and absenteeism, and tempts sabotage (Smelser & Reed, 2012, pp. 200–2002).

The severest difficulties arise when there is a clash between institutional arrangements and the prevailing culture or more accurately conflicting cultures (Caiden, 2012). These are situations where people are deeply split among themselves and at logger heads over almost everything. There is little meeting of the minds; intransigence prevails as few are willing to compromise and would rather sacrifice themselves instead. History has thrust them together but they are at odds over ideology, politics, religion and factions of the same religion, values, ideals, norms, and personal relationships. They cannot get on with one another. Without imperial authority to force them to live together, they would be at one another's throats, such is the undisguised enmity. Bordering on anarchy, corruption is rife as every separate community struggles to survive and prosper. This extreme is best examined by watching what people do when they think they are not being observed. The major causes of corruption are probably this deeply rooted.

A Society at War with Itself

A society that cannot live with itself can never properly govern itself. If it cannot reach agreement over anything important, there will always be incivility and dissent no matter what is done, as is the case in several African and Asian states (Dix & Jayawickrama, 2010). There has to be a prevailing spirit of compromise and consensus, a willingness to get along together no matter how wide the differences among its distinctive communities. Rivalries split people apart, competition divides, hatreds and backstabbing of the other intensify, discrimination and ostracism prevail, people suspect one another, and mutual trust is almost unknown. Each separate faction seeks to outdo the rest and exploit its advantages. The name of the game is winning, not losing, and too often winning at any price. Civilization is the antidote that keeps governance from getting out of hand. Unfortunately, unless civilized conduct is also deeply rooted and strictly enforced by social norms and discipline, the worst human instincts quickly emerge and corrupt "normal" behavior. People in an uncontrollable mob in panic have resorted to despicable acts that they could never imagine themselves doing otherwise.

Governance Lacking Trust

The civilizing influence of governance depends on trust without which there can be little loyalty, willing cooperation, enthusiasm, and drive. To some extent, some trust has to exist between leaders and followers, the rulers and the ruled, representatives and voters, the privileged and the underprivileged, the haves and the have-nots, parents and children, teachers and students, members of any association, and particularly between public authorities and their clientele and stakeholders. Followership does not necessarily reflect trust which has to be earned not imposed. People have to trust one another in some measure that they adhere to a widely understood social contract to preserve life, further the commonwealth, and improve the quality of life in a mutually beneficial relationship. Without such trust, there can be little willing cooperation, enthusiasm, and drive (Cook, Levi, & Hardin, 2009). Whenever governance becomes irregular, vulnerable, uncertain, inconsistent, morally irresponsible, self-enriching (kleptomanic), and cruel, it is in danger of forfeiting its trust and losing its effectiveness (Kornai, Rothstein, & Rose-Ackerman, 2004).

Unaccountable and Irresponsible Governance

Despotism accountable and responsible only to itself knows no bounds. It is capable of doing anything with its absolute power and makes for dishonesty, manipulation, and fraud (Cook et al., 2009). It is a source for barbarism and inhumanity, wreaking profound evil. Its propensity toward tyranny is unlimited as in the well-known quote that "power corrupts; absolute power corrupts absolutely" (Acton, 1887/2000). Public authorities and individual sociopaths commit atrocities that set such a bad example that vengeance and retribution wait their chance. Self-policing is unimaginable in such circumstances. Clear limitations over the exercise of absolute power together with governance in the sunshine (Vogl, 2012) are required to curb excesses. Failed states, like Afghanistan and Somalia, illustrate how poor governance relates to societies where rampant corruption is out of control. A comparison between the tables published annually by Transparency International on corruption and *Foreign Affairs* on failed states shows the close correlation.

Disrespect for Basic Human Rights

Treating any individual with indignity and disrespect is unworthy of governance. The cruelties of unchecked governance did finally result in the 1948 UN Universal Declaration of Human Rights, since followed up by numerous other international conventions, declarations, treaties, and protocols extending the identification of the "equal and inalienable rights of all members of the human family." People have these rights simply by virtue of being human. The work of emancipation is never done like that of those who compile aggregate governance indicators that provide new red lines that should not be crossed as they seek an end to atrocity, oppression, and inequity. If evidence is needed, one need only refer to the publications of several UN organizations that deal with human rights, crime, refugees, labor, and peacekeeping together with international non-governmental organizations that promote universal human rights.

Breaches of the Universal Rule of Law

Moral rights require the backing of legal enforcement to which all have access. The law should be applied without fear or distinction by independent judges who should not be prejudiced by any party in dispute, certainly not by public authorities whose actions and decisions are being challenged. There should be no double standards for anyone special, no possible exception. But the law is made and unmade by public authorities who can design what they want to weigh down the scales of justice to their own, their friends' and their supporters' benefit and advantage to the detriment of the weak, begrudged, ill-treated, violated, and scorned. Wrongdoing goes way beyond the reach of the law. Most legal studies dwell on the connection between disrespect for the rule of law and the prevalence of corruption, public law and morality, public regulation and enforcement, and judicial behavior and public ethics, and specifically on legal conduct and corruption (Treisman, 2000, 2006).

Gifting the Commons

Public authorities are guardians of resources held by the community to be used for the common good. These are precious natural resources, public property, public investments, public credits, and public goods and services that need to be carefully conserved and managed. Instead, they are treated as if they are the private preserves of public authorities that can be awarded to the highest bidder in an auction of public assets as if there were no tomorrow. The benefit goes to special interests and is not shared by all, especially when the bidding is secret, confined to narrow circles, and decided by revolving door cronies who bar access to anyone outside the charmed circle of the favored. In economic parlance, this phenomena is called "the resource curse" when applied to poor countries, like Mongolia and Congo (formerly Zaire), that are rich in natural resources and where the wealth is confined to the social apex.

Sheer Bad Governance

Sheer bad governance goes beyond even unaccountability and irresponsibility, it is government that is "ineffective and inefficient, not transparent, not responsive to the people, not held accountable for [its] actions, inequitable and exclusive to the elites, non-participatory, do [sic] not follow the rule of law and lacking policies that are consensus driven" (United Nations Economic and Social Commission for Asia and Pacific [UNESCAP], n.d.). There are governance systems so rotten to the core that they lack the capacity to do anything properly, wisely, rationally, competently, or credibly; they are likely to remain that way without drastic changes. Whatever help they receive makes little difference as it quickly disappears from view into the unknown (Spector, 2005). A ray of hope is that the signatories to the 2000 UN Compact and the 2003 UNCAC expect to do better by eventually attaining capable governance, not just within governmental circles.

Overlooking the Divide

The worst situation of all even beyond distrust and bad governance is the corrosion of the social fabric where the elites show virtually no concern for anybody else and use every means of suppression in their power to maintain their iron hold. Meantime, the elites race on ahead with little hope that rest can ever catch up. The elites enjoy envied comforts while the rest in comparison live a hard life. The latter resent their weaknesses being exploited by both fair means and foul sanctioned in effect by public authorities who are not seen as neutral but on the side of and part of the elites who rule. For those at the bottom of the social scale, life is hard and unforgiving, dependent on handouts that can be the difference between survival and death. Like the deprived everywhere, they long to share in whatever is available, not just welfare handouts whatever the source. They want an end to inequity, injustice, discrimination, and the conditions behind all forms of corruption (Dorling, 2011).

Studying just a fraction of the multiple factors behind the persistence of corruption shows how combating its many manifestations is no easy task and how many obstacles have to be overcome at all levels of governance and at every locality where public authority reaches. At the same time, many pointers to success are revealed and how much success has been, is being, and is expected to be made within the near future.

SOME COUNTRIES SUCCEED MORE THAN OTHERS

Indeed, some countries, societies, institutions, communities, and organizations have succeeded in overcoming corruption much more than others, success in terms of achieving the minimal level of how they define corruption, reducing wrongdoing and evil, pursuing the corrupt, encouraging exposure, warning possible victims, shaming offenders, and advocating and adopting anti-corruption reforms. The gap between the welfare democracies at one end of the scale and the kleptocratic mafia states (Naim, 2012) at the other is vast as is that between where corruption is an incidental *fact* of life and a *way* of life, and where corrupt practices are all too clumsy, obvious and unavoidable and where they are sophisticated, hidden, and avoidable. Just examining such key factors, some remedies suggest themselves as follows:

(a) *A country at peace with itself.* For some generations, there have been no major upheavals. The people get on well with one another; are hospitable, friendly, tolerant, and welcoming; behave with dignity, confidence, modesty, decency, and social respectability; share bonds of collective responsibility and high levels of interpersonal trust; like to be treated and respected as individuals; offer a helping hand and have a low tolerance of crime, wrongdoing, and corruption. They are hardworking, thrifty, and generous with a strong commitment to a sense of fairness, justice, goodwill, and democratization. They expect a voice, probably a strong voice, in governance. Such conditions may require several generations to inculcate for they require a lengthy spell of peace, reconciliation, identification, and harmony which most of the countries reputed to be the least corrupt have enjoyed.

(b) *Trusted governance.* People trust public authorities as long as they adhere to the implied social contract and give little cause for concern. The followers want to cooperate whole heartedly with their leaders; they do not want to be bullied, coerced, misled, or terrorized. They are reluctant to withdraw their support and confidence but their patience is limited. When upset, they protest. Should their complaints be ignored they seek ways of accommodating themselves, that is, of getting around the situation unofficially and informally (Garfinkel, 1967). This to their leaders may appear disruptive and corrupt but to their participants is a more productive, accommodating, and harmonious way of keeping the peace and promoting satisfaction if not happiness. Once again, the countries reputed to be the least corrupt enjoy trusted governance although some specific institutions may lack public confidence and credibility not always justified just as others may not be as deserving without further investigation behind the scenes.

(c) *Accountable and responsible governance* should prevent most excesses occurring before getting out of hand. Whenever absolutism threatens, swift action is required to step in and stop abuse in its tracks. This means keeping a vigilant watch and a permanent staff of skilled capable experts on hand ready to intervene on their own initiative and apply counter measures as quickly as possible. Here is where decentralization, redundancy, overlapping, and rivalry may be desirable to head off possible crises in the making (Caiden, 1970; Caiden & Wildavsky, 1974).

(d) *Respect for human rights* requires political will and effective implementation. Willing cooperation is much preferable to compulsion but where disrespect rules, corruption inevitably thrives wherever inhumanity and mistreatment occur without protest or anybody caring about its faceless victims.

(e) *Strict application of the rule of law* without fear or favor by impartial judges needs to be enforced throughout the legal and criminal justice systems from top to bottom. Manipulation of the rules is a misuse of public authority and undermines the credibility of public institutions as they decline in respect. The strict application of the rule of law is a crucial aspect of responsible and accountable governance.

(f) *Protecting the commons* against special interests has always been a contentious issue and will remain so as long as there are disputes about what constitute the commons, how best to protect the commons, and how its bounty can be shared equitably. The privatization of natural resources that have traditionally qualified as the commons such as land and water and otherwise collectively shared especially through confiscation and redistribution to cronies have always been disputed just as the denationalization of public services to private monopolists have been resented.

(g) *Sheer bad governance* requires large scale remodeling, reconstruction, reform, and reinvestment over a lengthy period of time probably under unfavorable circumstances and needs much external support. This quest is the key objective of the 2000 UNCB and 2003 UNCAC and remains a task of the UNDP.

(h) *Tackling the divide* is probably the hardest challenge of all. Narrowing the gap between the elites and the rest is an arduous task capping the rich to enable the poorest of the poor to catch up more than they otherwise could. This is the aim of the Millennium Development Goals that already lag well behind target despite the progress that has been achieved. Depending on what benchmarks and measures used, the gap widens and with it accusations of institutional corruption that blocks further progress (Dowling & Yap, 2013).

What is at stake involves a global transformation with anti-corruption ranking much higher in public policymaking. This means that curbing corruption has to compete for attention with all the other matters that are on the public agenda. It keeps being put off ("postponed into the future") because so many current emergencies require immediate action. As with other bold reforms, reaching an agreement is rarely a simple process. The timing has to be opportune, the ground prepared beforehand, vested interests in the status quo won over, enthusiasts cautioned not to oversell or promise too much raising unrealistic expectations, the appropriate details thrashed out, and the anticipated improvements considered worthwhile. All reforms are experiments and risky. They may not work at all or make matters worse than ever or circumstances change so quickly to outdate them or, having overcome resistance, they may induce a state of complacency that the issue has been settled once and for all. Their backers might be wrong or too timid or hoodwinked or outplayed (Caiden, 1969/2007). There is no telling, save to point out that corruption has remarkable staying power, the corrupt are ingenious, and whatever can go wrong does, frustrating attempt after attempt to combat it. Too often, the story tellers leave out crucial details because they do not know or do not want their listeners to know, relate half-truths as instructed, or conjecture an ending that listeners would enjoy. Hence, thoroughly researched studies of successes are the more valuable because they do reveal what can be achieved with persistence, hard labor, and luck.

SUCCESS STORIES

Most reputations are hard earned. Having a reputation for clean hands for a substantial period of time certainly indicates success in combating corruption both individually and systematically. Professional military officers have long been admired. So too have medical practitioners, diplomats, academicians, and high court judges among myriads of other professionals who have received public recognition for their unselfish devotion to furthering the public good. Their outstanding contributions to public service have shaped their organizations and instilled a noble tradition of selfless pride, reliability, and competence. Some notables go on to higher leadership positions but most remain modest backstage staff on whom their organizations rely to get things done that need doing. Every country is blessed by their presence, steadfastness, knowledge, skills, and integrity. Unheralded and often anonymous, they are the heart of good governance although others often take undeserved credit for their good deeds.

So what is it about the environment in certain parts of the globe such as Scandinavia, the Anglo-American democracies, western Europe, and several members of the Commonwealth that make them stand out for their long standing reputations over half a century for cleanliness? Within fairly close proximity to one another are Denmark, Sweden, Norway, Finland, the Netherlands, Belgium, Luxembourg, and Switzerland. Under British historical influence can be listed Australia, Barbados, Canada, Hong Kong, New Zealand, Singapore, and the United Kingdom. This is not purely coincidental (Treisman, 2000). They differ individually in countless ways. But if the eight key factors some of which clearly overlap that make *the* difference in combating corruption are considered, as the success stories in this book show they share much with one another and also with other countries outside this charmed circle which have not been as successful.

1. There is a common understanding of what constitutes misconduct derived from Western liberal democratic values with some parochial modifications. Moral integrity is highly prized in a meritocratic society that strictly polices itself and is severe on any members who let the side down by disgraceful conduct. Public duty comes first and last above all other considerations. Codes of public ethics prevail and are vigorously enforced despite lapses and omissions. The truly unfit are eventually weeded out and moved on. Public figures are always in the glare of harsh criticism for their shortcomings but when deserving they are also praised for their rectitude and public spirit.

2. The dignity of public authority is upheld. Uncaring, insensitive, and overly bureaucratic (officious) conduct is discouraged. Public authorities are expected to behave humanely, politely, tolerantly, and with kindly understanding. Officeholders are expected to be decent upstanding

members of the community, doing what is right but in a firm manner, commanding respect and emulation, and demonstrating fairness and concern. They try not to offend or cause harm without good cause. They are not expected to receive special privileges or rewards for doing what they do except for truly outstanding performance. They earn their trust by their actions and deeds.

3. The limitations on exercising public authority are respected at all times. All are expected to be law abiding and refrain from acting imperiously unless confronted with an emergency when speedy decisions and actions are needed. Otherwise, established guidelines and precedents count. The abuse and misuse of public authority are seen as sinful and likened to committing a crime. Governance is considered a partnership in common cause, not a bully pulpit taking advantage of the public trust reposed in it. Hectoring is not appreciated and likely to be interrupted by hecklers or quickly cut short.

4. Governance serves and enforces human rights, tries to give equal access and opportunity, and is mindful of social justice.

5. The rule of law exempts none. The benefit of any doubt errs on the side of innocence.

6. Public ethics are distinguished from private ethics, that is, public standards of conduct differ from private standards although they much overlap. What private organizations are allowed to do may be prohibited to public organizations and vice versa. Conflicts of interest are expected to be minimized to prevent ambiguities and what amounts to the legitimization of wrongdoing.

7. Bad governance, defined by the UN Economic and Social Commission for Asia and Pacific (UNESCAP, 2012) as "governments that are ineffective and inefficient, not transparent, not responsive to the people, not held accountable for their actions, inequitable and exclusive to the elites, non-participatory, do not follow the rule of law and lacking in policies that are consensus driven," is not tolerated. Any sign of this is immediately criticized and cause for concern when it is not rectified.

8. The one area where those reputed to be freest of corruption have fallen behind in recent years is in their commitment to communal welfare and their chipping away at their prized welfare states. The charge is that their elites have been using their political and economic power to favor themselves at the expense of the rest of society (Stiglitz, 2012). While this use of public authority may be legitimate, it allegedly corrodes the social fabric by restoring an aristocracy of wealth that is accused of causing rising structural unemployment, greater economic uncertainty

and instability, growing inequality, less opportunity and social mobility, an indifference toward social justice, and a decline in morality and a degradation of values "to the point where everything is acceptable and no one is accountable" (Stiglitz, 2012, p. xvii).

What is being insinuated is that the familiar stereotypes of corruption are being overtaken by a more sophisticated sinister form of systematic institutional corruption cleverly disguised as beneficial, a wolf in sheep's clothing. Stiglitz cites indictments of systemic institutional wrongdoing engineered through manipulative governance such as rent seeking, corporate welfare, lax law enforcement and regulation, presents of natural resources, tax concessions, money laundering, public sector contracting practices, shrinking non-corporate welfare benefits, international bribery, austerity policies, and public employment cutbacks, all of which weaken the enforcement of public ethics. He blames the ideological shift from Keynesian welfare model (regulated capitalism) to the liberal Hayek/Friedman market model (unregulated capitalism) (Wapshott, 2011). Public authorities are now just pieces in a very complicated high stakes game being played out globally. No country has been untouched or reacted in the same way.

As regards the first phase of adjustment to the new world of globalization, the Anglo-American democracies took the lead by moving away from public intervention toward more private entrepreneurialism, improving their competitiveness, tackling governmental financial shortfalls, making government more businesslike, viewing governance from the bottom as well as the top, and reducing the burdens being placed on government, the chief of which was the increasing cost of welfare (Caiden, 2013a). Their leadership in international economics enabled them to keep ahead, embrace the Washington consensus and muddle through economic downturns with varying degrees for some 30 years until the 2008 global financial crisis. Since then, their disagreement on how to overcome the resulting global recession, their hesitation over making bold decisions on fundamental issues and their inability to jump-start economic growth has enabled the Scandinavian democracies to take the initiative.

Although probably the most advanced of the welfare democracies, and having had that reputation from the 1930s, the Scandinavians have come through the current recession in better shape than most others in this second phase of adjustment. They seem to have avoided the systemic institutional wrongdoing cited by Stiglitz by being more disciplined, leaner, innovative, modest, unassuming, pragmatic, and *"willing to root out corruption and vested interests*" (*Economist*, 2013a, p. 9, emphasis added). They prize governance honesty and transparency. While they have their problems, corruption is not one of them. They stay faithful to their egalitarian ethos, public investment in human capital, and pride in the generosity of their welfare states in their version of welfare capitalism (or statist individualism) that focuses on outcomes not ideology although they are fraying at the edges when it comes to welfare recipients who take advantage of state largesse without contributing much in return.

What arouses concern is that greater emphasis on getting things done, obtaining results, and operating by the most effective means as implied by the embrace of the New Public Management movement between 1980 and 2000 by liberal democracies could signal a more ruthless riding roughshod over traditional public values. What most distinguishes public from private morality is that results increase the general happiness, enhance the collective good, improve the quality of life for all, minimize harm, and advance human ideals. These ideals are achieved by virtuous public authorities conscious of what constitutes wrongdoing in their personal as well as official life. They should never have to be reminded on how they set the tone for conducting public business as "moral agents, fiduciaries, and technicians, and for the nurturing of ethical competence."

> Only emphasizing operational skills, standards, and operational knowledge without paying attention to the need for individuals in public administration to be committed and socially embedded individuals, who are able to think for themselves, have proper judgment, a critical attitude, are reflexive as well as praxis-oriented, and developing themselves, is a threat to the quality of public administration. (Vries & Kim, 2011, p. 16)

This criticism of New Public Management is joined by political economists like Stigliz who believe that neo-liberalism has been carried too far. They are alarmed that consideration of public goods and services has been invaded too much by market values which have little place in the public sector. Social goods should not be determined just by the ability to pay detached from moral values. Technocratic managerial policies should not be allowed to take over and allow public goods and services to be degraded and corrupted by the short term, greed, and irresponsible risk taking, putting finance before people. There are some things that money should not buy. In a society where everything is for sale, inequality and corruption are inevitable simply because "commercialism erodes commonality ... people of affluence and people of modest means lead increasingly separate lives. ... It's not good for democracy, nor is it a satisfying way to live."

Democracy does not require perfect equality, but it does require that citizens share in a common life. What matters is that people of different backgrounds and social positions encounter one another, and bump up against one another, in the course of everyday life. For this is how we learn to negotiate and abide our differences, and how we come to care for the common good. (Sandel, 2012, pp. 202–203)

THE FUTURE PROSPECT

Nobody knows what the future holds and what the unexpected will do to wreck any forecast. But we also know that continuity remains a strong factor in looking ahead. As the French say, things change but they also stay much the same. The deep philosophical questions now being raised are unlikely to be resolved overnight, certainly not universally. Instead, each country will probably continue to go its own way regardless, doing what it decides is best for itself. The international community will stand by the 2000 UN Compact and the 2003 UNCAC and try to convince all-comers that adopting and improving on them is in everybody's interest. The least corrupt countries will presumably continue to try to deal with their most worrisome areas of corruption as they arise while the most corrupt countries without the capacity to tackle corruption will fall further behind global expectations. No doubt, ambitious reformers will make breakthroughs once they reassess unrewarding past attempts (Andrews, 2013), tackle systemic and systematic corruption, strengthen institutional safeguards against wrongdoing, and reduce incentives behind corrupt conduct.

Nothing that the reformers achieve will satisfy the doomsayers who point to the lack of success in dealing with greater issues facing humanity such as the spread of weapons of mass destruction, the prevention of global economic instability, and the relentless pursuit of material wellbeing that could well get the better of humanity's propensity for corruption (Redner, 2013). Against them, the optimists, looking at the brighter side, point to human ingenuity and how much improvement has been made in the human condition, accelerating with every generation. Corruption is worrisome and remains a cause for concern but it will not get the better of us. We know enough to understand that it is not inevitable and that it is not beyond human imagination and will to resolve (Ricci, 2013). Indeed, by comparison it is a much easier challenge than many others confronting humanity. Since 2000, a good start has been made to go beyond recognition to effective action (UNDP, 2004, 2008). Currently, several factors favor action.

First, global attitudes are changing now that corruption cannot be swept under the rug. Its dysfunctions are only too obvious and provoking resentment. International agreements are among many indications that corruption needs to be given greater attention and higher priority in public policymaking. Not a day passes when somewhere around the globe it is getting greater public attention and serious efforts are being made to find the right or better courses of action that should lessen its harm. Progress is not as fast as people would like to see and too often led to expect. True, those who stand to lose by curbing corruption block reforms and find new ways of getting around whatever is devised to curb it. Solutions cannot be conjured up overnight and may be outdated when they do eventuate but there is no want of trying. Ingrained cultural and religious opposition are quite difficult to overcome (Caiden, 2012). Progress is slow but it is not being hindered.

Second, the victims of corruption when awakened combine to demand action and when their patience is limited. What the corrupt may have gotten away with in the past is no longer so tolerated and accepted. People protest about the extremes of wealth and income, the contrast between luxury and suffering, security and fear, confidence and helplessness, access and denial, choice and compulsion, justice and injustice, sacrifice and greed, consumption and deprivation, respect and cruelty, and cooperation and hostility, all of which they connect to corruption. Broken promises rile. Resentment builds and awaits the opportunity to avenge. One spark can turn order into chaos. When it does, support quickly evaporates. Unless the victims of corruption stick together in common cause behind an implementable reform program and remain disciplined, they can defeat themselves. This is a risk all protest movements have to take but there may be no other way open to them. Even when crushed, such movements draw outside attention and support that stands them in good stead for a later attempt to curb corruption.

Third, institutional failure draws attention to the inadequacies of form without substance highlighted by systemic and systematic corruption. Neoliberal economics and globalization promised a new world order for global development. The bigger pie would enable bigger slices for all. But things have not quite worked out that way at all. Instead of sharing the rewards of economic development, much, perhaps too much, has ended up in the hands of elites. There has been more trickle up than trickle down. More and more people complain that they have been left out of public policymaking which has shifted to larger and larger bureaucracies dominated by experts and professionals who diligently serve the privileged elites, among whom they include themselves, while reducing the power and influence of everybody else. This has done little to help the poor, safeguard livelihoods, protect the environment, and improve the status of minorities, women and youth (who are still marginalized). Good governance as embraced by the international community is insufficient (Kurki, 2013).

What is required to make politics more inclusive, governments (indeed all large scale organizations) more responsive to societal needs, and public policies more sensitive to the quality of life for everyone is more *democratic governance* as interpreted by the UNDP in its annual reports on human development, the indicators of Freedom House (Freedom House, 2012), and the different conceptions of democracy of the "Varieties of Democracy" (V-Dem) project at the Kellogg Institute at Notre Dame University (see http://www.kellog.nd.edu/projects/ vdem/index.shtml). The call is for people, all peoples, to have a real say in the decisions that affect their lives and hold all decision-makers accountable on the basis of equal rights. Genuine democratic governance, as contrasted with hollow or sham democracy (Blunt, Turner, & Lindroth, 2013), would be more responsive to people's needs and aspirations, aim at eradicating poverty, expand choices, and respect the needs of future generations. A crucial ingredient of its agenda would be the assault on corruption. Since the UNDP established the Global Democratic Governance Forum in 2011 there appears to be backstage international pressure to incorporate this aspiration into the revised post-2015 Millennium Development Goals.

Fourth, since the advent of the 2008 global financial crisis and the austerity policies subsequently adopted, there are stronger calls for the revival of increased government intervention in economic development, the re-regulation of private enterprise, the redistribution of wealth and income, and renewed support for public enterprise. Implied is the restoration and strengthening of public ethics and their application to all bodies receiving financial help from government, the extension of public accountability and responsibility to the private sector (O'Sullivan et al., 2012, p. 354), and greater public participation in public policy and administration. Should these calls result in a change in attitudes (i.e., another switch in ideology), the expectation is that corruption should come under increasing scrutiny and action leading to its diminution.

The future looks promising if any of these trends persist. Meantime, the world has to cope with facts on the ground. As more information becomes available, so benchmarks can be instituted and better measures of success or failure can be constructed. Alas, too much of what is still being provided is suspect, partial, selected, biased, and just plain concocted by self-interested parties although the indices grow more elaborate and inclusive (Dowling & Yap, 2013) as do determinants to its vulnerability (Klasen & Waibel, 2013). People still don't know quite what to believe. Everyone likes to quote the country comparisons compiled by Transparency International based on perceptions. What is rarely mentioned is its Bribe Payers Index related to the bribery of low-ranking public officials, improper contributions to high-ranking politicians to achieve influence, and bribery between private companies as illicit financial out-flows from China, Russia, Mexico, Saudi Arabia, and Malaysia followed by the United Arab Emirates, Kuwait, and Qatar in the Middle East and Nigeria in Africa and Venezuela in South America (Vogl, 2012, p. 274), clearly implicated in money laundering to the benefit of the Netherlands, Switzerland, Belgium, Germany, Japan, Australia, Canada, and Singapore, and presumably all the other offshore tax shelters around the globe (*Economist*, 2013b, p. 13).

The continent of Africa is reputed to have the worst official corruption. Early in 2013, the *Economist* published a glowing report on how well it was doing generally and in combating corruption remarking in its gushing editorial that its correspondent "was not once asked for a bribe − inconceivable only ten years ago" although "bureaucrats and customs officers inflate the costs of getting anything done" (*Economist*, 2013c, p. 12). The whole continent with few exceptions is still plagued by political corruption, elite exploitation, gross inequality, bribery, communal conflicts, terrorism, insecurity, official oppression, white elephants, deficient public goods and services, and siphoned off public revenues.

> Incompetent governments will continue to build roads to nowhere, many pupils will still be taught in overcrowded classrooms, plenty of fields will be polluted and farmers will be pushed off their land to make room for investors … Fresh conflicts may arise when new wealth buys more weapons and begets more cross-border jealousies … Deadly droughts, flash floods and falling water tables are recurring themes … Joblessness is one reason for high crime rates. (*Economist*, 2013c, p. 18)

Not one word was said about illicit out-flows that robbed the continent of capital that could have fostered economic growth and development, estimated at some US\$1.3 trillion through clandestine channels without including bulk cash transfers by criminals such as drug runners and kidnappers (*Wall Street Journal*, 2013, p. A10). Nothing was said about the lenient treatment given to notorious convicted corrupt public leaders, exploitation of ill-paid employees, electoral fraud, the failure to implement universal human rights, and the difficulties recovering looted funds (*Economist*, 2013d, pp. 63−66).

One bright spot that raised hopes was the unexpected Arab Spring when several authoritarian regimes proved more fragile than their dictators believed.

> Corruption, nepotism, cronyism, and injustice have been the targets of mass protests. Appeals for dignity, human rights, and democracy have been among the protesters' most prominent slogans. (Brynen, Moore, Sallloukh, & Zohar, 2012, p. vii)

The uprisings were not the outcome of any Western-designated democracy promotion programs or any Western intervention until local popular uprisings threatened regional stability and then only selectively and in tandem with Western strategic interests. A combination of complex local, regional, and international factors have obstructed democratization creating "herculean statebuilding and socioeconomic challenges that may take precedence over democracy" proving that rights are "gained as a result of protracted and sometimes bloody popular struggles" (Brynen et al., 2012, pp. 300–301). The uprisings were the result of the accumulation of grievances against known evils and injustices and a universal longing for emancipation from tyranny, cruelty, deprivation, indifference, and ignorance. At heart, they were motivated by the ideals of democracy, human rights, respect for the individual, accountable and responsive governance, civilized conduct, and the abhorrence of wrongdoing. Alas, this does not appear to be the case at this time of writing but maybe one day soon these seeds may eventually germinate.

Alas, much the same story could be told about other continents where corruption exists as a way of life to which people have no other choice than to make the best of things and conform (Caiden, 2012). The impression is that despite successes in democratization and good governance, much seems to be business as usual with global corruption on the increase with much cooking of the books, both public and private, making things appear better than they really are, thereby misleading the public. Again, the same countries top the list where abuse was the least. There exists a global corruption perception gap in that people believe that corruption is more prevalent elsewhere than in their own country or industry (*New York Times*, 2013). As a result, attention will continue to be focused on how countries that have so far resisted the inroads of corruption continue to advocate action against corrupt practices and the corrupt. It remains to be seen what different paths will guided democracies, liberal democracies, and welfare democracies take in dealing with their own corrupt elements let alone extensive corrupt global networks. Unless humanity achieves greater success in curbing corruption, we will not be able to realize our full potential and we will all continue to lose.

REFERENCES

Acton, J. (1887/2000). Letters to Bishop Mandel Creighton. In J. Powell (Ed.), *The triumph of liberty*. New York, NY: Free Press.

Andrews, M. (2013). *The limits of institutional reform in development: Changing rules for realistic solutions*. New York, NY: Cambridge University Press.

Blunt, P., Turner, M., & Lindroth, H. (2013). Morton's fork: "Democracy" versus neopatrimonialism in developing countries. *International Journal of Public Administration*, *36*(1), 45–62.

Brynen, R., Moore, P., Sallloukh, B., & Zohar, M.-J. (2012). *Beyond the Arab spring: Authoritarianism and democratization in the Arab world*. Boulder, CO: Lynne Rienner Publishers.

Caiden, G. E. (1969/2007). *Administrative reform*. Chicago, IL: Aldine and Transaction Publishers.

Caiden, G. E. (1970). *Israel's administrative culture*. Berkeley, CA: Institute of Governmental Studies, University of California.

Caiden, G. E. (1991). What is public maladministration? *Public Administration Review*, *51*(6), 486–493.

Caiden, G. E. (2012). Culture and corruption. *Public Administration and Policy*, *15*(2), 93–128. Readers are advised to consult the more extensive lists of references contained in Caiden (2012) and Caiden (2013b).

Caiden, G. E. (2013a). Ideological differences in administrative reform: The current demotion of public service in key Anglo-Saxon democracies. In D. Argyriades & G. Timset (Eds.), *Moving beyond the crisis: Reclaiming and reaffirming our common administrative space* (pp. 95–138). Brussels: International Institute of Administrative Sciences and Brulant.

Caiden, G. E. (2013b). A checkered history of combating official corruption. *Adult Education and Development*, *2*(2), 92–111.

Caiden, G. E., & Caiden, N. J. (1977). Administrative corruption. *Public Administration Review*, *37*(3), 301–309.

Caiden, N.J., & Wildavsky, A. (1974). *Planning and budgeting in poor countries*. New York, NY: Wiley.

Cook, K., Levi, M., & Hardin, R. (2009). *In whom can we trust? How groups, networks and institutions make trust possible*. New York, NY: Russell Sage Foundation.

Dix, S., & Jayawickrama, N. (2010). *Fighting corruption in a post-conflict and recovery situation: Lessons from the past*. New York, NY: United Nations Development Programme.

Dorling, D. (2011). *Injustice: Why social inequality persists*. Bristol: Policy Press.

Dowling, J., & Yap, C.-F. (2013). *Happiness and poverty in developing countries: A global perspective*. New York, NY: Palgrave-Macmillan.

Economist. (2013a, February 2). Supplement on northern lights. *Economist*, 16pp.

Economist. (2013b, February 16). Supplement on offshore finance, *Economist*, 16pp.

Economist. (2013c, March 2). Aspiring Africa, p. 12, and Special Report on Emerging Africa: A hopeful continent. *Economist*, 18 pp.

Economist. (2013d, May 11). Making a hash of finding the cash. *Economist*, pp. 63–66.

Freedom House. (2012, September 13). *Freedom in the World 2012*. Washington, DC: Freedom House.

Friedman, M. (1970). A Friedman doctrine: The social responsibility of business is to increase its profits. *New York Times Magazine*, SM 17.

Garfinkel, H. (1967). *Studies in ethnomethodology*. Englewood Cliffs, NJ: Prentice Hall.

Graaf, G., Maravic, P., & Wagenaar, P. (2010). *The good cause: Theoretical perspectives on corruption*. Opladen and Farmington Hills, MI: Barbara Budrich Publishers.

Jancsics, D., & Javor, I. (2012). Corrupt government networks. *International Public Management Journal*, 15(1), 62–99.

Kahan, A. (1998). *Alexis de Tocqueville's the old regime and the revolution*. Chicago, IL: University of Chicago Press.

Klasen, S., & Waibel, H. (2013). *Vulnerability to poverty: Theory, measurement and determinants, with case studies from Thailand and Vietnam*. New York, NY: Palgrave Macmillan.

Kornai, J., Rothstein, B., & Rose-Ackerman, S. (2004). *Creating social trust in post-socialist transition*. New York, NY: Palgrave Macmillan.

Kurki, M. (2013). *Democratic futures: Revisioning democracy promotion*. New York, NY: Routledge.

Levine, D. (2013). *The capacity for ethical conduct: On psychic existence and the way we relate to others*. New York, NY: Routledge.

Marichal, J. (2012). *Facebook democracy: The architecture of disclosure and the threat to public life*. Farnham: Ashgate.

Mazower, M. (2012). *Governing the world: The history of an idea*. New York, NY: Penguin Press.

Naim, M. (2012). Mafia states. *Foreign Affairs*, 15(3), 100–111.

New York Times. (2013). A troubling survey on global corruption. *New York Times*, May 18, B 3.

O'Sullivan, P., Smith, M., & Esposito, M. (2012). *Business ethics*. New York, NY: Routledge.

Porta, D., & Vannucci, A. (2012). *The hidden order of corruption: An institutional approach*. Farnham: Ashgate.

Raadschelders, J. (1998). *Handbook of administrative history*. New Brunswick: Transaction Publishers.

Redner, H. (2013). *Beyond civilization: Society, culture, and the individual in the age of globalization*. New Brunswick: Transaction Publishers.

Ricci, G. (2013). *Culture and civilization: Cosmopolitanism and the global policy*. New Brunswick: Transaction Publishers.

Sandel, M. (2012). *What money can't buy: The moral limits of markets*. New York, NY: Farrar, Straus & Giroux.

Serra, D. & Wantchekon, L. (Eds) (2012). *New advances in experimental research on corruption*. Bingley: Emerald Group Publishing.

Smelser, N., & Reed, J. (2012). *Usable social science*. Berkeley, CA: University of California Press.

Spector, B. (Ed.) (2005). *Fighting corruption in developing countries: Strategy and analysis*. Bloomfield, CT: Kumarian Press.

Spector, B. (2012). *Detecting corruption in developing countries: Identifying causes/strategies for action*. Sterling, VA: Kumarian Press.

Stiglitz, J. (2012). *The price of inequality*. New York, NY: W.W. Norton.

Treisman, D. (2000). The causes of corruption: A cross-national study. *Journal of Public Economics*, 76(3), 399–457.

Treisman, D. (2006). *What have we learned about the causes of corruption from ten years of cross-national empirical research?* Los Angeles, CA: Department of Political Science, University of California.

UNDP (United Nations Development Programme). (2008). *Mainstreaming anti-corruption in development*. New York, NY.

UNDP. (2004). *Anti-corruption: Practice note*. New York, NY. Retrieved from http://www. undp.org/governsnce/account.htm. Accessed on February 2, 2013.

UNESCAP (United Nations Economic and Social Commission for Asia and Pacific). (n.d.). *UNESCAP Report 2012*. Retrieved from http:/www.unescap.org/pdd/prs/ProjectActivities/ Ongoing/

gg/governance.pdf. Accessed on February 2, 2013.

Vogl, F. (2012). *Waging war on corruption: Inside the movement fighting the abuse of power*. Lanham, MD: Rowman & Littlefield.

Vries, M., & Kim, P. (2011). *Value and virtue in public administration: A comparative perspective*. New York, NY: Palgrave Macmillan.

Wall Street Journal. (2013, March 13). Crimes found sapping billions from Africa. *Wall Street Journal*, A 10.

Wapshott, N. (2011). *Keynes Hayek: The clash that defined modern economics*. New York, NY: Norton.

CHAPTER 9

DIFFERENT PATHS TO CURBING CORRUPTION: A COMPARATIVE ANALYSIS

Jon S. T. Quah

ABSTRACT

Chapters 2−6 have dealt in turn with how Denmark, Finland, Hong Kong, New Zealand, and Singapore have been effective in curbing corruption, as manifested in their rankings and scores on the five international indicators of the perceived extent of corruption. In contrast, Chapter 7 focuses on India's ineffective anti-corruption measures and identifies the lessons which India can learn from their success in fighting corruption. The aim of this concluding chapter is twofold: to describe and compare the different paths taken by these six countries in their battle against corruption; and to identify the lessons which other countries can learn from their experiences in combating corruption. However, as the policy contexts of these six countries differ significantly, it is necessary to begin by providing an analysis of their contextual constraints before proceeding to compare their anti-corruption strategies and identifying the relevant lessons for other countries.

Different Paths to Curbing Corruption: Lessons from Denmark, Finland, Hong Kong, New Zealand and Singapore
Research in Public Policy Analysis and Management, Volume 23, 219−255
Copyright © 2013 by Emerald Group Publishing Limited
All rights of reproduction in any form reserved
ISSN: 0732-1317/doi:10.1108/S0732-1317(2013)0000023009

THE IMPORTANCE OF POLICY CONTEXT

The importance of the policy context was first highlighted by John Merriman Gaus (1947, p. 6) in his recommendation that "the study of public administration must include its ecology." According to him, the ecological approach was important in public administration because "it is within this setting that their instruments and practices of public housekeeping should be studied so that they may better understand what they are doing, and appraise reasonably how they are doing it." He identified these seven factors: "people, place, physical technology, social technology, wishes and ideas, catastrophe, and personality" to explain "the ebb and flow of the functions of government" (Gaus, 1947, p. 9).

Similarly, 14 years later, Fred W. Riggs (1961, pp. 2–3) had also advocated the use of the ecological approach in the comparative study of administrative systems. The basis of the ecological perspective is "the idea that public administrators operate in an environment which *constrains* them," but what they do, "may, in turn, affect the environment" (Richardson & Baldwin, 1976, p. 24). More recently, in applying his framework for assessing corruption in Honduras, Senegal, Timor-Leste, and Ukraine, Bertram I. Spector (2012, p. 275) concludes that "context can make a big difference in the capacity of countries, as well as their motivation, to seriously address corruption problems." In short, following the advice of these authors, the examination of the anti-corruption strategies of the six countries must begin with an analysis of their different policy contexts.

The most comprehensive definition of policy context is provided by Howard M. Leichter (1979, pp. 40–42) in his comparative study of health care policy in Germany, Great Britain, Japan, and the former Soviet Union. His comprehensive accounting scheme consists of 37 situational, structural, cultural, and environmental factors for analyzing the policy context in a country. On the other hand, Donald P. Warwick (1979, pp. 296–320) has relied on a narrower definition which focuses on the "remote and proximate environment" in his comparative analysis of the formulation and implementation of population programs in Egypt, Kenya, Mexico, and the Philippines.[1]

For this study, the policy context refers to these five factors: the geography, formative historical experiences, economy, demography (including cultural aspects), and political system, which influence the nature and style of the policy-making process in a country. Indeed, a country's policy context can promote or hinder its incumbent government's anti-corruption policies depending on whether the contextual factors are conducive or hostile to the effective implementation of these policies (Quah, 2011, p. 30).

More specifically, these five factors can assist or hinder the effective implementation of the anti-corruption measures in a country:

1. *Geography*, especially the size or land area as a large country or archipelago will face more problems in enforcing the anti-corruption measures in the provinces or outer islands than a small country or city-state.
2. *Formative historical experiences* or "those circumstances in the past with significant transference to the immediate environment" of public policy (Warwick, 1979, p. 307) as the historical origins of corruption in a country and its colonial legacy (if it was colonized) will have a significant impact on its anti-corruption strategy.
3. *Economic development* as reflected in the gross domestic product (GDP) per capita as a poor country will encounter more difficulties than a rich one in implementing the anti-corruption measures if it does not receive financial and technical assistance from donor agencies and other countries.
4. *Demography* as the nature and size of the population and their culture as a country with a small and homogeneous population will have less difficulty than a country with a large and multiracial population in implementing its anti-corruption measures.
5. *Political system* as the extent of corruption is influenced by its nature (whether democratic or authoritarian), its level of political stability, rule of law, government effectiveness, and control of corruption.

Table 1 shows the extent of diversity in the policy contexts in the six countries, with the greatest variation manifested in their land areas, varying

Table 1. Policy Contexts of Six Countries.

Country	Land Area (sq km)	Colonial Legacy	Population (2011)	GDP Per Capita (2011)	Political System
Denmark	43,075	NA	5.8 m	US$59,928	Democracy
Finland	338,145	Swedish Russian	5.6 m	US$49,350	Democracy
Hong Kong	1,075	British	7.4 m	US$34,049	SAR, China
New Zealand	270,534	British	4.6 m	US$36,648	Democracy
Singapore	715.8	British	5.3 m	US$49,271	Democracy
India	3,287,263	British	1,250.2 m	US$1,389	Democracy

Sources: Economist (2012, pp. 140, 146, 154, 158, 186, 208) and Schwab (2012, pp. 383–384).

from India (the seventh largest country in the world) to the tiny city-state of Singapore. Finland is the second largest country, followed by New Zealand, Denmark, and Hong Kong. This means that it will be easier to enforce the anti-corruption laws in the city-states of Singapore and Hong Kong than in the sub-continent of India or the larger countries of Finland, New Zealand, and Denmark.

Second, in terms of GDP per capita, Denmark, Finland, Singapore, New Zealand, and Hong Kong are high-income countries with their GDPs per capita ranging between Hong Kong's US$34,049 and Denmark's US $59,928, which is 43 times larger than India's GDP per capita of US$1,389. This huge difference in GDP per capita between the five affluent countries and poorer India means that the former, unlike the latter, will be able to allocate the required resources for the effective implementation of their anti-corruption measures.

Third, the five richer countries also have smaller populations between 4.6 million and 7.4 million unlike India, which has the second largest population in the world with 1.25 billion in 2011. It should be noted that their combined population of 28.7 million in 2011 is smaller than the populations of these 14 states in India: Uttar Pradesh (199.6 million); Maharashtra (112.4 million); Bihar (103.8 million); West Bengal (91.3 million); Andhra Pradesh (84.7 million); Madhya Pradesh (72.6 million); Tamil Nadu (72.1 million); Rajasthan (68.6 million); Karnataka (61.1 million); Gujarat (60.4 million); Odisha (41.9 million); Kerala (33.4 million); Jharkhand (33.0 million); and Assam (31.2 million) (Dreze & Sen, 2013, pp. 298−299). This vast difference in population size means that the task of curbing corruption in India is much more challenging and difficult than in the other five countries with their smaller populations.

Fourth, all the countries are parliamentary democracies except Hong Kong, which is a Special Administrative Region (SAR) of China. However, Table 2 shows that Finland has the highest average percentile rank for political stability, followed by New Zealand, Denmark, Singapore, Hong Kong, and India, which is highly unstable politically with an average percentile rank of only 14.2. Similarly, as can be seen in Table 3, Finland also scores the highest average percentile rank for rule of law, followed by Denmark, New Zealand, Singapore, Hong Kong, and India, which also has the lowest average percentile rank of 56.1. For government effectiveness, Table 4 shows that Denmark is the most effective, followed by Finland, Singapore, New Zealand, and Hong Kong. However, unlike these five countries, India's government is less effective because its average percentile rank for government effectiveness from 1996 to 2011 is 54.2. Thus, Denmark, Finland, Hong Kong, New Zealand, and Singapore are politically more

Table 2. Political Stability in Six Countries, 1996–2011.

Year	Denmark	Finland	Hong Kong	New Zealand	Singapore	India
1996	98.1	97.6	59.6	93.8	85.1	19.2
1998	97.6	99.0	64.4	94.2	75.0	14.4
2000	96.2	99.5	76.0	94.2	81.3	18.3
2002	97.1	100.0	74.5	94.7	88.5	15.4
2003	89.9	100.0	77.4	89.4	77.9	8.7
2004	83.2	100.0	86.5	99.0	87.0	13.5
2005	83.2	100.0	92.8	89.9	87.0	17.8
2006	83.2	100.0	88.0	92.8	93.3	16.3
2007	87.0	100.0	85.6	93.8	91.8	13.5
2008	86.1	99.5	87.1	90.0	96.2	13.9
2009	85.3	95.7	83.4	84.8	90.0	10.4
2010	85.8	94.8	78.8	90.6	89.6	10.8
2011	86.8	97.6	77.8	97.2	90.1	12.7
Average	89.2	98.7	79.4	92.6	87.1	14.2
Rank	3	1	5	2	4	6

Source: Retrieved from http://info.worldbank.org/governance/wgi/mc_chart.asp.

Table 3. Rule of Law in Six Countries, 1996–2011.

Year	Denmark	Finland	Hong Kong	New Zealand	Singapore	India
1996	97.6	99.0	68.4	98.6	89.5	59.3
1998	98.1	100.0	80.4	98.6	90.0	60.3
2000	97.1	100.0	72.2	96.2	87.6	59.8
2002	99.0	99.5	87.1	96.2	90.9	51.2
2003	99.0	100.0	91.9	96.7	93.3	55.0
2004	98.6	99.5	92.8	96.7	94.7	54.1
2005	99.0	99.5	92.8	97.1	95.7	57.9
2006	100.0	99.0	91.9	96.7	92.3	56.9
2007	100.0	98.6	90.9	96.7	92.3	56.0
2008	99.5	98.1	90.9	97.1	92.3	56.3
2009	98.6	100.0	90.5	99.1	92.4	55.0
2010	98.6	100.0	91.0	98.1	92.9	54.5
2011	99.1	100.0	90.6	98.6	93.4	52.6
Average	98.8	99.5	87.0	97.4	92.1	56.1
Rank	2	1	5	3	4	6

Source: Retrieved from http://info.worldbank.org/governance/wgi/mc_chart.asp.

stable, with a higher degree of rule of law and government effectiveness than India, according to the World Bank's indicators on these three aspects. Hence, it is not surprising that these five countries have also performed better than India in terms of control of corruption, as can be seen in Table 5.

Table 4. Government Effectiveness in Six Countries, 1996–2011.

Year	Denmark	Finland	Hong Kong	New Zealand	Singapore	India
1996	96.6	94.1	86.8	97.1	100.0	53.7
1998	98.5	99.0	86.8	91.2	100.0	54.1
2000	97.6	99.5	88.3	89.8	100.0	51.2
2002	99.5	100.0	89.3	92.7	93.7	51.7
2003	99.5	100.0	91.7	93.7	96.6	55.1
2004	100.0	99.0	91.7	95.6	96.1	55.1
2005	99.5	100.0	91.7	94.1	99.0	55.1
2006	100.0	99.0	97.1	92.7	99.5	54.1
2007	99.5	97.6	96.6	93.2	100.0	56.8
2008	99.5	99.0	97.1	93.7	100.0	53.4
2009	100.0	99.0	96.2	97.6	99.5	54.5
2010	99.0	99.5	94.7	97.1	100.0	55.5
2011	99.5	100.0	94.3	98.1	99.1	54.5
Average	99.1	98.9	92.5	94.4	98.7	54.2
Rank	1	2	5	4	3	6

Source: Retrieved from http://info.worldbank.org/governance/wgi/mc_chart.asp.

Table 5. Control of Corruption in Six Countries, 1996–2011.

Year	Denmark	Finland	Hong Kong	New Zealand	Singapore	India
1996	100.0	99.5	90.7	98.0	96.6	40.0
1998	99.5	100.0	91.7	98.0	96.1	43.9
2000	99.5	100.0	90.7	98.5	96.6	46.3
2002	99.5	100.0	92.7	99.0	98.5	38.0
2003	99.5	100.0	93.2	99.0	98.0	42.9
2004	99.5	100.0	94.1	99.0	98.5	43.4
2005	99.0	100.0	93.2	98.5	98.0	43.9
2006	99.5	100.0	93.7	99.0	97.6	46.3
2007	100.0	99.5	93.7	99.0	97.6	40.8
2008	100.0	99.0	94.2	98.5	98.1	44.2
2009	100.0	98.6	94.3	99.5	98.1	37.8
2010	100.0	98.1	94.7	99.5	98.6	35.4
2011	100.0	98.6	94.3	99.5	96.2	35.1
Average	99.7	99.5	93.2	98.8	97.6	41.4
Rank	1	2	5	3	4	6

Source: Retrieved from http://info.worldbank.org/governance/wgi/mc_chart.asp.

In short, the analysis of the different policy contexts in the six countries demonstrates clearly that India has the most unfavorable policy context for implementing its anti-corruption measures effectively because it has the largest land area and population with the lowest GDP per capita, and a lower level of political stability, rule of law, government effectiveness, and control of corruption than the other five countries. Table 6 shows that Finland has performed best overall on the four governance indicators, followed by Denmark, New Zealand, Singapore, Hong Kong, and India. Hence, it is not surprising why India has been less effective in curbing corruption than these five countries because of its unfavorable policy context and lack of political will.

THREE PATHS TO CURBING CORRUPTION

A comparison of the different paths taken by the six countries to curb corruption reveals that they have relied on three methods, depending on whether their anti-corruption measures rely on anti-corruption laws without an anti-corruption agency (ACA), a single ACA or multiple ACAs to implement the anti-corruption laws as depicted in Table 7. Unlike Singapore and Hong Kong, which rely on the Corrupt Practices Investigation Bureau

Table 6. Average Ranking of Six Countries on Four Governance Indicators.

Country	Political Stability	Rule of Law	Government Effectiveness	Control of Corruption	Overall Ranking
Finland	98.7 (1)	99.5 (1)	98.9 (2)	99.5 (2)	1.50 (1)
Denmark	89.2 (3)	98.8 (2)	99.1 (1)	99.7 (1)	1.75 (2)
New Zealand	92.6 (2)	97.4 (3)	94.4 (4)	98.8 (3)	3.00 (3)
Singapore	87.1 (4)	92.1 (4)	98.7 (3)	97.6 (4)	3.75 (4)
Hong Kong	79.4 (5)	87.0 (5)	92.5 (5)	93.2 (5)	5.00 (5)
India	14.2 (6)	56.1 (6)	54.2 (6)	41.4 (6)	6.00 (6)

Source: Compiled from Tables 2–5.

Table 7. Three Paths to Curbing Corruption in Six Countries.

Path	Features	Countries
1	Reliance on anti-corruption laws without an ACA	Denmark, Finland, New Zealand
2	Reliance on a single ACA to implement anti-corruption laws	Singapore, Hong Kong
3	Reliance on multiple ACAs to implement anti-corruption laws	India

(CPIB) and Independent Commission Against Corruption (ICAC) respectively to curb corruption, Denmark, Finland, and New Zealand have relied instead on other watchdog institutions to implement their zero-tolerance policy toward corruption. On the other hand, India has relied on multiple ACAs to implement its anti-corruption laws.

CURBING CORRUPTION WITHOUT A SINGLE ANTI-CORRUPTION AGENCY

Finland's Ombudsman and Chancellor of Justice

In her insightful and comprehensive analysis of governance and corruption in Finland, Paula Tiihonen (2003, pp. 108–111) has provided 13 reasons to explain why corruption is not a serious problem in Finland. Among the reasons cited by her, is the important role played by the Ombudsman and the Chancellor of Justice, who are "the highest and most highly regarded jurists in Finland" (Tiihonen, 2003, p. 110). According to Finland's Ministry of Foreign Affairs (2006, p. 7), the efficiency and high public profile of these two individuals, who have the authority to monitor and investigate the actions of public servants and political leaders at the highest levels, has prevented abuses and contributed to the country's low level of perceived corruption.

The institution of the Justice Ombudsman was first established in Sweden in 1809 to supervise public administration by investigating public complaints of official wrongdoing (Caiden, Macdermot & Sandler, 1983, p. 10). The Ombudsman was introduced in Finland on February 7, 1920 and he served on a part-time basis during the first 12 years and was inadequately assisted by only a legal secretary.[2] Initially, the Ombudsman was overshadowed by the better known Chancellor of Justice as it received only 106 complaints in 1928. However, in 1963, the situation was reversed as the Ombudsman received 1,029 complaints while the Chancellor received only 479 complaints. By 1999, the number of complaints lodged with the Ombudsman increased to 2,788 with the Chancellor receiving only 1,138 complaints (Modeen, 2000, p. 319). During the first 59 years, the number of complaints investigated by the Ombudsman increased from 75 complaints during his first year of operation in 1920 to 2,725 complaints in 1979 (Aalto, 1983, p. 95). According to Ari Salminen, in Chapter 3 on Finland, the Ombudsman's workload has increased further in recent years with the number of complaints exceeding 4,000 complaints annually.

The Chancellor of Justice was created earlier in 1919 to ensure that the government observes the law by supervising the actions of the President, Cabinet members, and other public officials (Kastari, 1968, p. 60). Unlike the Ombudsman, who is appointed by Parliament, the Chancellor is appointed by the President and reports to the Government and Parliament. As the Ombudsman and Chancellor of Justice are both responsible for the legal regulation and supervision of legality in Finland, Ari Salminen in Chapter 3 points out that the Chancellor focuses on the misconduct of public servants while the Ombudsman deals with cases involving violations of the principles of equality and impartiality.

In their comparative analysis of the corruption-related cases investigated by both institutions from 2000 to 2005, Salminen, Viinamaki, and Ikola-Norrbacka (2007, pp. 89—90) found that the top five types of the 538 cases handled by the Ombudsman involved delayed issues, violating the principle of equality, negligence, improper justification of decisions, and lack of publicity. In contrast, among the 188 cases investigated by the Chancellor of Justice, the top five topics were delayed issues, disqualification, inadequate hearing of the parties involved, insufficient advice, and misuse of public office. In spite of their different emphasis, Table 8 shows that there is overlapping in five types of the corruption-related cases investigated by both agencies. However, Walter Gellhorn (1966, p. 64) has noted that in spite of their overlapping duties, and the "broad opportunity thus presented for conflict between these high offices, no friction seems to have occurred."

Thus, the small number of corruption-related cases investigated by both the Ombudsman and Chancellor of Justice during 2000—2005 confirms

Table 8. Common Types of Corruption-Related Cases Investigated by Finland's Ombudsman and Chancellor of Justice, 2000—2005.

Type of Case	No. of Cases Investigated by the Ombudsman	No. of Cases Investigated by the Chancellor of Justice
Delayed issues	129	73
Improper justification of decisions	53	8
Lack of publicity	49	12
Inadequate hearing of the parties involved	43	20
Insufficient advice	29	15

Source: Compiled from Tables 3 and 4 in Salminen, Viinamaki, and Ikola-Noorbacka (2007, pp. 89—90).

that corruption is not a serious problem in Finland. Furthermore, while both institutions are responsible for investigating corruption-related cases, the Ombudsman's role appears to be more important as its workload is almost three times heavier than that of the Chancellor of Justice during these six years. In short, what Walter Gellhorn (1966, p. 87) wrote 47 years ago that their role as "the public's watchmen against official mistakes" was "generally regarded as a valuable shield against oppression" remains valid today.

Denmark's Ombudsman and Audit Institutions

The Ombudsman was established in Denmark by Parliament in December 1954 and the first Ombudsman, Stephan Hurwitz, Professor of Criminal Law at the University of Copenhagen, was elected on March 29, and assumed office on April 1, 1955 (Gellhorn, 1966, p. 5; Pedersen, 1968, p. 77). According to the Danish Constitution of June 1953, the Ombudsman's role is to "supervise the civil and military administration of the state and the administration of local government authorities." The Ombudsman Act of 1954 states specifically that the Ombudsman's duty is to "see whether any person coming within his sphere of authority commits faults or acts of negligence in the performance of his duties." Investigations are initiated by the Ombudsman on the basis of complaints received or on his own initiative (Nielsen, 1983, pp. 73–75). The current Ombudsman, Jorgen Steen Sorensen, said that the Parliamentary Ombudsman was introduced to "meet the individual citizen's need for an independent, free and easily accessible appeal body" and to "monitor the administration's use of the rules that had been passed" (Danish Parliamentary Ombudsman, 2012, p. 10).

The complaints dealt with by the Ombudsman were wide ranging and classified into 12 categories by a Judge of the City Court of Copenhagen, I. M. Pedersen (1968, pp. 84–90), based on her analysis of the cases presented in the annual reports: (1) qualifications of those officials making decisions; (2) bias or conflict of interest; (3) completeness and correctness of evidence; (4) failure to provide applicants with information about evidence and sufficient opportunity to argue their case; (5) other procedural rights of the applicants; (6) information on reasons for decisions; (7) information on an applicant's right to appeal; (8) administrative standards; (9) unnecessary delay; (10) other errors; (11) questions of law; and (12) discretionary powers. However, the 4,922 cases concluded by the Ombudsman in 2011 are distributed into these nine administrative areas: labor market and social law (34.3 percent); justice and aliens (25.3 percent); environment, building, and housing law (9.9 percent); local and regional authorities, health, foreign affairs, and defense (8.6 percent); personnel cases (6.1 percent); business and energy (4 percent); education, research, ecclesiastical affairs, and culture (4 percent); and transport, communications, and roads (2.6 percent) (Danish Parliamentary Ombudsman, 2012, p. 99).

The Ombudsman's workload has increased greatly over the years. During 1955−1970, the average number of cases investigated per year was 1,100, ranging from 964 cases in 1970 to 1,370 cases in 1964 (Nielsen, 1983, p. 76). Table 9 shows that the number of cases investigated by the Ombudsman has increased from 3,725 in 2002 to 4,909 in 2011. With only 88 employees and a budget of DKK 54,527,000 (US$9,482,957[3]) the Ombudsman's heavy workload has put a severe strain on its limited resources, and requires it to "prioritize ruthlessly" those cases it can investigate to ensure the optimal use of its resources (Danish Parliamentary Ombudsman, 2012, pp. 13, 81, 83).

The Ombudsman's role in ensuring good governance (including combating corruption) in Denmark is supplemented by the Public Accounts Committee (PAC) and Auditor General's Office (AGO), both of which supervise the use of public resources and report to Parliament and the public. The PAC consists of six members appointed by Parliament and is responsible for reviewing the AGO's annual report and presenting its findings to Parliament. It can also request the AGO to investigate various matters. The AGO is an independent agency that audits the state's accounts to prevent mistakes and ensures that its finances are spent properly.

Table 9. Number of Cases Investigated by the Danish Ombudsman, 2002−2011.

Year	Cases Investigated
2002	3,725
2003	4,298
2004	4,093
2005	4,266
2006	4,110
2007	3,976
2008	4,229
2009	4,379
2010	4,994
2011	4,909

Source: Danish Parliamentary Ombudsman (2012, p. 23).

The Auditor General, who heads the AGO, is appointed by the Speaker of Parliament on the PAC's recommendation (Danish Parliament, 2013).

While the Danish Parliamentary Ombudsman has squeezed "the arrogance out of government" by usefully disposing of "dissatisfactions engendered by an official's having strayed from common patterns of rightful conduct," he is not "a panacea for the cure of governmental ills" (Gellhorn, 1966, pp. 44–47). Nevertheless, as pointed out by Judge Pedersen (1968, p. 94), the Danish Ombudsman "has proved to be an extremely useful institution" by supplementing control without "hampering the efficiency or independence of the administration" through its reliance on "a small personnel" and responding quickly to the complaints received. In sum, the effectiveness of the Ombudsman, PAC and AGO, in promoting good governance in Denmark has contributed to its low level of perceived corruption.

New Zealand's Ombudsman and Serious Fraud Office

New Zealand is the first country outside the Scandinavian countries to introduce the Ombudsman on October 1, 1962 (Northey, 1968, p. 127; Satyanand, 2005, p. 213). The Parliamentary Commission (Ombudsman) Act of 1962 was amended in 1975 to extend the Ombudsman's jurisdiction to include local government organizations and to provide for the appointment of more than one Ombudsman (Lundvik, 1983, p. 136). The two Ombudsmen are Officers of Parliament appointed by the Governor-General on the recommendation of Parliament. They are also accountable to Parliament through the Speaker of the House of Representatives and their budget is provided by Parliament. These arrangements ensure their independence and enhance their ability to withstand pressure from government departments or ministers (Satyanand, 2005, p. 215).

In Ghana and Papua New Guinea, the Ombudsman is responsible for investigating allegations of corruption. However, in New Zealand the Ombudsmen's role in curbing corruption is indirect because of their role in enhancing the Government's transparency and accountability by acting on complaints about maladministration or by providing, where appropriate, official information. This means that the Ombudsmen can, in the course of their work, "become aware of evidence of corruption and can be in a position to recommend action regarding it" (Satyanand, 2005, p. 224).

Describing the New Zealand's Ombudsman as "a striking personal success," Walter Gellhorn (1966, pp. 152–153) cited a friendly civil servant who revealed that "when the Ombudsman began, we wondered whether he was going to be a blasted thorn in our side; but now we are glad to have him." Sir Ronald Algie, a former Speaker of the House of Representatives, has provided several reasons for the Ombudsman's success in New Zealand:

> The ombudsman system probably would not work well everywhere. It works well in New Zealand because we have a fine public service. Corruption is so rare as to be deemed virtually non-existent. Officials generally seek to serve rather than to defeat citizens. … Our Ombudsman may stimulate officials to be even a little bit better than they have been. But the ombudsman system is succeeding here precisely because, really, there isn't a staggering lot for it to do. (Gellhorn, 1966, p. 153)

In other words, Algie has attributed the Ombudsman's success in New Zealand to its fine public service, low level of corruption, and its light workload.

Unlike the Ombudsman's indirect role in combating corruption, the Serious Fraud Office (SFO) was established in 1990 to combat serious economic crime because the New Zealand Government realized the need to "create a new and highly efficient organization to deal with corrupt business practices expeditiously" after the economic crisis in the late 1980s (Sturt, 1996, p. 305). The SFO's website describes it as "a small, highly specialized government department responsible for complex or serious fraud investigations and prosecutions" (SFO, 2013a).

The SFO differs from its counterpart in the United Kingdom because its Director is not seconded from the police and has the power to obtain and execute search warrants. Furthermore, the SFO's lawyers provide advice as prosecutors throughout the investigation of cases but do not participate in the investigatory process. More importantly, the SFO is an independent government department as its Director is not responsible to the Attorney General and is "free from political direction or influence" regarding the investigations and prosecutions undertaken by the SFO (Sturt, 1996, pp. 306–307).

The SFO (2013b, p. 9) uses these four indicators to assess the impact of its activities: (1) increasing business and investor confidence; (2) increasing public confidence that those who commit financial crime are held to account; (3) minimizing the impact of financial crime on the regulatory environment; and (4) maintaining New Zealand's international reputation for low levels of corruption. The number of cases investigated by the SFO has increased from 134 cases in 2009/2010 to 465 cases in 2011/2012. With a staff of 52 personnel and a budget of NZ\$7.89 million in 2012, the SFO has performed well as reflected in its 100 percent conviction rate from 2010 to 2012 and the positive survey findings on the public confidence in its role[4] (SFO, 2013b, pp. 14, 17, 47, 79).

In short, the SFO and Ombudsman are two important institutions responsible for ensuring good governance and maintaining the low level of perceived corruption in New Zealand.

CURBING CORRUPTION WITH A SINGLE ANTI-CORRUPTION AGENCY

Singapore's Corrupt Practices Investigation Bureau

During the British colonial period, corruption was a way of life in Singapore and the task of corruption control was delegated in December 1937 to the Anti-Corruption Branch (ACB) within the Criminal Investigation Department of the Singapore Police Force (SPF), even though police corruption was rampant and documented by the 1879 and 1886 Commissions of Inquiry. The fallacy of this ineffective method of relying on the ACB to curb corruption was exposed 14 years later by the Opium Hijacking scandal in October 1951 when it was discovered that several police detectives were responsible for stealing 1,800 pounds of opium worth S$400,000 (US$133,133). The investigations of the scandal resulted in the dissolution of the ACB and its replacement by the CPIB in October 1952.

Thus, Singapore's breakthrough in corruption control can be traced to this important decision to transfer the function of combating corruption from the SPF to a separate agency outside its purview. However, the CPIB was not effective during its first eight years because of its small number of personnel (most of them being seconded from the SPF) and its inadequate legal powers. The CPIB's initial handicaps were removed in June 1960, when the Prevention of Corruption Act (POCA) was enacted, one year after the People's Action Party (PAP) government assumed office after winning the May 1959 general election. The CPIB was given a new lease of life by the POCA, which empowered it to perform its anti-corruption functions effectively.

Even though the CPIB comes under the purview of the Prime Minister's Office, it operates independently and has investigated many corruption cases involving senior civil servants and political leaders, including members of the ruling government. Indeed, the PAP government's zero tolerance for corruption is reflected in the CPIB's impartial enforcement of the POCA, which means that corrupt offenders, regardless of their status or position, are punished according to the law if found guilty. Furthermore, the PAP government's political will in combating corruption is reflected in the increase in the CPIB's personnel from 13 to 138 persons during 1952−2011, and its budget from S$1.02 million in 1978 to S$34.07 million in 2011.

Singapore's status as the least corrupt Asian country is confirmed by its consistently good performance on the five international indicators of the perceived extent of corruption and the small number of corruption cases (about 200 cases per year during 2008−2012) investigated by the CPIB. Apart from attracting worldwide attention as reflected in the 13,031 foreign delegates visiting the CPIB from 2005 to 2012, the CPIB's effectiveness in curbing corruption has also resulted in the adoption of a single ACA in many Asian countries since its inception in October 1952 (Quah, 2011, pp. 27−28).

Hong Kong's Independent Commission Against Corruption

As a British Colony, Hong Kong had also relied on the Anti-Corruption Branch (ACB) within the Royal Hong Kong Police Force (RHKPF) from 1948 to 1971 to curb corruption even though police corruption was rampant. The ACB was upgraded into the Anti-Corruption Office (ACO) in 1971, but the ACO was ineffective even though it was given more manpower. The escape of a corruption suspect, Chief Superintendent of Police Peter F. Godber, on June 8, 1973 to Britain angered the public and undermined the ACO's credibility (Quah, 2011, p. 252). The Blair-Kerr Commission of Inquiry appointed by the government to investigate Godber's escape recommended that the ACO should not remain within the RHKPF for "political and psychological" reasons. Accordingly, Governor Murray MacLehose accepted the Commission's recommendation to create a new ACA that was independent of the RHKPF. According to H. J. Lethbridge (1985, p. 98):

> Godber's activities had thus awakened and illuminated the Governor as to the serious-
> ness of the problem [of corruption]. Godber had fortified his resolve to create an anti-
> corruption organization that would be independent of the police, a force which had
> sheltered Godber comfortably for so many years.

Thus, the revelation of Godber's corrupt activities and the adverse publicity on his escape to Britain was the catalyst that made the governor accept the risk of breaking the RHKPF's control over the investigation of corruption. Lethbridge (1985, pp. 101−102) has described Governor MacLehose's decision as "path-breaking" because many previous governors and committees "had deferred to the police for a variety of reasons but principally because they feared a collapse of police morale if the control of corruption was handed over to an independent body." Governor MacLehose informed the members of the Legislative Council on October 17, 1973 that an independent ACA separate from the RHKPF was necessary because the public would have more confidence in such an agency. Four months later, the ICAC was formed on February 15, 1974.

Section 12 of the ICAC Ordinance of 1974 describes the Commissioner's duties as the investigation and prevention of corruption including the "education of the public against the evils of corruption and the enlisting and fostering of public support in combating it" (Lethbridge, 1985, p. 104). Ian Scott has provided a comprehensive analysis of the ICAC's important community relations strategy in Chapter 4, which focuses on its prevention and education functions. The ICAC's three-pronged strategy focusing on investigation, prevention, and education has contributed to its success in curbing corruption because it has (1) inculcated fear among corrupt offenders by enforcing the anti-corruption laws impartially; (2) reduced opportunities for corruption by streamlining procedures and management processes to prevent corruption; and (3) changed the population's attitudes toward corruption through community education and publicity (Cheung, 2008, p. 106).

The ICAC's success in minimizing corruption is reflected in Hong Kong's favorable performance on the five international indicators of corruption, which makes it the second least corrupt territory in Asia after Singapore. John R. Heilbrunn (2006, p. 136) describes the ICAC as the universal model of anti-corruption commissions because of its emphasis on the "investigative, preventive and communicative functions" and its "resounding success in fighting corruption." Like Singapore's CPIB, the ICAC has also attracted worldwide interest as 891 foreign delegates from 47 countries and five international organizations visited the ICAC during 2012 (ICAC, 2013, pp. 89–90).

CURBING CORRUPTION WITH MANY
ANTI-CORRUPTION AGENCIES: THE CASE OF INDIA

India initiated her fight against corruption in 1941 with the establishment of the Delhi Special Police Establishment (DSPE) to "investigate cases of bribery and corruption in transactions" involving the War and Supply Departments because the growth in expenditure during the early years of World War II increased the opportunities for corruption. In 1948, the DSPE was placed under the charge of the Inspector General of Police, and in April 1963, the government formed the Central Bureau of Investigation (CBI) by incorporating the DSPE as one of its six divisions, namely, the Investigation and Anti-Corruption Division (Quah, 2011, pp. 92−94).

As the lead ACA in India, the CBI today has seven divisions and is responsible for these three functions: (1) combating corruption in public life, and curbing economic and violent crimes through meticulous investigation and prosecution; (2) help fight cyber and high-technology crime; and (3) play a leading role in the war against national and transnational organized crime (CBI, 2010, p. iv). However, the CBI is not the only ACA in India as the Central Vigilance Commission (CVC) was established in February 1964 on the recommendation of the Santhanam Committee to "investigate any complaint or suspicion of improper behavior" against a civil servant.

The CBI is organized into 16 zones and 60 branches to cater for India's vast territory. Each state has at least a branch or unit of the CBI at the state capital or at a major city (CBI, 2010, p. 6). The 28 states in India have their own State Vigilance Commissions (SVCs) and Anti-Corruption Bureaus (ACBs) for dealing, respectively, with vigilance and anti-corruption work, but these ACBs derive their powers of investigation from the Police Act as they are regular police units. The SVCs are patterned after the CVC and are assisted by the special police establishments in conducting investigations. They investigate those transactions where public servants are suspected or alleged to be involved in corrupt behavior (Sharma & Sharma, 2009, pp. 437−438).

In his negative assessment of India's multiple ACAs, especially the CBI, S. S. Gill, a former senior civil servant, lamented that:

> Looking at the number of agencies created to tackle corruption, it would appear that the government was in dead earnest to eradicate this malady.... Yet this elaborate and multi-layered apparatus to control administrative corruption has hardly made a dent on the situation. The CBI is the star investigation and prosecuting agency of the government.... Yet, the public perceives it to be a pliable tool of the ruling party, and its investigations tend to become cover-up operations for the misdeeds of the ministers.... That the CBI goes only after the small fry is shown by the fact that only one gazetted officer was dismissed as a result of its endeavors in 1972 and two in 1992.... Much more dismal is its record in its investigation into mega scams from Bofors onwards. (Gill, 1998, pp. 237−238)

Table 10. India's Performance on Five Indicators, 2011–2013.

Indicator	Rank	Score	No. of Countries
Corruption Perceptions Index 2012	94th	36	176
PERC Survey on Corruption 2013	17th	8.95	17
Control of Corruption 2011	35.1	−0.56	215
Ease of Doing Business Rank 2013	132nd	NA	185
Public Trust of Politicians 2012	106	2.2	144

Sources: Retrieved from http://cpi.transparency.org/cpi2012/results/; PERC (2013, p. 6); http://info.worldbank.org/governance/wgi/mc_chart.asp; World Bank (2013, p. 3); and Schwab (2012, p. 391).

Furthermore, Gill's (1998, p. 127) harsh indictment that corruption has infected the whole system in India, with every level devising "its own methods of extortion," confirms the failure of its ACAs, which is reflected in its low rankings and scores on the five international indicators, as shown in Table 10.[5]

FIVE LESSONS FOR OTHER COUNTRIES

What lessons can other countries learn from the three different paths to curbing corruption taken by Finland, Denmark, New Zealand, Singapore, Hong Kong, and India? As the policy contexts of these six countries differ from the policy contexts of other countries, these contextual differences must be taken into account as "the nature of a particular bureaucracy is linked to the system of government and the society in which it operates" because its options are limited by the social and political context (Sayre, 1967, p. 354).

Lesson 1: Political Will and Good Governance Are Needed for
Effective Corruption Control

Why are Denmark, Finland, Hong Kong, New Zealand, and Singapore more effective than India in curbing corruption? The short answer is: good governance and political will, which Sahr J. Kpundeh (1998, p. 92) has defined as "the demonstrated credible intent of political actors (elected or appointed leaders, civil society watchdogs, stakeholder groups, etc.) to attack perceived causes or effects of corruption at a systemic level." He further contends that political will is "a critical starting point for sustainable and effective programs" because "without it, governments' statements to reform civil service, strengthen transparency and accountability, and reinvent the relationship between government and private industry remain mere rhetoric" (Kpundeh, 1998, p. 92). Indeed, without political will, anti-corruption measures will fail as they are not supported by the political leaders in a country. According to Ian Senior (2006, p. 184), who was also quoted in Chapter 6 on Singapore, that political will is indispensable for effective corruption control because politicians have the power to "change a culture of corruption" as they "make the laws and allocate the funds that enable the laws to be enforced."

The governments of the five richer countries are committed not only to minimizing corruption, but also to ensuring good governance. Corruption is closely related to governance in two ways. As the independent variable, corruption is an important factor determining the governance of a country, which is the dependent variable. From this perspective, curbing corruption constitutes a necessary but insufficient prerequisite for good governance. Conversely, if corruption is the dependent variable, poor governance is an important independent variable, as highlighted by Gerald E. Caiden in his analysis of the major causes of corruption in Chapter 8.[6] In other words, corruption is not only an important cause of poor governance, but is also a serious consequence of poor governance in a country (Quah, 2009, pp. 125–126).

If a country is well governed like the five countries, it is less likely to suffer from corruption if the government implements impartially the anti-corruption measures. On the other hand, if a country is poorly governed like India, it is more likely to be afflicted by rampant corruption because the government lacks the political will to implement impartially the anti-corruption measures. In Chapter 2, Michael Johnston argues that Denmark's good record in corruption control is also a reflection that it has governed well and effectively. Similarly, Paula Tiihonen (2003, pp. 100, 112) observes that as corruption is viewed as a crime and "a part of bad governance and/or politics," Finland's consensus system and "fairly unanimous" power elite "support good governance and prevent corruption." In Chapter 5, Robert Gregory and Daniel Zirker attribute New Zealand's low level of perceived corruption to its "strong egalitarian ethos" and its staunch "commitment to impartiality and rule of law in the administration of public policy." Tables 2–6 confirm that Finland, Denmark, New Zealand, Singapore, and Hong Kong (in descending order) have much higher percentile ranks on the four governance indicators on political stability, rule of law, government effectiveness, and control of corruption, than India.

The linkage between poor governance and rampant corruption is demonstrated clearly by the poor performance of several Asian countries and the superior performance of the five countries on the 2013 Failed States Index (FSI) and 2012 CPI, as depicted in Table 11. As failed states are "consumed by internal violence and cease delivering positive political goods to their inhabitants," it is not surprising that corruption "thrives on an unusually destructive scale" in these states because there is both widespread "petty or lubricating corruption" and "escalating levels of venal corruption" (Rotberg, 2004, p. 8). Table 11 shows that the failed states of Afghanistan, Pakistan, North Korea, Myanmar, Sri Lanka, and Bangladesh have much lower CPI scores than Finland, Denmark, New Zealand, and Singapore,[7] which have the lowest scores on the 2013 FSI. India's ranking and score on

Table 11. Performance of Selected Countries on the Failed States Index of 2013 and Corruption Perceptions Index of 2012.

Country	Failed States Index 2013 Rank and Score[a]	Corruption Perceptions Index 2012 Rank and Score[b]
Afghanistan	7th (106.7)	174th (8)
Pakistan	13th (102.9)	139th (27)
North Korea	23rd (95.1)	174th (8)
Myanmar	26th (94.6)	172nd (15)
Sri Lanka	28th (92.9)	79th (40)
Bangladesh	29th (92.5)	144th (26)
China	66th (80.9)	80th (39)
India	79th (77.5)	94th (36)
Singapore	158th (34.0)	5th (87)
New Zealand	173rd (22.7)	1st (90)
Denmark	174th (21.9)	1st (90)
Finland	178th (18.0)	1st (90)
No. of countries	178	176

Sources: Retrieved from http://ffp.statesindex.org/rankings_2013-sortable; and http://cpi.transparency.org/ cpi2012/ results/.
[a]The Failed States Index of 2013 score ranges from 0 to 120, with a higher score indicating a higher degree of state failure. The score is based on a country's performance on these 12 indicators: demographic pressures; displacement of refugees; group grievances; human flight; uneven development; economic decline; delegitimization of the State; public services; human rights; security apparatus; fractionalized elites; and external intervention.
[b]The CPI 2012 score ranges from 0 (highly corrupt) to 100 (very clean).

the 2013 FSI is better than China's but pales in comparison with the lowest 2013 FSI scores of the other four countries.

In short, Finland, Denmark, New Zealand, Singapore and Hong Kong are more effective than India and other Asian countries in corruption control because of the political will of their governments in curbing corruption and their good governance.

Lesson 2: Rely on a Single ACA Instead of Many ACAs for Effective Corruption Control

As discussed above and in Chapter 6, the Opium Hijacking scandal of October 1951 in Singapore, which made the British colonial government realize the futility of relying on the ACB when police corruption was rampant, was the triggering event that led to the CPIB's formation one year later. Similarly, the escape of Chief Superintendent of Police, Peter Godber, from Hong Kong to Britain on June 8, 1973, triggered a chain of events which culminated in the creation of the ICAC in February 1974. The subsequent effectiveness of the CPIB and ICAC has confirmed that the British colonial governments in Singapore and Hong Kong made the correct decision in abandoning their reliance on the police to curb corruption in 1952 and 1974, respectively.

As the CBI is a police agency and the state ACBs derive their investigation powers from the Police Act, India has unfortunately not learnt this important lesson from Singapore's and Hong Kong's success in curbing corruption namely: "do not rely on the police to curb corruption" especially when the police are corrupt because this "would be like giving candy to a child [and] expecting that it would not be eaten" (Quah, 2004, pp. 1—2). As police corruption remains a serious problem in India today, it is indeed surprising that the Government of India has continued to rely for the past 50 years on the CBI as the lead ACA to curb corruption even though this traditional British method of relying on the police for corruption control has been shown to be ineffective.

The CPIB's and ICAC's success in corruption control has also led to a proliferation of single ACAs in 13 other Asian countries. However, unlike the CPIB and ICAC, these ACAs have failed to curb corruption effectively because of their lack of political will and unfavorable policy contexts (Quah, 2013, pp. 21—22). In other words, the strategy of relying on a single ACA in a country will only be effective if the incumbent government provides it with sufficient legal powers, budget, personnel, and operational autonomy, and if the policy context is favorable.

Assuming that there is political will and a favorable policy context, the policy-makers in a country can follow the examples of Finland, Denmark, and New Zealand of not relying on a single ACA but on other institutions like the Ombudsman, Chancellor of Justice, and SFO, to maintain good governance. Their success in corruption control shows that the establishment of a single ACA is not always necessary. For example, the National Integrity Assessment of Finland conducted by Ari Salminen, Rinna Ikola-Norrbacka, and Venla Mantysalo in 2011 for Transparency Suomi (2012, p. 7) has concluded that even though Finland does not have an ACA, "the system functions well for the most part." In their view, an ACA is not needed in Finland because "establishing [such] a new agency would require additional resources, with no guarantees of effectiveness."

An ACA is a specialized agency created by a government to minimize corruption in the country by providing centralized leadership in these core areas of anti-corruption activity: "policy analysis and technical assistance in prevention, public outreach and information, monitoring, investigation, and prosecution" (Meagher, 2005, p. 70). Consequently, an ACA has many advantages over other less specialized agencies formed to deal with corruption, namely: reduced administrative costs; reduced uncertainty over jurisdiction by avoiding duplication of powers and work; a high degree of specialization and expertise; a high degree of autonomy; separateness from the agencies and departments that it will be investigating; high public credibility and profile; established security protection; political, legal, and public accountability; clarity in the assessment of its progress, successes, and failures; and swift action against corruption because task-specific resources are used and officials are not subjected to the competing priorities of general law enforcement, audit, and similar agencies (Nicholls, Daniel, Polaine & Hatchard 2006, p. 476; UNODC, 2004, pp. 89−90).

Perhaps the key advantage of creating an ACA highlighted by the United Nations Office on Drugs and Crime (UNODC) (2004, p. 90) is that it sends a powerful signal to the citizens in the country that the government is committed to fighting corruption. But, this asset will be lost if the government does not provide the new ACA with sufficient legal powers, adequate human and financial resources, and operational autonomy to enable its officers to investigate those accused of corrupt offenses, regardless of their status or position. More importantly, the advantages of establishing a single ACA listed in the previous paragraph are not applicable if a country relies instead on several ACAs because of the conflict and competition between these multiple agencies.

India's reliance on the ineffective CBI, CVC, and its state agencies is not unique as the Philippines, China, Vietnam, and Taiwan have also depended on ineffective multiple ACAs to curb corruption. The reliance on five ACAs[8] by the Philippines has resulted in "resource and effort-dilution in the anti-corruption efforts due to duplication, layering and turf wars" (Quimson, 2006, p. 30). There is also no coordination or cooperation among these ACAs, which compete for recognition, staff, and resources because they are understaffed and poorly funded. Furthermore, their overlapping jurisdictions not only diffuse anti-corruption efforts but also result in "poor coordination in policy and program implementation, weak management and wastage of resources" (Oyamada, 2005, p. 99).

In China, the lack of coordination among several ACAs has compelled the Central Commission for Disciplinary Inspection, Supreme People's Procuratorate, and the Ministry of Supervision to improve cooperation among themselves from 1993. Similarly, in Vietnam, the National Anti-Corruption Steering Committee was created in 2006 to coordinate the anti-corruption activities of the six ACAs (Quah, 2007a, pp. 4–6). Finally, the establishment of the Agency Against Corruption in Taiwan on July 20, 2011 to supplement the anti-corruption efforts of the existing Ministry of Justice Investigation Bureau and the Public Prosecutors Offices has not resolved the problems of lack of coordination, overlapping of functions, and competition for resources between these three ACAs (Quah, 2011, pp. 195–196).

In other words, the second lesson is that if a government decides to establish an ACA instead of relying on other institutions to curb corruption and ensure good governance, it should establish a single ACA instead of multiple ACAs, and provide it with the necessary resources, legal powers, and operational autonomy to implement the anti-corruption laws effectively.

Lesson 3: Importance of Cultural Values in Minimizing Corruption

Culture contributes to corruption in those countries where cultural practices like gift-giving, *guanxi* (connections), and family ties influence individuals to give or receive bribes (Quah, 2011, p. 21). According to Peter Larmour (2012, p. 116), culture has often been used "to explain, or excuse, acts of corruption." For example, the tradition of gift-giving in Japan,

Mongolia, and South Korea has encouraged bribery among those civil servants, who accept gifts (or bribes) given by those wishing to cut red tape or to obtain licenses or permits improperly. In Taiwan, gift-giving is also an important social tradition and voters do not object to vote-buying because of their close *guanxi* with the candidates and view the money offered as a gift and not as a bribe for their votes. In Thailand, giving gifts to civil servants for services provided is not viewed as bribery but as *sin nam jai* or gifts of goodwill. In the Philippines, corruption is rampant because the importance of family ties has been reinforced by the *compadre* system and the cultural value of *utang na loob* (debt of gratitude) (Quah, 2011, pp. 49–54, 131–133, 178–179, 290–291, 320–321, 421–422). Corruption in India has been attributed to Hinduism because of its forgiving nature, lenient attitude toward offenders, and encouragement of a fatalistic attitude among Indians that it would be difficult to curb corruption (Tummala, 2002, pp. 46–47; Raghunathan, 2006, pp. 44–46).

In a recent article, Gerald E. Caiden (2012, p. 96) noted that "the cultural dimension of corruption has been for too long a poor relative of other studies." The studies cited in the previous paragraph have focused on the negative effects of cultural values as contributing to corruption as very little research has been done on how cultural values prevent or inhibit corruption. An exception is the pioneering research by Grant Richardson (2006) on the influence of culture on fiscal corruption in 47 countries. He tested four hypotheses on the relationship of Hofstedt's four cultural dimensions of power distance, individualism, uncertainty avoidance, and masculinity on fiscal corruption and found that

> ... power distance and uncertainty avoidance have significant relationships with fiscal corruption after controlling for economic development, democracy and government size. The higher the level of power distance (reflecting higher inequality of power and wealth) and uncertainty avoidance (reflecting a cultural tendency towards certainty and low tolerance of ambiguity) and the lower the level of economic development, democracy and government size, the higher is the level of fiscal corruption across countries. (Richardson, 2006, p. 136)

As high power distance and uncertainty avoidance are associated with higher levels of fiscal corruption, Richardson (2006, p. 137) recommends that governments can minimize the negative consequences of these cultural dimensions by improving economic development, democracy, and the size of government. Economic development curbs fiscal corruption by providing better compensation and education for civil servants in the tax administration to reduce their temptation to extract bribes from the public. Fiscal corruption is more easily detected in democracies where the tax administrations are more transparent and publicly accountable. Finally, fiscal corruption can also be reduced by increasing the size of government.

Richardson's finding that those countries with significant inequalities in income and wealth are more likely to experience fiscal corruption especially when there are also low levels of economic development and democracy lends credence to Robert Gregory and Daniel Zirker's argument in Chapter 5 that the most important factor for New Zealand's corruption-free record is its "strong egalitarian ethos that underwrote one of the world's first welfare states." To reinforce their argument, they referred to the recent comparative study by David H. Fischer (2012, pp. 27–28) who found that, unlike Americans, New Zealanders are more concerned with fairness than freedom. Indeed, the "feeling for fairness" is prominent in New Zealand's culture and evident in law, business, sport, and language (Fischer, 2012, pp. 10–11).

Similarly, in the case of Finland, Paula Tiihonen (2003, p. 108) contends that the emphasis on equality and absence of class distinctions in Finnish society have "reduced the necessity of bribing civil servants, or the need for civil servants to take a bribe." Matti Joutsen and Juha Keranen (n.d., p. 8) also point out that the four administrative principles of equality, objectivity, proportionality, and appropriate action, have contributed to the rule of law in Finland as Finns handle "most legal problems very pragmatically." Finland's Ministry of Foreign Affairs (2006, p. 5) has indicated that the emphasis on the values of moderation, personal restraints, and the common good discourage "the pursuit of private gains at the expense of others" and build mutual trust among the Finnish population. Two key aspects should be noted here. First, "the moral and legal condemnation of power centralization and socio-economic disparities, combined with the promotion of a culture of governance fostering the common good" is an important strength in combating corruption in Finland. The second important aspect is that the moral example of the officials and executive decision-makers is indispensable for nurturing the development of an ethical culture of governance, which includes a culture of accountability in public administration, in Finland as "good civil servants do not vaunt their powers or boast about their positions" (Ministry of Foreign Affairs, Finland, 2006, pp. 5, 15).

In Chapter 2, Michael Johnston focuses on Denmark's consensual, communal, and egalitarian political culture, which is an important factor contributing to its effective corruption control that will be difficult for other countries to emulate. Eric M. Uslaner (2008, pp. 42–43) asserts that "corruption reflects low levels of generalized trust and high levels of economic inequality." More specifically, he argues that "inequality breeds corruption" by "leading ordinary citizens to see the system as stacked against them"; making them dependent and pessimistic for the future, and unlikely to treat their neighbors honestly; and "distorting the key institutions of fairness in society, the courts, which ordinary citizens see as their protectors against evildoers." However, it will be difficult for those countries with "high levels of inequality, low trust, and elevated rates of corruption" to avoid "the inequality trap" because those countries with "low levels of inequality, high levels of trust, and honest governments" are more likely to adopt policies to reduce inequality (Uslaner, 2008, p. 247). The experiences of Finland, New Zealand, and Denmark have confirmed the accuracy of Uslaner's thesis. Furthermore, given the importance of equality in these three countries, it is not surprising that their Gini coefficients are much lower than those of India, Singapore, and Hong Kong, as shown in Table 12.

Thus, the effectiveness of corruption control in Finland, Denmark, and New Zealand has shown the importance of such values as equality, fairness, and moderation in promoting good governance and curbing corruption. In other words, the third lesson to be learnt is that culture does not only necessarily lead to corruption as emphasized in the literature, but can also contribute to minimizing corruption.

Lesson 4: Adequate Salaries Are Necessary But Insufficient for Effective Corruption Control

As low salaries constitute an important cause of corruption in many Asian countries (Quah, 2011, pp. 15−16), an obvious solution is to raise the "starvation wages" of their public officials. Robert S. Leiken (1996/1997, p. 68) has recommended that "when the people pay government functionaries

Table 12.   Gini Coefficients of Six Countries.

Rank	Country	Score[a]	Year
11th	Hong Kong	53.7	2011
26th	Singapore	47.8	2012
78th	India	36.8	2004
84th	New Zealand	36.2	1997
127th	Finland	26.8	2008
132nd	Denmark	24.8	2011

Source: Compiled from http://www.cia.gov/library/publications/the-world-factbook/.
[a]The score ranges from 0 (perfect equality) to 100 (perfect inequality).

decent salaries, they are buying a layer of insulation against patronage and bribery." In the same vein, Paulo Mauro (1997, p. 5) warns that "when civil service pay is too low, civil servants may be obliged to use their positions to collect bribes as a way of making ends meet, particularly when the expected cost of being caught is low." However, raising the low salaries of public officials will not necessarily curb corruption without other safeguards.

The salaries of civil servants and political leaders in Singapore and Hong Kong are the highest in the world as the annual basic salary of Singapore's Prime Minister was US$2,183,516 in 2010 and Hong Kong's Chief Executive's annual basic salary for the same year was US$513,245 (Economist, 2010). When the PAP government assumed office in June 1959, corruption was a way of life in Singapore and it also inherited a budgetary deficit of S$14 million, which was reduced by removing the variable allowances of senior civil servants and resulted in a savings of S$10 million (Bogaars, 1973, p. 80). The allowances of these bureaucrats were restored by the government in September 1961 as the budgetary situation had improved. In 1968, the Harvey Report on public sector salaries recommended salary increases for five grades in the Division I superscale salaries. However, the government did not accept this recommendation because the economy could not afford a major salary revision, and more importantly, there was no serious exodus of talented civil servants to the private sector (Quah, 2007b, p. 27).

The situation changed during the 1970s as the rapid economic growth increased private sector salaries and resulted in many civil servants leaving for jobs in the private sector. Accordingly, the National Wages Council recommended the payment of an additional 13th month salary to all civil servants in 1972 to reduce the gap between salaries in the public and private sectors. As the PAP government could not afford to raise the salaries of civil servants and ministers during its first 12 years from June 1959 to December 1971, it relied solely on the CPIB to enforce the POCA impartially. Public sector salaries were periodically increased from March 1972 to January 1994 to stem the brain drain of civil servants to the private sector. From 1995, the salaries of civil servants and ministers were benchmarked to the salaries of six private sector professions to minimize the salary gap and attraction of private sector jobs (Quah, 2007b, pp. 27–29).

As the CPIB has succeeded in minimizing corruption in Singapore during 1959–1971 without raising the salaries of civil servants and ministers, it is necessary to reiterate that Singapore's success in combating corruption cannot be attributed solely to the "egregiously high salaries of its public officials" as claimed by Darren C. Zook (2009, p. 166), who is unaware that the purpose of paying competitive salaries to senior civil servants and political leaders is to attract the "best and brightest" citizens to the civil service and government and to retain them by reducing the salary gap in the public and private sectors.

In Hong Kong, the high public sector salaries can be attributed to the British colonial legacy of providing such generous perks and benefits as "housing, chauffeur-driven limousines for personal use, passages, local and overseas education allowances" for the Chief Executive, Chief Justice, and senior civil servants, but not for the legislators. These generous pay packages were introduced during the colonial period to attract expatriates from Britain to work in Hong Kong, and were gradually extended to local civil servants, and have been retained after Hong Kong's handover to China in July 1997. As private sector salaries in Hong Kong are also higher than those of the civil service, it is not surprising that "top bureaucrats have begun to resign from the civil service for greener pastures." Thus, Hong Kong's low level of perceived corruption should not be attributed solely to the high pay of its public officials but also to its stringent regulations and severe penalties for corrupt civil servants (Lee, 2003, pp. 130, 140–142).

In contrast to the high public sector salaries in Singapore and Hong Kong, civil servants and ministers in India earn much lower salaries as reflected in their Prime Minister earning a basic salary of US$4,106 during 2010 (Economist, 2010). However, unlike Singapore and Hong Kong, the salaries of public officials and politicians in Finland, Denmark, and New Zealand are lower but adequate to prevent corruption. Paula Tiihonen (2003, pp. 108–109) has observed that Finnish civil servants are honest as their salaries, although not high, are "good enough" as they are taken care of after their retirement. The emphasis on moderation and restraint is reflected in the low-income disparities in Finland and the payment of reasonable wages to its public officials, which do not differ greatly from those of other Finnish wage-earners (Ministry of Foreign Affairs, Finland, 2006, p. 10).

In Denmark, salaries of civil servants are also adequate but not high because the official incomes policy is based on egalitarian principles and the "strict and centralized rules regulating public sector pay did not allow civil servants to keep pace with the rapid increase in private sector wages" (Christensen, 1994, pp. 72, 87). The total compensation packages of middle managers and executive secretaries in the Danish public service are slightly above the Organisation for Economic Co-operation and Development (OECD) average, while those of economists and policy analysts are slightly lower (OECD, 2011a, p. 2). In New Zealand, public sector salaries are also adequate as the total compensation packages of middle managers in the public service are in line with the OECD average, while the salaries of economists, policy analysts, and executive secretaries are somewhat below the average (OECD, 2011b, p. 2).

The importance of egalitarian principles in Denmark, Finland, and New Zealand is reflected most vividly in the modest lifestyles of politicians. In the case of Denmark, Michael Johnston refers in Chapter 2 to the example of the Speaker of Parliament, who rides a bicycle to work. Such modest behavior not only reinforces the values of egalitarianism, accountability, and service, but also discourages politicians from increasing their own salaries or displaying their wealth. Indeed, Danish politicians earn much lower salaries than senior bureaucrats because voters' distrust and fear of a populist backlash threaten their re-election and prevent them from raising their salaries to meet the rising cost of living. According to J. G. Christensen (1994, p. 85), Danish politicians have failed to protect their own economic interests because Members of Parliament (MPs) regained their 1969 income level from 1986, but Ministers have "suffered a decline in income because their pay has been unchanged since 1969." They are "modest people" as "their income does not compare well with that of other decision makers" like senior civil servants or private sector managers. Moreover, the salaries of MPs from Denmark, Norway, Sweden, and Switzerland are among the lowest in a comparative study of several OECD countries (Christensen, 1995, pp. 105, 108, 112).

Civil servants and political leaders are more vulnerable to corruption if their salaries are meager or not commensurate with their positions or responsibilities. It is therefore unrealistic to expect them to remain honest if they are paid low salaries which are insufficient to meet their daily needs. Thus, they should be paid adequate salaries instead of "starvation wages" to insulate them from bribery and patronage. The success of Finland, Denmark, and New Zealand in corruption control reaffirms the importance of paying public officials adequate but not high salaries. Furthermore, as raising public sector salaries is expensive, only those countries that have sustained economic growth like Singapore and Hong Kong can afford to do so. More importantly, the CPIB's and ICAC's success in curbing corruption shows that it is not necessary to increase the salaries of bureaucrats and politicians if the anti-corruption laws are enforced impartially. As private sector salaries in Singapore and Hong Kong are much higher than public sector salaries, their governments increased the salaries of senior civil servants and politicians to minimize the outflow of talent from the public to the private sectors and not to curb corruption.

Two further *caveats* on the efficacy of salary revision as an anti-corruption strategy must be noted. First, increasing the salaries of civil servants minimizes petty corruption as it reduces the incentives for corruption among junior officials but does not eliminate grand corruption among senior civil servants and politicians, which is motivated by greed rather than need. The second *caveat* is that raising salaries alone will be ineffective in solving the problem of corruption if the incumbent government lacks the political will to do so, if the ACA is ineffective, if corrupt officials are not punished, and if the opportunities for corruption are not reduced in vulnerable public agencies. In other words, the fourth lesson is that paying adequate salaries to civil servants and politicians is a necessary but insufficient condition for curbing corruption if other reforms are not undertaken also.

Lesson 5: Constant Vigilance Is Needed for Sustained Success in Corruption Control

The consistently good performance of the five countries on Transparency International's CPI from 1995 to 2012 and the World Bank's Control of Corruption from 1996 to 2011 confirms the effectiveness of their anti-corruption measures during the past 15–17 years. However, these countries should not "rest on their laurels" or be complacent in view of some emerging trends.

In his analysis of corruption control in Denmark in Chapter 2, Michael Johnston has pointed out that Denmark's future CPI rankings and scores might be adversely affected if Greenland, which is under Danish control, were included as part of Denmark because of the ample opportunities for corruption in its mining and growing wind power industries. Transparency Greenland has alleged that there is corruption in Alcoa's aluminium smelter in Maniitsoq. Some wind-power companies based in Greenland were reported to have falsified data on the environmental effects of power generation windmills to win construction approvals and pay affected landholders lower compensation.

As Finland "has taken a long time to construct a good governance and administrative system," Paula Tiihonen (2003, p. 117) has wisely cautioned that this system is "very fragile" and can "easily be destroyed — suddenly or slowly, intentionally or unintentionally." In similar vein, Ari Salminen, the author of Chapter 3, suggests that Finland's control system needs to be redefined and reformed to meet three emerging challenges even though its anti-corruption measures are effective. While there is no urgent need to introduce additional anti-corruption laws, or set up an ACA, he recommends more active participation of civil society organizations, the prevention of distorted networking in politics, business, and public administration, and the introduction of codes of ethics for Finnish civil servants, politicians, and those working for local authorities to deal with these challenges.

In Chapter 5, Robert Gregory and Daniel Zirker suggest that with changing circumstances, "there is no guarantee that either corruption generally or governmental corruption specifically will not become significant problems in New Zealand." Indeed, New Zealanders should not be complacent about their country's corruption-free record because of three recent trends, the most important of which is the rising income equality, which threatens New Zealand's egalitarian ethos. Table 12 shows that New Zealand's Gini coefficient for 1997 was 36.2. While this figure is lower than the more recent figures for Hong Kong and Singapore, the gap between New Zealand and the two city-states appears to be narrowing as an article in *NZ Fairfax News* by L. Nichols (2011) reported that the richest New Zealanders, who constitute only one percent of the population, are three times richer than the poorest 50 percent. The other two troubling trends are the increased incidence of financial fraud, and the extensive media coverage of corruption scandals in various sectors in New Zealand during the past five years.

While there is less emphasis on equality in Hong Kong and Singapore, Table 12 shows that the high Gini coefficients of 53.7 for Hong Kong in 2011, and 47.8 for Singapore in 2012, indicate the widening income gap between the rich and poor in both city-states. Even though Singapore and Hong Kong have escaped the "inequality trap" mentioned by Uslaner (2008, p. 242), their rising income inequality does not bode well for the future if appropriate measures are not introduced to redress it. Furthermore, the high profile corruption scandals involving senior civil servants in both territories in recent years are a cause for concern even though the number of corruption cases investigated annually by the CPIB and ICAC remains small and come mainly from the private sector.

As the majority of corruption cases investigated by the CPIB and ICAC in recent years come from the private sector, the most important challenge facing both ACAs is tackling the increasing trend of private sector corruption in Singapore and Hong Kong without alienating the members of the business community. The increasing incidence of financial fraud in New Zealand, the distorting influence of old boys' networks in Finland, and the growing importance of Greenland's mining and wind power industries indicate that these three countries will not be immune and must also redouble their anti-corruption efforts to meet the growing challenge of private sector corruption. As corrupt individuals are highly intelligent and capable of finding legal loopholes or other methods to circumvent anti-corruption laws, Alexandra Wrage (2013) has advised those responsible for combating corruption in the public and private sectors to "think like a criminal to stay ahead of the bad guys" and their five "schemes for creative corruption."

As "anti-corruption reform is a marathon, not a sprint" (Millennium Challenge Corporation [MCC], 2007, p. 8), Finland, Denmark, New Zealand, Singapore, and Hong Kong should not remain complacent about their success in combating corruption. Rather, these five countries should be constantly vigilant to identify potential future threats to their corruption-free records, and to address these threats with appropriate measures to sustain their effectiveness in minimizing corruption for the long term.

CONCLUSION

Corruption is "alive and well" today in spite of the strong rhetoric against corruption in many countries (Berkman, 2008, p. 5). Gerald E. Caiden contends in Chapter 8 that most anti-corruption efforts around the world are ineffective as reflected in the extensive media coverage of corruption scandals. As success stories are few, the three alternative paths to curbing corruption by the six countries analyzed in this book and the five lessons identified in the previous section should be instructive for those policymakers, anti-corruption practitioners, and civil society activists who are concerned with ameliorating the corruption situation in their countries.

If the government and citizens of a country afflicted by rampant corruption wish to improve the status quo, what can they do? They have three options. The first option, which should be avoided, is not to follow the examples of countries like China, India, Philippines, Taiwan, and Vietnam, which have continued to rely for many years on ineffective multiple ACAs to address the problem of rampant corruption, without success. The second option, which is practised by Finland, Denmark, and New Zealand, is to strengthen existing institutions in the country to enhance good governance without creating an ACA. The final option in combating corruption was initiated by the creation of the CPIB in Singapore in 1952, and emulated by the formation of the ICAC in Hong Kong in 1974. The CPIB and ICAC were established by the British colonial government in both colonies to rectify the serious mistake it made in making their corrupt police forces responsible for curbing corruption. The Opium Hijacking scandal of October 1951 in Singapore and the June 8, 1973 escape of corruption suspect Peter Godber from Hong Kong to Britain confirmed the futility of relying on the police to combat corruption when they were corrupt.

While the adoption of a single ACA is a popular option as reflected in the proliferation of ACAs around the world, it should be remembered that the CPIB and ICAC are effective because of the strong political will of their governments and their favorable policy contexts. In other words, the establishment of a single ACA is not a magic bullet or panacea for minimizing corruption in a country if there is weak political will and an unfavorable policy context. Furthermore, the experiences of Finland, Denmark, and New Zealand show that it is possible to curb corruption effectively without relying on an ACA if there are other institutions to ensure good governance. In short, while the creation of an ACA is not necessarily the best option for combating corruption, those countries which decide to rely on this option should realize that they will only succeed if there is strong political will and a favorable political context. Without these prerequisites, the single ACA established will be ineffective in curbing corruption.

NOTES

1. The "remote environment" refers to the "physical, historical, sociocultural, ecological, and technological conditions with distant effects on the policy process" and the "proximate environment" includes "those actors, issues, and conditions with an immediate and/or direct influence on the policy processes" (Warwick, 1979, pp. 304, 310).

2. For a comprehensive treatment of the first 50 years of Finland's Ombudsman, see Hiden (1973).

3. The exchange rate at the end of 2011 was US$1 = DKK5.75 (Economist, 2012, p. 140).

4. Surveys commissioned by the SFO in 2011 and 2012 have shown that the SFO is well-regarded by all of its stakeholders, with 67 percent of the respondents indicating that they have trust and confidence in it, and 66 percent of them saying that the SFO has done a good job in bringing offenders to account (SFO, 2013b, pp. 22–24).

5. For a recent evaluation of the effectiveness of the CBI and CVC, see Quah (2011, pp. 99–108).

6. See also Caiden (1997, pp. 1–22).

7. As a Special Administrative Region of China, Hong Kong is not included in the 2013 Failed States Index. However, China's 66th rank and score of 80.9 do not reflect accurately Hong Kong's rank and score if it were included as Hong

Kong's performance on the World Bank's 2011 governance indicators surpasses that of China's.

8. These five ACAs are the Office of the Ombudsman (which is the lead ACA), Presidential Commission on Good Governance, Inter-Agency Anti-Graft Coordinating Council, Presidential Committee on Effective Governance, and Governance Advisory Council (Quah, 2011, pp. 26, 151).

REFERENCES

Aalto, J. S. (1983). Finland. In: G. E. Caiden (Ed.), *International handbook of the Ombudsman: Evolution and present function* (pp. 93–103). Westport, CT: Greenwood Press, Chap. 5.

Berkman, S. (2008). *The World Bank and the gods of lending*. Sterling, VA: Kumarian Press.

Bogaars, G. E. (1973). Public services. In *Towards tomorrow: Essays on development and transformation in Singapore*. Singapore: National Trades Union Congress.

Caiden, G. E. (1997). Undermining good governance: Corruption and democracy. *Asian Journal of Political Science, 5*(2), 1–22.

Caiden, G. E. (2012). Culture and corruption. *Public Administration and Policy, 15*(2), 93–128.

Caiden, G. E., Macdermot, N. & Sandler, A. (1983). The institution of the Ombudsman. In G. E. Caiden (Ed.), *International handbook of the Ombudsman: Evolution and present function* (pp. 3–21). Westport, CT: Greenwood Press, Chap. 1.

CBI. (2010). *Annual report 2009*. New Delhi.

Cheung, A. B. L. (2008). Evaluation of the Hong Kong integrity system. In L. Huberts, F. Anechiarico, & F. Six (Eds.), *Local integrity systems: World cities fighting corruption and safeguarding integrity* (pp. 105–115). The Hague: BJu Legal Publishers, Chap. 7.

Christensen, J. G. (1994). Denmark: Institutional constraint and the advancement of individual self-interest in HPO. In C. Hood & B. G. Peters (Eds.), *Rewards at the top: A comparative study of high public office* (pp. 70–89). London: Sage Publications, Chap. 4.

Christensen, J. G. (1995). Denmark. In F. F. Ridley & A. Doig (Eds.), *Sleaze: Politicians, private interests and public reaction* (pp. 102–114). Oxford: Oxford University Press.

Danish Parliament. (2013). *Institutions of the Danish Parliament. Copenhagen.* Retrieved from http://www.thedanishparliament.dk/About_the_Danish_Parliament/Institutions_of_the_Danish_Parliament.aspx. Accessed on July 10, 2013.

Danish Parliamentary Ombudsman. (2012). *Annual report 2011*. Copenhagen.

Dreze, J. & Sen, A. (2013). *An uncertain glory: India and its contradictions*. London: Penguin Books.

Economist. (2010). Politicians' salaries, Leaders of the fee world: How much a country's leader is paid compared to GDP per person. *Economist*, July 5.

Economist. (2012). *Pocket world in figures 2013 edition*. London: Profile Books.

Fischer, D. H. (2012). *Fairness and freedom: A history of two open societies, New Zealand and the United States*. New York, NY: Oxford University Press.

Gaus, J. M. (1947). *Reflections on public administration*. University, AL: University of Alabama Press.

Gellhorn, W. (1966). *Ombudsmen and others: Citizens' protectors in nine countries*. Cambridge, MA: Harvard University Press.

Gill, S. S. (1998). *The pathology of corruption.* New Delhi: HarperCollin Publishers India.

Heilbrunn, J. R. (2006). Anti-corruption commissions. In R. Stapenhurst, N. Johnston, & R. Pelizzo (Eds.), *The role of parliament in curbing corruption* (pp. 135–148). Washington, DC: World Bank, Chap. 9.

Hiden, M. (1973). *The Ombudsman in Finland: The first fifty years* (A. Bell, Trans.). Berkeley, CA: Institute of Governmental Studies, University of California.

ICAC. (2013). *Annual report 2012.* Hong Kong. Retrieved from http://www.icac.org.hk/file manager/en/Content_1238/2012.pdf. Accessed on July 10, 2013.

Joutsen, M & Keranen, J. (n.d.) *Corruption and the prevention of corruption in Finland.* Helsinki: Ministry of Justice.

Kastari, P. (1968). Finland's guardians of the law: The Chancellor of Justice and the Ombudsman. In D. C. Rowat (Ed.), *The Ombudsman: Citizen's defender* (pp. 58–74). London: George Allen & Unwin, Chap. 2.

Kpundeh, S. J. (1998). Political will in fighting corruption. In S. J. Kpundeh & I. Hors (Eds.), *Corruption and integrity improvement initiatives in developing countries* (pp. 91–110). New York, NY: United Nations Development Programme, Chap. 6.

Larmour, P. (2012). *Interpreting corruption: Culture and politics in the Pacific Islands.* Honolulu: University of Hawaii Press.

Lee, G. O. M. (2003). Hong Kong – institutional inheritance from colony to special administrative region. In C. Hood, B. G. Peters, & G. O. M. Lee (Eds.), *Reward for high public office: Asian and Pacific rim states* (pp. 130–144). London: Routledge, Chap. 8.

Leichter, H. M. (1979). *A comparative approach to policy analysis: Health care policy in four nations.* Cambridge: Cambridge University Press.

Leiken, R. S. (1996/1997). Controlling the global corruption epidemic. *Foreign Policy, 105* (Winter), 55–73.

Lethbridge, H. J. (1985). *Hard graft in Hong Kong: Scandal, corruption, the ICAC.* Hong Kong: Oxford University Press.

Lundvik, U. (1983). New Zealand. In G. E. Caiden (Ed.), *International handbook of the Ombudsman: Evolution and present function* (pp. 135–146). Westport, CT: Greenwood Press, Chap. 10.

Mauro, P. (1997). *Why worry about corruption?* Washington, DC: International Monetary Fund.

MCC. (2007). Building public integrity through positive incentives: MCC's role in the fight against corruption. Working Paper. MCC, Washington, DC.

Meagher, P. (2005). Anti-corruption agencies: Rhetoric versus reality. *Journal of Policy Reform, 8*(1), 69–103.

Ministry of Foreign Affairs, Finland. (2006). *Combating corruption: The Finnish experience.* Helsinki.

Modeen, T. (2000). The Swedish and Finnish parliamentary Ombudsman. In: R. Gregory & P. Giddings (Eds.), *Righting wrongs: The Ombudsman in six continents* (pp. 315–322). Amsterdam: IOS Press.

Nichols, L. (2011). Revealing the gap between NZ's rich and poor. *Fairfax NZ News,* November 18.

Nicholls, C., Daniel, T., Polaine, M., & Hatchard, J. (2006). *Corruption and misuse of public office.* Oxford: Oxford University Press.

Nielsen, L. N. (1983). Denmark. In G. E. Caiden (Ed.), *International handbook of the Ombudsman: Evolution and present function* (pp. 73–79). Westport, CT: Greenwood Press, Chap. 3.

Northey, J. F. (1968). New Zealand's parliamentary commissioner. In: D. C. Rowat (Ed.), *The Ombudsman: Citizen's defender* (pp. 127–143). London: George Allen & Unwin, Chap. 6.

OECD. (2011a). *Government at a Glance 2011, Country Note: Denmark*. Paris. Retrieved from http://www.oecd.org/gov/indicators/govataglance. Accessed on July 10, 2013.

OECD. (2011b). *Government at a Glance 2011, Country Note: New Zealand*. Paris. Retrieved from http://www.oecd.org/gov/indicators/govataglance. Accessed on July 10, 2013.

Oyamada, E. (2005). President Gloria Macapagal-Arroyo's anti-corruption strategy in the Philippines: An evaluation. *Asian Journal of Political Science, 13*(1), 81–107.

Pedersen, I. M. (1968). Denmark's Ombudsmand. In D. C. Rowat (Ed.), *The Ombudsman: Citizen's defender* (pp. 75–94). London: George Allen & Unwin, Chap. 3.

PERC (Political and Economic Risk Consultancy). (2013). Corruption's impact on the business environment. *Asian Intelligence*, No. 871, March 20.

Quah, J. S. T. (2004). Best practices for curbing corruption in Asia. *The Governance Brief, 11*, 1–4.

Quah, J. S. T. (2007a). *National integrity systems Transparency International regional overview report: East and Southeast Asia*. Berlin: Transparency International.

Quah, J. S. T. (2007b). *Combating corruption Singapore-style: Lessons for other Asian countries*. Baltimore, MD: School of Law, University of Maryland.

Quah, J. S. T. (2009). Governance and corruption: Exploring the connection. *American Journal of Chinese Studies, 16*(2), 119–135.

Quah, J. S. T. (2011). *Curbing corruption in Asian countries: An impossible dream?* Bingley: Emerald Group Publishing.

Quah, J. S. T. (2013). Combating corruption in Asian countries: What lessons have we learnt? *Public Administration and Policy, 16*(1), 15–34.

Quimson, G. (2006). *National integrity systems Transparency International country study report: Philippines 2006*. Berlin: Transparency International.

Raghunathan, V. (2006). *Games Indians play: Why we are the way we are*. New Delhi: Penguin Books India.

Richardson, G. (2006). The influence of culture on fiscal corruption: Evidence across countries. In M. Stewart (Ed.), *Tax law and political institutions* (pp. 124–142). Annandale: Federation Press.

Richardson, I. L. & Baldwin, S. (1976). *Public administration: Government in action*. Columbus, OH: Charles E. Merrill Publishing Company.

Riggs, F. W. (1961). *The ecology of public administration*. Bombay: Asia Publishing House.

Rotberg, R. I. (2004). The failure and collapse of nation states: Breakdown, prevention, and repair. In R. I. Rotberg (Ed.), *When states fail: Causes and consequences* (pp. 1–49). Princeton, NJ: Princeton University Press, Chap. 1.

Salminen, A., Viinamaki, O.-P., & Ikola-Norrbacka, R. (2007). The control of corruption in Finland. *Revista Administrati si Management Public* [Administration and Public Management Review], *9*, 81–95.

Satyanand, A. (2005). The role of Ombudsman and its connection with the control of corruption. In UNAFEI, *Resource Materials Series*, No. 65 (March), 213–228. Retrieved from http://www.unafei.or.jp/english/pdf/RS_No65/No65_18VE_Satyanand.pdf. Accessed on July 10, 2013.

Sayre, W. S. (1967). Bureaucracies: Some contrasts in systems. In N. Raphaeli (Ed.), *Readings in comparative public administration* (pp. 341–354). Boston, MA: Allyn & Bacon.

Schwab, K. (Ed.) (2012). *The global competitiveness report 2012–2013*. Geneva: World Economic Forum.

Senior, I. (2006). *Corruption – the World's big C: Cases, causes, consequences, cures*. London: Institute of Economic Affairs.

SFO (Serious Fraud Office). (2013a). Our purpose and role. Auckland. Retrieved from http://www.sfo.govt.nz/about. Accessed on July 10, 2013.

SFO. (2013b). *Annual report 2012*. Auckland. Retrieved from http://www.sfo.govt.nz/f55, 18661/SFO_Annual_Report_2012.pdf. Accessed on July 10, 2013.

Sharma, P. D. & Sharma, B. M. (2009). *Indian administration: Retrospect and prospect*. Jaipur: Rawat Publications.

Spector, B. I. (2012). *Detecting corruption in developing countries: Identifying causes/strategies for action*. Sterling, VA: Kumarian Press.

Sturt, C. (1996). The fight against corruption: New Zealand's answer. In Academic Office of the 7th International Anti-Corruption Conference Secretariat (Ed.), *Anti-corruption for social stability and development* (pp. 305–311). Beijing: Hong Qi Publishing House.

Tiihonen, P. (2003). Good governance and corruption in Finland. In S. Tiihonen (Ed.), *The history of corruption in central government* (pp. 99–118). Amsterdam: IOS Press.

Transparency Suomi. (2012). *National integrity assessment: Finland*. Helsinki.

Tummala, K. K. (2002). Corruption in India: Control measures and consequences. *Asian Journal of Political Science, 10*(2), 43–69.

UNODC (United Nations Office on Drugs and Crime). (2004). *The global program against corruption: United Nations anti-corruption toolkit*. 3rd ed. Vienna.

Uslaner, E. M. (2008). *Corruption, inequality, and the rule of law: The bulging pocket makes the easy life*. New York, NY: Cambridge University Press.

Warwick, D. P. (1979). Cultural values and population policies: Cases and contexts. In J. D. Montgomery, H. D. Lasswell, & J. S. Migdal (Eds.), *Patterns of policy: Comparative and longitudinal studies of population events* (pp. 295–337). New Brunswick: Transaction Books, Chap. 11.

World Bank. (2013). *Doing business 2013*. Washington, DC.

Wrage, A. (2013). Five schemes for creative corruption. *Forbes*, March 12.

Zook, D. C. (2009). The curious case of Finland's clean politics. *Journal of Democracy, 20*(1). 157–168.